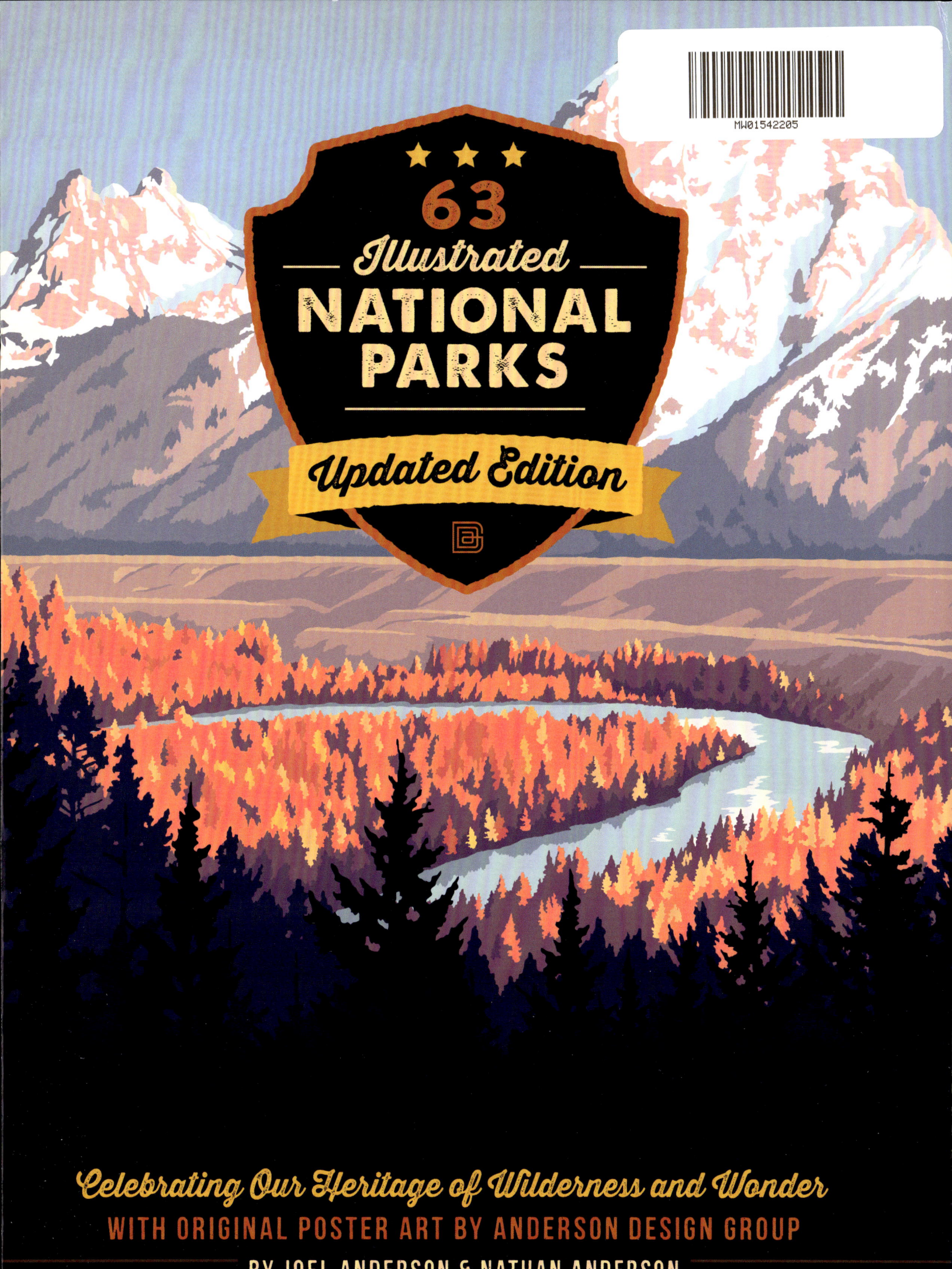

SPECIAL THANKS TO:

David Anderson, Derek Anderson, Julian Baker, Kai Carpenter, Andy Gregg, Aaron Johnson, and Michael Korfhage: for collaborating as a team to create such a beautiful and comprehensive collection of National Park poster art.

Kai Carpenter: for collaborating with us to produce a series of gorgeous oil paintings.

Edward Patton: for your expert typography, design, and layout of the book interior.

Dawn Verner: for your many hours of research, photo searching, and proofreading.

Jamie "Flip" Blaine: for editing Nathan's writing and adding creative direction to the narrative.

Dick Koonce: for your keen eye as a proofreader and your encouragement as a friend.

Dr. Matt Hearn: for offering your time, insight, and fresh eyes on the revised manuscript.

Rick Smith, Former Superintendent and Ranger for 5 National Parks: for helping us connect with other retired Park officials who provided a wealth of information and wonderful quotes.

Retired National Park Officials: for fact-checking, offering insight, perspective, and years of service.

All of our prints are available in standard frame sizes, including: 11"x 14" and 18"x 24". They are available as canvases, too.

To purchase our classic gallery prints and gifts, please visit:
www.ADGstore.com

Library of Congress Control Number: 2020911674
Updated Edition 1st printing, March 2021
© 2021 Joel Anderson. All rights reserved. No portion of this book may be reproduced in any form for any reason without express written consent.

Cover, interior design, and all posters created by Anderson Design Group, Inc.
116 29th Avenue North, Nashville, Tennessee 37203 • Phone: 615-327-9894 • www.AndersonDesignGroup.com • www.ADGstore.com
All photos used by permission. Printed & bound in the U.S.A.

Published by Anderson Design Group, Inc.

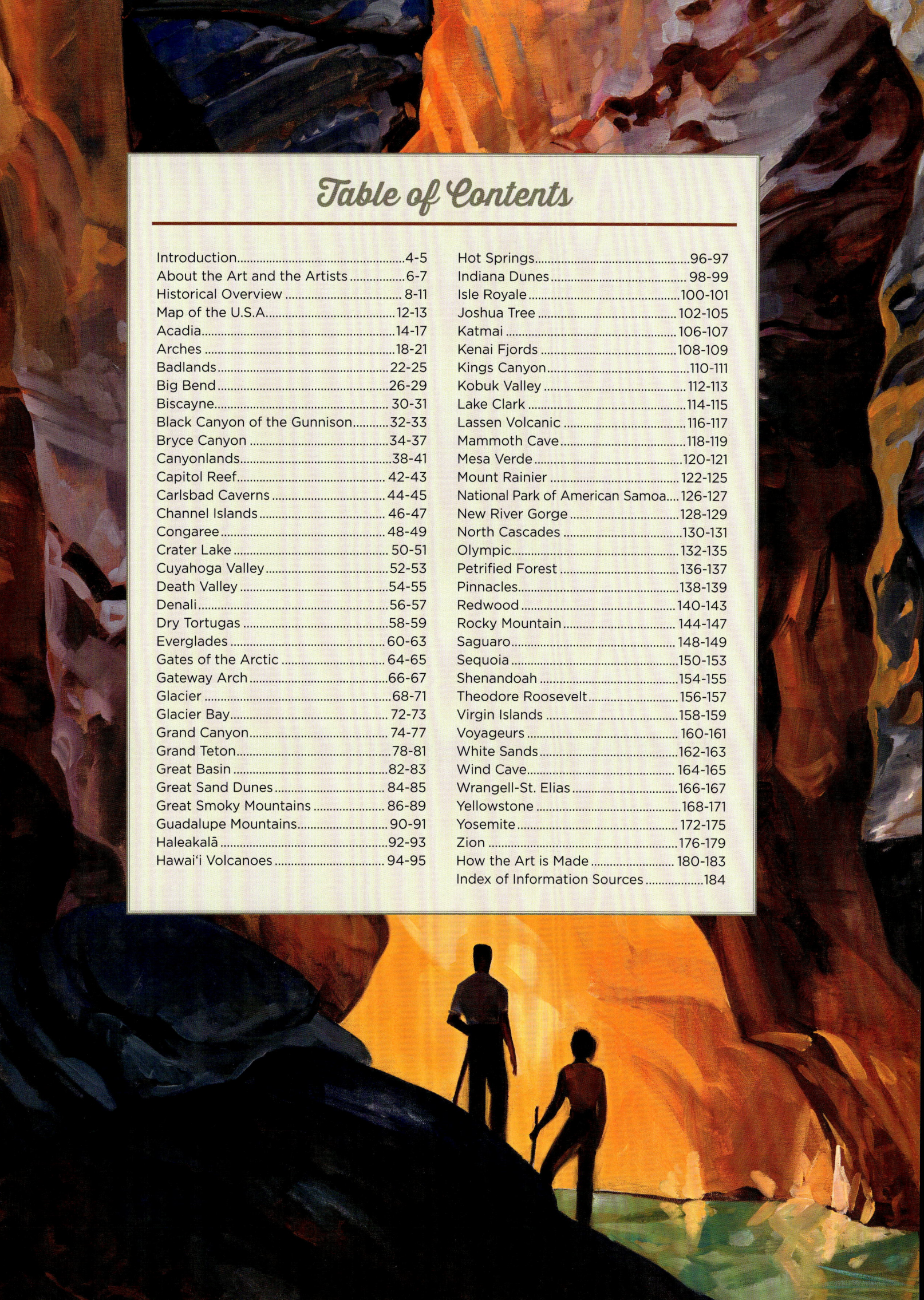

Table of Contents

Introduction...4-5	Hot Springs...96-97
About the Art and the Artists.............6-7	Indiana Dunes....................................98-99
Historical Overview.............................8-11	Isle Royale..100-101
Map of the U.S.A................................12-13	Joshua Tree......................................102-105
Acadia..14-17	Katmai...106-107
Arches..18-21	Kenai Fjords.....................................108-109
Badlands..22-25	Kings Canyon....................................110-111
Big Bend..26-29	Kobuk Valley......................................112-113
Biscayne...30-31	Lake Clark..114-115
Black Canyon of the Gunnison..........32-33	Lassen Volcanic................................116-117
Bryce Canyon.....................................34-37	Mammoth Cave................................118-119
Canyonlands.......................................38-41	Mesa Verde.......................................120-121
Capitol Reef..42-43	Mount Rainier..................................122-125
Carlsbad Caverns..............................44-45	National Park of American Samoa....126-127
Channel Islands.................................46-47	New River Gorge..............................128-129
Congaree..48-49	North Cascades...............................130-131
Crater Lake..50-51	Olympic..132-135
Cuyahoga Valley................................52-53	Petrified Forest................................136-137
Death Valley.......................................54-55	Pinnacles...138-139
Denali..56-57	Redwood...140-143
Dry Tortugas......................................58-59	Rocky Mountain...............................144-147
Everglades...60-63	Saguaro..148-149
Gates of the Arctic............................64-65	Sequoia..150-153
Gateway Arch.....................................66-67	Shenandoah.....................................154-155
Glacier...68-71	Theodore Roosevelt........................156-157
Glacier Bay..72-73	Virgin Islands...................................158-159
Grand Canyon....................................74-77	Voyageurs..160-161
Grand Teton.......................................78-81	White Sands.....................................162-163
Great Basin..82-83	Wind Cave...164-165
Great Sand Dunes.............................84-85	Wrangell-St. Elias............................166-167
Great Smoky Mountains..................86-89	Yellowstone......................................168-171
Guadalupe Mountains......................90-91	Yosemite..172-175
Haleakalā..92-93	Zion..176-179
Hawai'i Volcanoes..............................94-95	How the Art is Made.......................180-183
	Index of Information Sources.................184

A Word from the Author...

"**WHEN I WAS VERY** young and the urge to be someplace else was on me, I was assured by mature people that maturity would cure this itch. When years described me as mature, the remedy prescribed was middle age. In middle age I was assured greater age would calm my fever and now that I am fifty-eight perhaps senility will do the job. Nothing has worked…. I fear this disease is incurable." - John Steinbeck

One of my favorite parts about writing this book was the dreaming. Between feverish bursts of typing copy and tearing through *The Synonym Finder* were moments of internal adventure. I visualized myself somewhere else, doing all that I was writing, experiencing the thrills and the challenges involved with any visit to a National Park. As I researched each Park, my mind would swim with trip itinerary ideas ("We could fly into Salt Lake City, rent an SUV, drive to Moab, and stay in this awesome AirBnB / campground / Airstream…"). The disease, as Steinbeck writes, is incurable.

The disease is also transmissive. I'm a husband and a father now, and my wife is even more well-traveled than I am. We both long for our two daughters to enjoy their American heritage. Yosemite! Arches! Zion! Glacier! Our girls have gotta see these places. They need to know that deep sense of awe and wonder that occurs in the most spectacular of settings. I got a late start; my wife, before she met me, conquered the summit of Mount Whitney (coordinating the whole trip herself). She camped beneath the stars at 9,000 feet. She stood on the roof of California, for pete's sake. I was probably at home watching hockey and eating a pizza. I want my daughters to be like their mother. There's a solemn connection that happens between loved ones in the wild, especially in the midst of such grandeur as our National Parks.

Back during the railroad heyday of the early 1900s, rail promoters saw the addition of National Parks as a prime business opportunity. They coined a phrase that still rings true today: "See America First." Many American families were crossing the Atlantic to see the Old World, unaware of the fact that a vast landscape of untouched beauty was waiting in their own backyard. This "See America First" concept isn't meant to diminish the architectural and cultural splendor of Europe

but rather to celebrate America's diverse natural glory. And it has never been easier to see this vast country of ours. You don't need a passport to visit the world's oldest and tallest trees at Kings Canyon National Park. You don't need approval from a customs officer to stand at the edge of the Grand Canyon or whale-watch at Schoodic Point or drive Trail Ridge Road over the Rocky Mountains.

The 100th anniversary of the National Park Service brought a massive amount of attention to America's wilderness (and to the first edition of this book - thanks y'all!). Since 2016, more and more families are visiting the Parks.

New generations of Americans are now experiencing their birthright for the very first time. Congress has also added three more National Parks to the fold, giving us three more reasons to get outside and explore. But all of this, more than ever before, forces us to consider: how do we enjoy, promote, and share these incredible blessings without "loving them to death"? How do we teach new visitors to "leave no trace" in our National Parks and to respect the sometimes deadly powers of nature? Talking to a Park Ranger is a good place to start. These brave folks decided against having a cushy desk job to live in inconvenient splendor. The Ranger quotes scattered throughout these pages offer a perspective of the National Parks that I will never have. But their sense of appreciation and devotion to the Parks is downright contagious.

The book you hold in your hands has many functions. It is first and foremost a collection of original poster art created by our team of illustrators. It is also a story about our country, a narrative of the fearless Americans who made the idea of a National Park possible. Third, it is a travel guide filled with some of my favorite hikes and sights, plus plenty more that are on my bucket list. My hope is that as you flip through this book, your imagination will transport you and get your heart aching to be out there. That's what it's done to me. Sixty-three times.

We'll see you out there.

—*Nathan Anderson,* Author

The Anderson brothers (left to right) Nathan, David, and Benji

Brothers hiking in a slot canyon

A Word from the Artist...

DRIVING AN RV was just one of the fun/scary/crazy experiences that helped shape this book. A few months before I finished producing the first edition, my amazing wife Patty and I took turns driving a borrowed RV (affectionately dubbed "Large Marge") from Nashville to the Grand Canyon, Zion, Bryce Canyon, Petrified Forest, and back. I relished days of conversation with my wife of 34 years, who is also my best friend and the mother of our kids. I dedicate this book to her (to Patty—not Large Marge!). While our four kids relaxed in the 90s-era upholstered living room on wheels, Patty and I watched the scenery change through the windshield. The green rolling hills of Tennessee gave way to the open plains of Arkansas and Oklahoma, which gradually morphed into the painted deserts of New Mexico, Arizona, and Utah. At each stop, my family explored canyons, rafted rivers, and stood in awe of jaw-dropping sunsets and panoramic vistas. We laughed and hiked and ate and posed for family photos. We took full advantage of the wonderful National Park visitor centers, scenic roads and trails, exhibits, and coin-operated campground showers (with 7-minute limits). Thanks to dedicated people we have never met, we enjoyed unspoiled, expertly-managed Parks full of natural wonders, protected and preserved as our national heritage. We shared a universal human and Divine experience walking in reverent silence along the rim of the Grand Canyon with people from all over the globe. It was the greatest family adventure we've ever had.

I was a king for those 2 weeks, enjoying the things I love most in life—the great outdoors, my country, and my family. It was also a much-needed break from the long hours I'd been spending in the studio creating poster art and running my design firm. After working for more than 5 years

to create a complete series of National Park poster art, this was the perfect way to celebrate the final stretch of a long process.

My oldest son Nathan, an avid hiker, history buff, and a very talented writer, agreed to help me produce an NPS coffee table book that would feature dozens of the National Park posters and oil paintings my team had created. He also added his own compilation of insights, facts, travel tips, and historical information.

During and after our RV trip, Nathan worked tirelessly to research information, check facts, and write a rich narrative about each of the National Parks. He tackled the task of summarizing the 100-year history of the National Park Service, making it both accessible and interesting. As a father/son duo, we visited Parks and pored over dozens of books, travel guides, maps, and websites. We watched the National Parks documentary by Ken Burns which we found to be one of the finest compilations of history, narrative, and imagery ever assembled on the subject.

Finally, I engaged my design firm's all-star team to help me lay out the book. The result is a celebration of our national heritage expressed in poster art, oil paintings, photography, and the written word. It is a love letter to America by a group of creative people, outdoor enthusiasts, and history lovers. It is a call to our fellow citizens to venture out and experience the wilderness and wonder that has been set aside for us to enjoy. America's natural sanctuaries have been made accessible to everyone thanks to the sacrifice, foresight, and dedication of Park Rangers, politicians, philanthropists, naturalists, and ordinary people. Our National Parks exist today thanks to public servants who have worked ceaselessly to protect and preserve some of the most beautiful outdoor spaces on our planet. I hope this book will inspire you to visit as many National Parks as possible, to share the experiences with people you love, and to leave each place as good (or better than) you found it.

—*Joel Anderson,* Graphic Artist and founder of Anderson Design Group, Inc.

The Anderson family (left to right) Joel, Nathan, David, Patty, Benji, Mimi

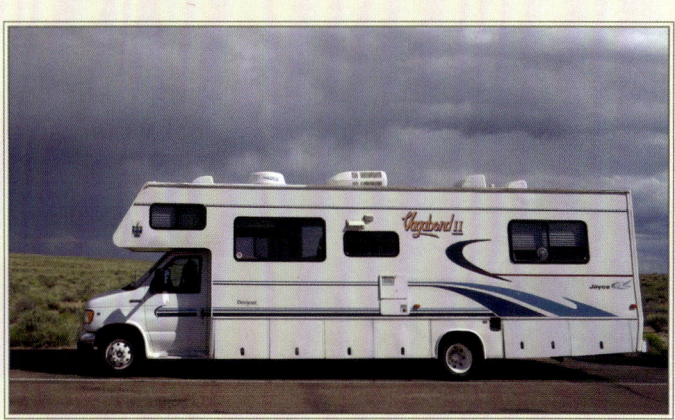

"Large Marge," the Mother Ship for our 2015 National Park adventure

About the Art and the Artists...

OUR POSTERS LOOK OLD, as if they were produced generations ago and then recently discovered in an estate sale. Folks often assume our creations are vintage posters from the 20th-Century. That's because we have spent years studying the rendering techniques, typography, color palettes, and art styles of the 1920s, '30s and '40s. We create original poster art, but we strive to make our designs look like they were done by artists from another era.

During my first year as an illustration major in art school, I fell in love with the iconic imagery created during the Golden Age of Poster Art—a glorious era of commercial art from the late-1800s to the mid-1900s. I was especially captivated by the romance and adventure of travel poster art. Back before the age of photography or computers, designers and illustrators used their masterful hand-rendering and hand-lettering skills to catch the attention of viewers, to draw them into a scene, and inspire them to take a trip to some exotic destination. The colors, fonts, rendering styles and general aesthetic were beautiful even though these posters were in their day nothing more than everyday advertisements created to be pasted up on a wall out in a public space. (In those days, architecture, packaging, even street lamps were ornate, intricate, and crafted with artistic attention to the smallest detail).

Today, in an era of computerized art, photography and cost-conscious efficiency, our culture craves simplicity and vintage craftsmanship. We desire authenticity, excellence, and anything hand-crafted. So it's no surprise that we now decorate with yesterday's ordinary advertising art and accept it as historic and beautiful, a legitimate, nostalgic and emotionally engaging art form.

One of my favorite series of prints from the Golden Age of Poster Art was created in a response to a crisis. During the Great Depression, the Works Progress Administration sought to help unemployed artists by commissioning posters that were intended to inspire Americans to visit National Parks. I still remember the very first time I saw a WPA National Parks print. I was with my son Nathan in the Visitor Center at

Above: The first WPA print I ever bought. Below: The first National Park print my team produced.

Yellowstone National Park, and my eye was drawn to a simple yet iconic poster that was screen printed in a limited color palette. The clean composition drew my eye to Yellowstone Falls and summed up the experience my son and I had enjoyed earlier that week. I had taken lots of photos, but this poster did what no camera could—it eliminated all the unnecessary details and it focused my attention on the canyon, the majestic waterfall and the open sky above, adding a typographical appeal to see the sights and experience the wonder of Yellowstone. I immediately bought that poster, and I took it home as a treasured souvenir of the amazing week I spent with my son.

Visiting National Parks with my family inspired me to collect more WPA poster art that would capture the awe and wonder of America's most beautiful places. I began to notice the powerful compositions, the selective focus on iconic imagery and the integration of hand-lettering. These classic posters promoted the Parks, romanticized nature, and inspired Americans to travel and explore our great country. But as I soon discovered, only a few of these National Parks prints were ever created, and many of the ones that were produced had been lost or damaged over the decades. For the surviving WPA National Park posters we enjoy today, we owe a debt of thanks to seasonal Park ranger Doug Leen, who in 1973 found a WPA Grand Teton poster in a pile of trash being hauled out during NPS renovations. He began scouring the country for other surviving prints and negatives. As it turns out, only 14 Parks had ever commissioned a WPA poster, and of those 14 Parks, only 11 poster designs have survived. After years of searching, Doug and his team carefully restored and reproduced the designs they had salvaged, saving a treasure trove of delicate and deteriorating art from extinction, and making fresh reproductions available to the public once more. I will always be grateful to Ranger Doug for having the foresight to hunt down the WPA Park posters and for making the designs available to a new generation.

Once I realized that no one had ever

Shown above are a few of the original oil paintings by Kai Carpenter in collaboration with Joel Anderson.

created a complete collection of National Parks posters, I had an idea. Why not create a whole new generation of original poster art inspired by those classic WPA prints? Why not produce an original illustrated poster design for each of the 59 Parks? As an artist, an outdoor enthusiast, and a proud American, I couldn't think of a more inspiring or exciting way to merge my passion and talents.

I decided to pick up where the WPA artists left off by creating a few prints of my own favorite Parks. I shared the list with my illustration team, who at the time included staff artist Andy Gregg, intern Julian Baker, and free-lance artist Michael Korfhage. Over a five-year period, I assigned specific Park posters to each of my artists, providing them with direction, reference and inspiration. In the last few months before assembling this book, Michael Korfhage created 20 of the designs at a pace that resembled the buzzing productivity of the old WPA poster art studios. Kai Carpenter produced 12 oil paintings in a classic, romantic travel style. My son David Anderson was working as an intern at my studio while he was in art school, so he worked on a few of the prints along with staff illustrator Aaron Johnson. We surpassed my original goal of 59 posters and produced a series of National Parks prints that now includes 360+ designs!

All along the way, we kept the designs iconic, simple, and beautiful. Our goal was to produce art that would catch your eye from a distance, and then speak to your soul upon closer inspection. We wanted to inspire everyone to fall in love with adventure, to protect and preserve nature, and to celebrate the rich heritage that is ours as citizens of this grand and beautiful country.

After working on this series with the aid of modern technology, I am amazed at the beautiful prints the WPA artists cranked out in an era before photography was widely used in advertising art. They did their jobs creating temporary art that was produced to be pasted onto a wall or taped up in school classrooms. By necessity, their art had to be bold, iconic, emotive, and easily read in a split second. It had to be created in a very limited color palette. Ironically, the WPA artists were just glad to have work to do during the Great Depression. They never dreamed that their work would be collected and prized by future generations like ours.

We use the computer as a finishing tool, but I still insist that my artists draw and sketch to create art that is as authentic and iconic as the classic 20th century works that inspire us. There is no quick or simple way to do this kind of art. Just like in the old days, each of our posters starts with a clever idea and takes 30 to 60 hours to render. Years ago, poster art was disposable (that is why the few surviving vintage posters are so rare and valuable today). And that is why we are creating a new generation of poster art which hopefully will not suffer the same fate of being pasted up on a wall, only to fade in the sun, peel in the wind, and disintegrate in the rain!

As you'll see in this book, everything we do is a labor of love, rooted in our appreciation of classic American advertising art. I hope you enjoy the art as much as we enjoyed creating it!

JOEL ANDERSON *was born in Denver, Colorado in 1965. His family moved every few years to places such as Texas, Curacao, El Salvador, New York, and South Carolina. Joel studied at Ringling School of Art & Design in Sarasota, Florida where he concentrated on Illustration and Design. After graduating with honors in 1986, Joel moved to Nashville and worked for 7 years at Carden & Cherry advertising agency. While there, Joel won several ADDYS and an Emmy Award for his work on a Saturday morning TV show; independently, he exhibited & sold his paintings in local galleries. Joel co-founded Anderson Thomas Design in 1993 with David Thomas. The firm worked on numerous award-winning projects for clients like Universal Studios, DreamWorks, Hasbro, and Harper Collins. After David retired in 2007, Joel retooled the company as Anderson Design Group and narrowed the focus to illustrative design, publishing and poster art. Joel has published over 2,000 posters and 14 books.*

Celebrating the History of our National Parks

IT ALL BEGAN with a strange, bubbling region in the remote territory of northern Wyoming. Established in 1872, Yellowstone National Park was America's first National Park, featuring a vast and mysterious frontier laced with geysers, hot springs, waterfalls, and lonely stretches of wilderness. It was also an area that could have been easily exploited: hunters massacring Yellowstone's bison population while crafty businessmen purchased scenic plots of land and charged tourists a hefty toll to see the Park's wonders. This National Park would exist to protect Yellowstone's wilderness from and for mankind. The historic Senate bill read: "Be it enacted … that the tract of land … lying near the headwaters of the Yellowstone river … is hereby reserved and withdrawn from settlement, occupancy, or sale under the laws of the United States, and dedicated and set apart as a public Park or pleasuring ground for the benefit and enjoyment of the people."

Though Yellowstone was created 44 years before the National Park System was born, this initial Park set the precedent for the 62 that followed. It was the conception of the National Park idea, answering these questions: what is the function of a National Park? What is its purpose? Why do we intentionally set aside vast areas of our own land that could otherwise be used for commercial or agricultural development? Yellowstone was the seed planted into the American consciousness, pointing out not only our fleeting existence but the fragility of nature. Yellowstone caused us to look at ourselves and think ahead. What will be left of this country for our children? For

our grandchildren? The first Park made us consider the natural wonders we possessed, and asked us how we, as a nation, would care for these gifts. The ancient canyons, geysers, waterfalls, and mudpots pointed out our youth in the shadow of the Earth's age. We did not create the land, but we became

"It is not what we have that will make us a great nation; it is the way in which we use it."
-- Theodore Roosevelt

stewards of it.

The origins of the National Park System would be incomplete without mentioning a humble Scottish sheepherder named John Muir. A self-taught naturalist, fearless mountain climber, poet, prophet, and champion for exploited wilderness, John Muir's life and work borders on an American legend. He was a simple man who surrendered his life to Nature, to experience the living world like very few "Westernized" people ever would. He climbed Douglas fir trees, slept on Alaskan glaciers, sledded down an avalanche, and scaled slippery waterfalls out of an unquenchable curiosity for the natural world. Yosemite Valley was Muir's backyard, classroom, and playground in the later years of the 1800s. It was here that John Muir studied the plants and animals of the Sierra Nevada Mountains with a religious fervor. He taught Yosemite's visitors to appreciate what was free for all humanity to enjoy. He wrote essays and letters celebrating the vibrant life that poured down from the peaks and pleading for their protection. He was a defender of the defenseless, a voice crying out in the wilderness.

Muir studied America from the woods, where he gained a unique perspective on American greed. Enterprising lumber companies decimated irreplaceable groves in California and Washington State. Hunters and sportsmen killed

---

A 149-Year Timeline of the National Parks: 1872 - 2021*

Sixty-three current Parks have been formed since our nation began preserving land for the enjoyment of future generations. Nine of them were set aside before the National Park Service was created in 1916 to manage the Parks. Over the years, Presidents protected tracts of land by designating them as National Monuments. Often in the face of opposition by corporations and private citizens, Congress acted to establish these protected areas as National Parks, creating a legacy of wilderness and wonder for all of us to cherish.

1875

1872 Yellowstone

1890 Sequoia
1890 Yosemite

* It was surprisingly difficult to determine the actual order of when each of the 63 Parks were established. Since all of our sources varied, this timeline portrays the most recently established dates for each current National Park (as opposed to authorization dates). Parks that have been dissolved and reestablished are dated accordingly.

thousands upon thousands of bison on the Great Plains. Gray wolves and grizzly bears were shot to near extinction. Ancient pre-Columbian artifacts were stolen from ancestral Indian homes as souvenirs. Miners lusted for gold and blasted into mountains (no matter how scenic) in search of precious minerals. Muir observed a young country that, though exploding with industry and achievement, was gouging itself with unbridled commercialism. We were quickly becoming victims of our own success, and Muir watched as we consumed our timeless and fragile wilderness spaces in the name of progress. The eccentric mountain man of Yosemite sounded the alarm, and his psalms of natural splendor resonated in the hearts of countless Americans. Because of early advocates such as John Muir, the National Park idea caught momentum in our nation's capitol. We needed a system to save us from desecrating ourselves irreparably.

The bones of the National Park Service began to assemble with the passing of the Antiquities Act in 1906. This ruling gave the President of the United States the ability to designate land as National Monuments. Theodore Roosevelt would sign this Antiquities Act into law, and he carried out his new capacity with relish. Many of our National Parks today originated as National Monuments, including the Grand Canyon, Zion, Acadia, and Carlsbad Caverns. Roosevelt's passion for conservation set the tone for future Americans as the National Parks idea came to fruition. By the end of his presidency, Theodore Roosevelt had created five National Parks, 18 National Monuments, and placed over 280,000 square miles of U.S. land under federal preservation. The Antiquities Act now allowed the federal government to begin collecting and protecting places of national and natural significance for the country's enjoyment.

What's the difference between a National Monument and a National Park? A National Monument usually contains one primary resource of cultural, scientific, or historic interest worth preserving. This could be a recreational area, a wilderness or forested area (such as Muir Woods or Glen Canyon), a military site (such as Pearl Harbor),

pre-Columbian ruins (at Chaco Canyon), or a patriotic site (Mount Rushmore or the Statue of Liberty). A National Park is composed of several resources and scenery (wildlife, forests, canyons, geysers, waterfalls) that are all federally protected from any private commercial use. National Monuments could be created without Congressional approval, so many early champions of the National Park idea went straight to the President with their requests to protect America's uniquely beautiful landscapes.

A magnetic, wildly successful businessman named Stephen Mather would become the first director of the National Park Service. With his enthusiastic

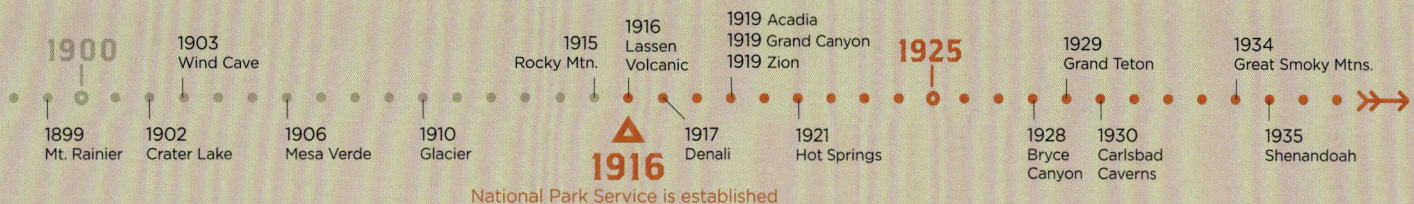

knack for promotion and love for National Parks, Mather would convince the country of the need for one department to oversee the country's greatest natural treasures. Accompanied by his young assistant Horace Albright, Mather convinced congressmen, railway barons, and average American families to first familiarize themselves, then cherish the National Parks. Touring the country, Mather and Albright brought the Parks into the public limelight, promoting tourism and encouraging more convenient lodging and travel options for Park guests. Their tireless efforts gave Ameri-

cans a sense of ownership and responsibility for these beautiful places. And, on August 25, 1916, President Woodrow Wilson would sign an Organic Act bringing the National Park Service into existence. Its fundamental purpose would be to "conserve the scenery and the natural and historic objects and the wild life" of the Parks, and "provide for the enjoyment of the same in such manner … as will leave them unimpaired for the enjoyment of future generations." The National Park System was born, and Stephen Mather would lead the way into a new age of natural preservation, building the first Park system of its kind on the planet.

With this new conservation administration in place, the National Parks Service now had the written power to protect America's precious landscapes from commercial abuse. Enforcing this authority, however, would prove to be an enormously difficult task. As World War I raged on, calls to support the troops with federally-protected lumber, minerals, and livestock grew louder and louder. Private logging companies eyed the forests of the Great Smoky Mountains and Mount Rainier. Ranchers pushed to raise sheep and cattle on the lush fields of Yosemite. But Mather and Albright withstood the attacks, and the National Park Service continued to add

more Parks to the fold from all over the country, wilderness wonders from Utah, Alaska, Maine, Colorado, North Carolina, and Tennessee. Roadways and railways were developed to bring more

> "We have fallen heirs to the most glorious heritage a people ever received, and each one must do his part if we wish to show that the nation is worthy of its good fortune."
> -*Theodore Roosevelt*

and more visitors into the Parks. When Stephen Mather passed away in 1930, an experienced Horace Albright championed Mather's legacy to preserve and promote America's National Park System in the midst of a financial crisis.

As America plunged into the Great Depression of the 1930s, President Franklin Delano Roosevelt did his part to keep the Park system alive too. He reorganized federal protection of National monuments, forests, war memorials, and preservations by placing them under National Park jurisdiction. This expansion

A 149-Year Timeline of the National Parks: 1872 - 2021

- 1938 Olympic
- 1940 Kings Canyon
- 1940 Isle Royale
- 1941 Mammoth Cave
- 1944 Big Bend
- 1947 Everglades
- **1950**
- 1956 Virgin Islands
- 1960 Haleakalā
- 1961 Hawai'i Volcanoes
- 1962 Petrified Forest
- 1964 Canyonlands
- 1968 North Cascades
- 1968 Redwood
- 1971 Arches
- 1971 Capitol Reef
- 1972 Guadalupe Mtn.
- **1975**
- 1975 Voyageurs
- 1978 Badlands
- 1978 Theodore Roosevelt

of power added incalculable significance to the National Park Service. They were now sole stewards of America's historical and natural treasures. A new Wildlife division was added, with a greater emphasis on protecting the Park's animal populations, spearheaded by young zoologist George Melendez Wright. When 1 out of every 4 American workers lost their jobs during the Depression, Roosevelt's New Deal programs put more than 3 million people back to work. Groups such as the Civilian Conservation Corps improved roads and campsites, built trails and visitor centers, and planted trees throughout the Park system.

Progress slowed as the nation entered World War II and many young men were sent overseas, but the Parks continued to

be a place of solace as the war raged on until 1945. With a renewed sense of patriotism and relief, Americans flooded back into the National Parks after the war. By 1955, annual visitor attendance topped 62 million. In response to this massive influx of tourism, National Parks Director Conrad Wirth proposed a 10-year, $787 million plan to dramatically develop the Parks' infrastructure and keep the Parks from being "loved to death." This proposal was named Mission 66 and would be completed by the Park System's 50th birthday in 1966.

The grooming and growing of Mission

66 paid off, and the Parks continued to add valuable landmarks and wilderness regions to its ever-widening fold. Secretary of the Interior Stewart Udall led the charge, urgently persuading Congress to create Parks such as North Cascades, Redwood, Canyonlands, and Guadalupe Mountains. He would also help establish protected waterways, seashores, and trailways such as the Appalachian Trail and the Pacific Crest Trail. Udall embodied the National Park's motto of preservation for future generations, stating: "Each generation has its own rendezvous with the land, for despite our fee titles and claims of ownership, we are all brief tenants on this planet. By choice, or by default, we will carve out a land legacy for our heirs."

Udall's efforts would take the National Park Service to new heights; over 165 million people would visit the 38 National Parks and 200 historic sites and monuments by 1972. In 1980, President Jimmy Carter would invoke the Antiquities Act in Alaska, controversially setting aside 47 million acres of pristine Alaskan wilderness. Seven enormous National Parks would be carved out of America's Last Frontier.

Since then, Congress has established 15 more National Parks, bringing the Park Service's total to 63 as of early 2021. Each place is a unique depiction of American freedom: a refuge for wildlife, geological phenomena, and vast woodlands. They are also our playgrounds, where people of all backgrounds, races, and creeds can enjoy communion with nature. The tension between tourism and preservation continues to affect how the Parks are managed. As our world changes, these areas of timeless beauty must be maintained to protect that healthy balance. The National Park Service has fought to keep the "legacy of the land" for future generations, and as Americans we should embrace our Park heritage. Go and enjoy these 63 wonders of nature. They were set aside just for you.

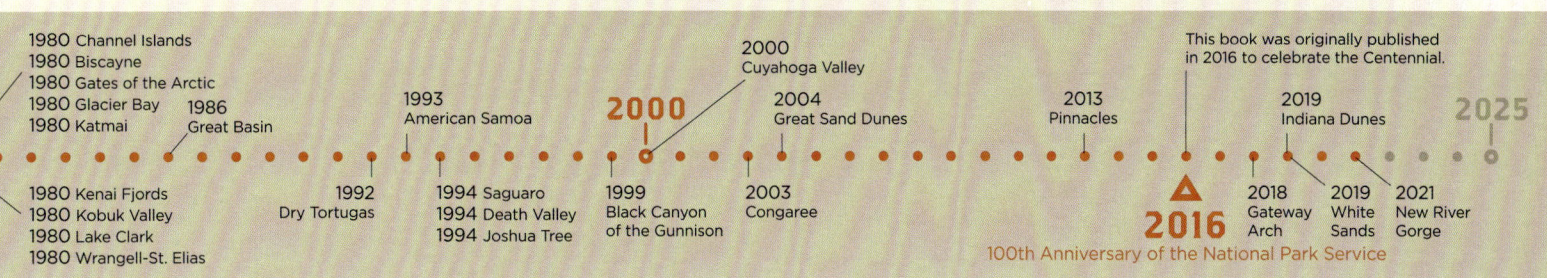

ACADIA

WITH ITS GRANITE clifftops and thick pine trees jutting right up to the craggy coastline, Acadia is a New England paradise. What once was a rich man's summer playground has become a quiet public refuge from the busy and crowded city life of the Northeast. Left in the wake of an earth-shaping icesheet, Acadia National Park (located on Mount Desert Island) features one of the largest mountains on the East Coast and America's only known fjord in the Atlantic Ocean. Acadia is not just a place of natural phenomena, however. It is also a living story of an American ideal: selflessness for the benefit of future generations. What was long a fertile hunting and gathering place of the native Abenaki ("People of the Dawn"), Mount Desert Island was spotted and claimed by French sea captain Samuel de Champlain in 1604. Champlain, seeing the

> "The sea, once it casts its spell, holds one in its net of wonder forever"
> -*Jacques Yves Cousteau*

bald tops of the granite cliffs, christened the place "l'Isle des Mont Déserts" or "the island of the bare mountains." The name stuck throughout the years, and Mount Desert Island (MDI) remained nothing more than a remote hiking and fishing destination until painters Thomas Cole and Frederic Church began capturing Acadia's wild beauty in the mid-19th century. Their powerful images of the Atlantic coastland enticed many of New England's upper-class families, seeking a secluded vacation spot not too far from home. Many of these wealthy elite purchased large tracts of land to build their summer getaways (or "cottages" as they called them). And yet from the aristocrats would arise a willingness to sacrifice their slices of paradise so that millions of future Americans could enjoy them as well. John D. Rockefeller Jr., son of the billionaire oil baron, spent his summers playing in the

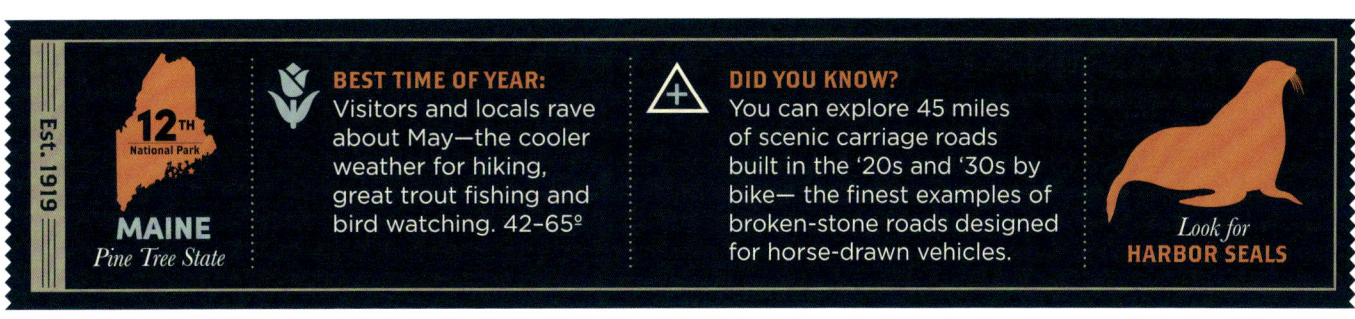

BEST TIME OF YEAR: Visitors and locals rave about May—the cooler weather for hiking, great trout fishing and bird watching. 42-65°

DID YOU KNOW? You can explore 45 miles of scenic carriage roads built in the '20s and '30s by bike— the finest examples of broken-stone roads designed for horse-drawn vehicles.

Look for **HARBOR SEALS**

Est. 1919 · 12TH National Park · MAINE *Pine Tree State*

<**ACADIA** 18" X 24" Poster art created in 2013 by Michael Korfhage & Joel Anderson

Photo by Boundless Blue

lush forests and sea-soaked puddles of Mount Desert Island. As an adult, he recognized the need to protect Acadia's pristine wilderness. He spent over $3.5 million to expand the Park, donating some 11,000 acres while also building 57 miles of broken-stone carriage roads for public use. These roads gave hikers, bikers, and horseback riders a uniquely Acadian experience without the interruption of motorized vehicles (still banned from the carriage roads to this day).

Another key individual to the creation of Acadia National Park was George Dorr. Dorr grew up in a family of wealthy "cottagers" who spent their summers on MDI. As he grew older, Dorr realized that his beloved Acadia, currently divided up into the hands of private owners like himself, would be safer from exploitation if given over to the fledgling National Park Service. With the idea of preserving this natural wonder for future generations, Dorr convinced scores of his wealthy neighbors to donate their vacation home property to create this patchwork Park. In 1919, Acadia National Park was officially recognized and George Dorr would spend the next 25 years as the Park's

Superintendent, earning a monthly wage of $1. During this time, Dorr blazed many of the hiking trails still enjoyed today. The tallest mountain in the Park was named after Dorr to honor his tireless efforts to conserve Maine's majestic coast. When George Dorr passed away in 1944, his ashes were scattered from a seaplane over MDI, the island he had devoted his life to protect. Park visitors now have a divine New England shoreline to savor thanks to people like Rockefeller and Dorr.

Early birds should grab a blanket with some coffee and hike (or drive) up **Cadillac Mountain** to watch the sun rise over the Atlantic. Take in the dramatic coastal vista from **Schoodic Point** via **Schoodic Head Trail.** Wander with your thoughts down the tranquil **carriage roads**. Face your fears and witness Maine's rugged coastline from an incomparable angle atop **Champlain Mountain** via **Precipice Trail**. Don't forget to check out the 19th-century lighthouse (and the view that inspired our Acadia poster) from **Bass Harbor Head.**

"Acadia National Park is truly a National treasure steeped in beauty for all seasons. Fall colors grace the mountain landscape, winter snows cap Cadillac Mountain, tireless waves crash the craggy shoreline, and a maze of carriage paths and trails provide ample opportunities to experience this natural wonder. All this coupled with a touch of 'down east hospitality' on Mt. Desert Island provide both a natural and cultural experience beyond compare."
— Roger Rudolph, Former Park Ranger at Acadia from 1979-1981
(total years of NPS service: 34)

ACADIA: PUFFIN 18" X 24" Poster art based on an oil painting created in 2017 by Kai Carpenter >

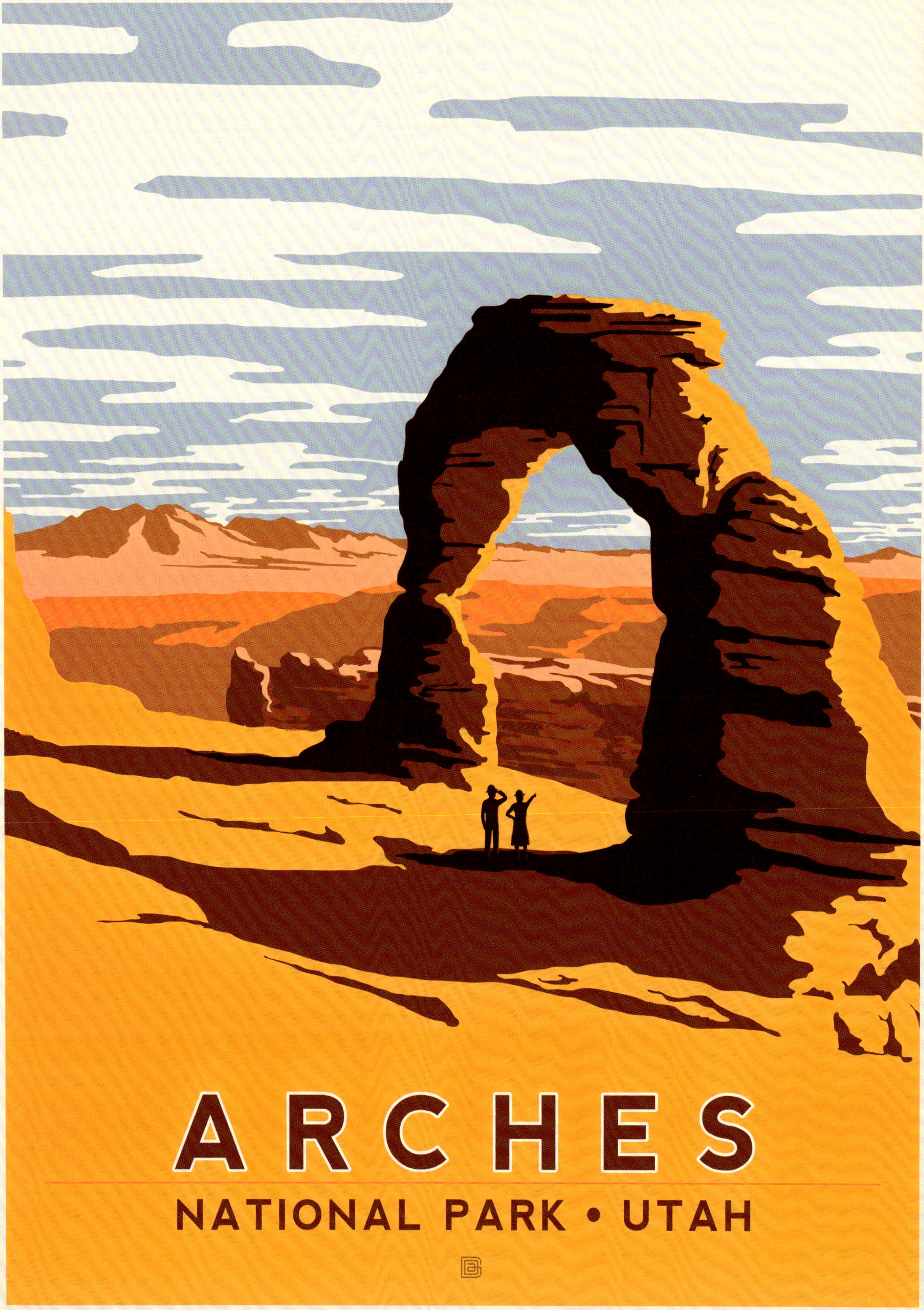

ARCHES

LOCATED IN THE HIGH desert country of the Colorado Plateau, Arches National Park is like wandering into a natural stone arch convention. Spires, balancing rocks, stone fins, and the namesake arches all abound here, congregating together underneath a sweeping Utah sky. No other place in the world offers such a high concentration of stone arch work: more than 2,000 of these natural formations populate the park. This region is home to a variety of celebrity arches, such as **Landscape Arch** (longest arch in North America, second longest in the world) and the rockstar of all natural arches, the **Delicate Arch** (as seen on many a Utahn license plate as well as our poster art). Thanks to diligent planning, many of these stone celebrities can be admired up-close. One main Park road delves deep into the heart of the region, introducing guests to new curved skylines at every turn. Whether you are an avid hiker or prefer seeing the sights by car, the main characters of this panoramic Park beckon to be explored.

Famed nature writer Edward Abbey was a Park Ranger at Arches in the 1950s. His lucid and lonesome accounts of wilderness life helped spark a movement towards greater environmental awareness, to protect vulnerable places like Arches from pollution and irresponsible use of natural resources. He understood humanity's desperate need for nature. From the silence of the Utah desert, Abbey penned *Desert Solitaire*, and with Muir-like cognizance he wrote: "Wilderness is not a luxury but a necessity of the human spirit, and as vital to our lives as water and good bread. A civilization which destroys what little remains of the wild, the spare, the original, is cutting itself off from its origins and betraying the principle of civilization itself."

Abbey recognized that few places on Earth contain more originality than Arches. And sadly, time is limited. As the years roll on, the creative force of the arches will also destroy them: erosion will one day bring its fragile

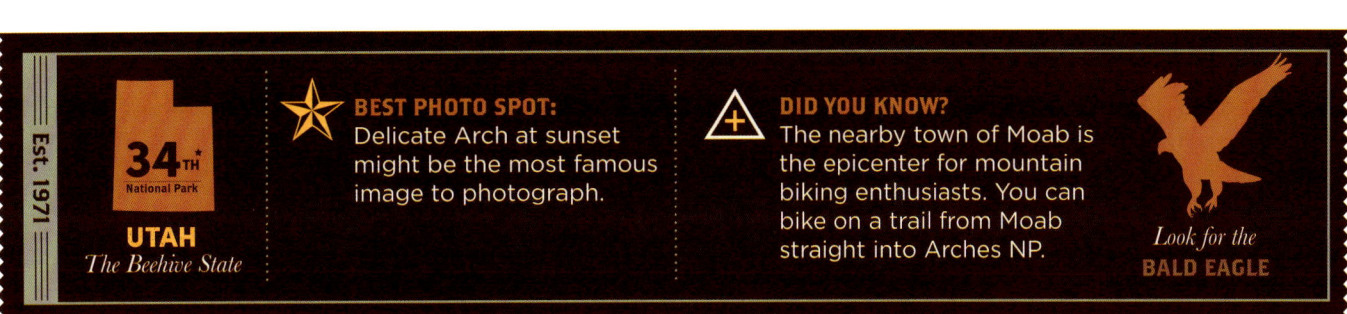

BEST PHOTO SPOT: Delicate Arch at sunset might be the most famous image to photograph.

DID YOU KNOW? The nearby town of Moab is the epicenter for mountain biking enthusiasts. You can bike on a trail from Moab straight into Arches NP.

Est. 1971 · 34TH National Park · **UTAH** *The Beehive State* · *Look for the* **BALD EAGLE**

<**ARCHES** 18" X 24" Poster art created in 2010 by Julian Baker & Joel Anderson

handiwork crumbling back to earth. No one knows for sure how much longer we will have these incredible feats of nature, so Park Rangers are especially adamant on visitor responsibility.

Carefully-laid trails lead to many of the popular formations throughout the Park, several of which are only a short hike from the main road. The payback for exploring Arches is great: one hike usually packs in several photogenic spots. Trails such as **Park Avenue** and **Devils Garden** are loaded with can't-miss moments. The illustrious (and especially fragile) Landscape Arch is accessible from the Devils Garden Trailhead. This Golden Gate of stone bridges is the longest arch in North America at 306 feet from base to base. The **Windows Section** features an easy climb to the awe-inspiring **Double Arch**, a natural phenomena where visitors may scramble up under its sinuous arms and experience the arches from directly beneath.

Perhaps the most iconic image in all of Utah is the Delicate Arch. A three-mile, strenuous hike will bring you to the foot of this sandstone beauty. Especially gorgeous at sundown, this arch lives up to the hype. Bring plenty of water and patience: the trail to Delicate

> *"The farther one gets into the wilderness, the greater is the attraction of its lonely freedom."*
> *-Theodore Roosevelt*

Arch is one of the Park's most popular. Make time for some memorable meandering through the stone maze at **Fiery Furnace**. This beloved section of Arches is a Ranger-led adventure and will put your all-terrain skills to the test.

"The location of the greatest concentration of stone arches and the largest free standing arch in the world is a wonderland of mystical rock formations that should be viewed not only in daylight but by moonlight."
— Walt Dabney, Former General Superintendent of Arches from 1991-1999 (total years of NPS service: 30)

ARCHES: DOUBLE ARCH 18" X 24" Poster art created in 2017 by Michael Korfhage & Joel Anderson ∧
ARCHES: ARCH OF TRIUMPH 18" X 24" Poster art based on an oil painting created in 2015 by Kai Carpenter >

BADLANDS

LIFE, DEATH, and the solemn beauty of decay are themes represented on the rugged plains of Badlands National Park. Just off I-90 in southwestern South Dakota, Badlands entertains over one million guests a year with stories of its tumultuous geologic past. The largest protected prairie in the National Park System is found here, as is one of the richest fossil beds of mammals on the planet. The treasures of the past are buried beneath a landscape so harsh and stubborn that Spanish explorers, French fur trappers, and Lakota Sioux Indians all called it the same name: "the bad lands". Despite the hostile environment, this northern prairie feeds and shelters over 250 species of wildlife within the Park. And thanks to the ancient forces of deposition and erosion, the Badlands continues to surprise and delight paleontologists, naturalists, and tourists with its natural treasures each day.

The air and earth at Badlands are thick with the past. What is now a canyon with spires of limestone and soft mudstone was once a shallow sea. The water teemed with fish, turtle, and squid. As geological forces changed the landscape of the American Great Plains, the water drained out of the area, leaving an abundant subtropical environment. Fossils of sabertooth tigers, giant lizards, mammoths, camels, and hornless rhinos reveal a once vibrant population.

Badlands National Park is divided into two sections. The North Unit is by far the most visited section of the Park, featuring the Badlands Wall, Loop Road, and nearly all of the maintained hiking routes. The South "Stronghold" Unit lies on the Pine Ridge Indian Reservation and is virtually undeveloped. However, few places on Earth are richer with mammal fossils than the banks of the **White River**, which runs through the South Unit.

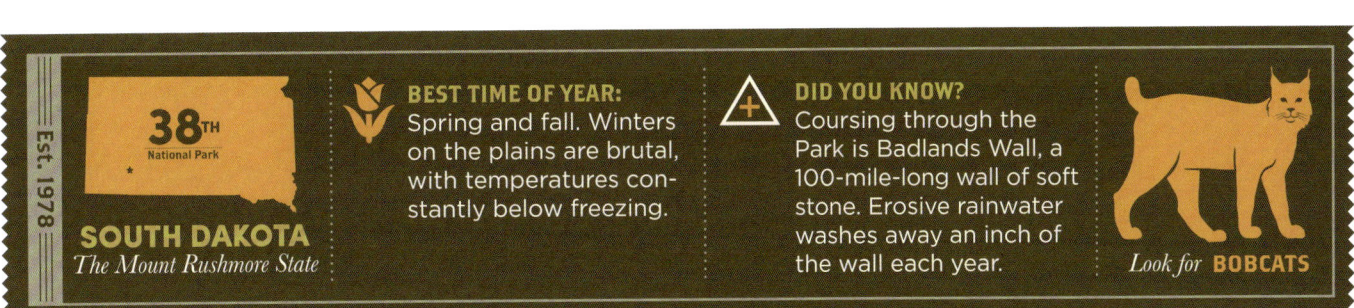

Est. 1978 · 38TH National Park · **SOUTH DAKOTA** *The Mount Rushmore State*

BEST TIME OF YEAR: Spring and fall. Winters on the plains are brutal, with temperatures constantly below freezing.

DID YOU KNOW? Coursing through the Park is Badlands Wall, a 100-mile-long wall of soft stone. Erosive rainwater washes away an inch of the wall each year.

Look for **BOBCATS**

<BADLANDS 18" X 24" Poster art created in 2013 by Michael Korfhage & Joel Anderson

Thousands of cars, motorcycles, and RVs travel the 42-mile **Badlands Loop Road** each year to experience the barren beauty of the **Badlands Wall**. Stop-offs and overlooks punctuate the scenic drive, beginning with the **Big Badlands Overlook** just within the Park's Northeast Entrance off Interstate 90. Pay a visit to the **Ben Reifel Visitor Center** to get oriented and to check with rangers for trail closures.

The semi-arid climate of the Badlands limits the range of tree and plant species. Only the hardiest plants can survive the extreme shifts in this region's weather, year-in year-out. Roasting heat during the summer brings drought and wildfire, torrential downpours create flash flooding, and the long winter entails frequent subzero temperatures and blizzards. The sole forest you'll find at Badlands National Park is one of grass: 244,000 acres of it, growing one to two feet high. Thus the views from atop the Badlands Wall are inhibited only by the streaked sedimentary cliffs that undulate across the prairie. Otherwise, the fields seem to roll on into the infinite.

A fantastic network of hiking trails are located in the first section of Badlands Loop Road. Gain a quick multidimensional perspective of the Badlands Wall and the surrounding prairies from short trails such as **Door**, **Window**, and

Notch (the latter includes an adventuresome clamber up a wooden ladder into the wall itself). Hoof it up the steep **Saddle Pass** trail for remarkable views of the White River Valley. **Castle Trail** is a five-mile connection hike across the Badland formations to the **Fossil Exhibit Trail**, a short, informative boardwalk highlighting the strange and fearsome creatures that once roamed this part of the Earth.

Erosive rainwater frequently reveals buried treasure hidden throughout Badlands National Park. It is not uncommon for visitors to stumble (sometimes literally) upon fossilized bones of a long-extinct animal. Be sure to never touch or remove any fossils you may find in the Park. Report your findings to a Park Ranger and experience the pleasure of contributing to the Badlands' rich tradition of prehistoric discoveries.

The Park also contains a thriving population of living creatures: bison, pronghorn, bighorn sheep, prairie dogs, black-footed ferrets, and swift fox all dwell in the Badland prairies. The best opportunities for animal spotting are along the unpaved **Sage Creek Rim Road**. Evening stops at the **Badland Wilderness Overlook** and **Roberts Prairie Dog Town** are excellent locations for a wildlife watching experience as well.

BADLANDS: LIVING THE GOOD LIFE 18" X 24" Poster art based on an oil painting created in 2017 by Kai Carpenter >

BIG BEND

DEEP in the sunbaked desert of southwestern Texas lies a limestone canyon carved out by the Rio Grande. The river serves as the boundary between the United States and Mexico, and the isolated wilderness surrounding its banks reinforces the idea of a no-man's land. Big Bend, named after the horseshoe curve of the river around the Park, is lightly visited throughout the year because of its remote location. But this is no mere desert: Big Bend National Park is home to over 5,000 species of plants, trees, and animals, including some 450 types of migratory birds. The highlands of the Chisos Mountains combined with the floodplains of the Rio Grande make for a diverse and highly enjoyable landscape when visiting in the cooler seasons of fall or spring. Climb up into these secluded Texas canyonlands to see how life blossoms in the desert.

For centuries, Big Bend's territory belonged to the Native Americans as an oasis in the Chihuahuan Desert. The Indians survived by farming and hunting the river valley's abundant wildlife. As the years went by, the Rio Grande would eventually soak the shoes of many different types of people, wading across with various ambitions. The conquest-driven Spanish crossed the river from Mexico in the late 16th century, searching for gold and new lands. Comanche Indians later blazed a trail through the Park at **Persimmon Gap** and across the river, traversing back and forth while raiding Mexican villages. Mexican and American settlers established homesteads and ranched on both sides of the Rio Grande. Dangerous outlaws, bandits, and Mexican revolutionaries fled through Big Bend's canyons to avoid arrest. The region was also a place of epiphany for rancher Everett Ewing Townsend in the early 1900s. The Texas mountains roused Townsend to political action, and he would spend the next two decades lobbying for a Park at Big Bend. Roosevelt's New Deal sent a CCC team to the Rio Grande in the 1930s, where the workers faced a daunting task: to bring infrastructure and access to a desolate area with no electricity and blazing summer heat. Despite the challenge, the men got it done and Townsend's dream was realized in 1944. Thanks to Townsend and the CCC, Big Bend National Park's remote grandeur is now accessible to visitors by river, road, and trail.

Few bodies of water provide such unparalleled access to a National Park like the Rio Grande does. From high up in the Rocky Mountains of Colorado, the Rio Grande wanders nearly 1,900 miles down to the Gulf of Mexico. Forming the southern border of the Park, the river flows like an artery through this barren region of Texas, providing life and relief from an intense desert sun. A float down

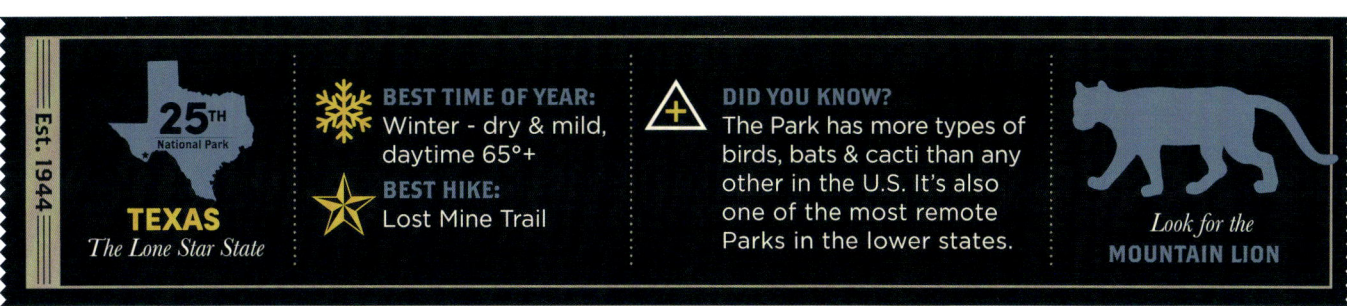

Est. 1944 — **25TH** National Park — **TEXAS** *The Lone Star State*

BEST TIME OF YEAR: Winter - dry & mild, daytime 65°+
BEST HIKE: Lost Mine Trail

DID YOU KNOW? The Park has more types of birds, bats & cacti than any other in the U.S. It's also one of the most remote Parks in the lower states.

Look for the **MOUNTAIN LION**

<BIG BEND 18" X 24" Poster art created in 2014 by Michael Korfhage & Joel Anderson

the Rio Grande in a canoe or kayak is one of the top ways to experience the immense splendor of the **Santa Elena Canyon**. Towering 1,400 feet over the river in the Park's western end, Santa Elena's staggering views from below make this section a favorite among paddlers.

The Santa Elena Canyon Trail serves as a gratifying endpoint for roadway travelers who take the 30-mile **Ross Maxwell Scenic Drive** down to the Rio Grande. **Mule Ear Peaks**, a peculiar set of rock pinnacles in the Chisos Mountains, is a popular spot to stretch your legs along the way as well.

The **Chisos Basin** is the starting point for many hiking adventures in the Chisos Mountains. Several popular hiking trails stem from this region, drawing the majority of Big Bend's traffic during the busy season. The tallest mountain in the Park (**Emory Peak**, 7,825 ft.) can be ascended here via a rugged 10.5-mile round-trip hike which includes a slippery scramble near the top. Those looking to enjoy Big Bend's gorgeous desert landscape without the exertion should visit **Window View Trail**, an easy 0.3-mile stroll along a paved pathway. Folks can sit on Park-provided benches and enjoy a sunset over the Chihuahuan Desert. **Lost Mine Trail** may perhaps be the most popular trail in the Park and, at 4.8 miles round-trip, makes for an ideal day hike. The Lost Mine offers a wide range of scenery, from highland forests of juniper and pine to the breathtaking vistas above Casa Grande, Pine Canyon, and the Sierra del Carmen in Mexico.

While rafters and hikers flock to the western end of the Park, birds and "birders" swarm the eastern end. The **Rio Grande Village** offers some of the best bird-watching opportunities in North America. **Boquillas Canyon** is a pleasant 1.4-mile hike that descends from a cliff overlooking the Rio Grande to the bird-friendly slopes of the river. The **Cottonwood campground** near Santa Elena Canyon and **Boot Canyon Trail** in Chisos Basin are prime birding locations as well. Big Bend's unique blend of mountain forests, lush river banks, and desert ecosystems create the perfect environment for migrating birds of all shapes and sizes. Colima Warblers, Peregrine Falcons, Lucifer Hummingbirds, Vermilion Flycatchers, Bewick's Wrens, and Mexican Mallards are all notable visitors of Big Bend National Park. Visit in the springtime for the most variety.

Stargazing is another must-do activity for visitors to Big Bend National Park. Thanks to the Park's distance from any major source of light pollution, the night skies here are impeccable. Spend the night in the backcountry (perhaps at **Balanced Rock** in the **Grapevine Hills**) and stare into an infinite tapestry of Texas starlight. Or wind down from a long day of desert hiking in a bathtub beneath the stars at **Hot Springs natural spa**. It's hard to imagine a place farther from the convenience of the city and closer to the heart of nature than Big Bend.

BIG BEND: DESERT PERCH 18" X 24" Poster art based on an oil painting created in 2017 by Kai Carpenter >

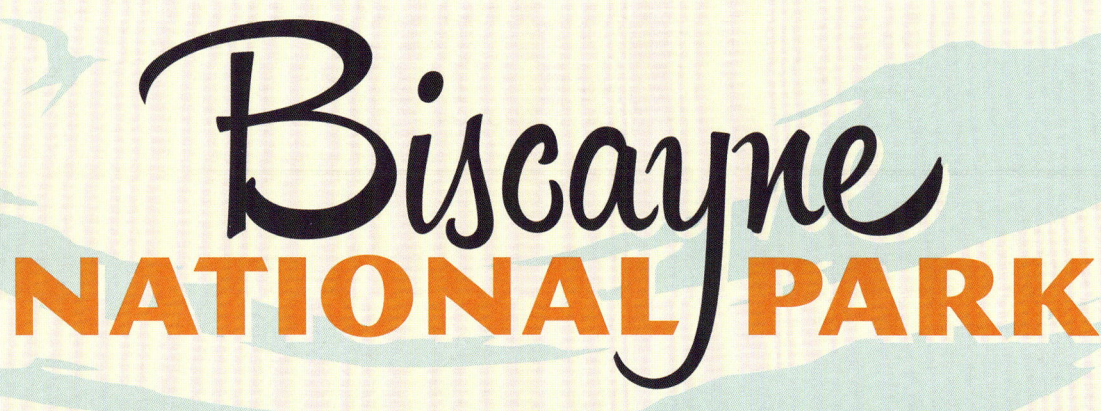

BISCAYNE

A FRAGILE South Florida metropolis lies just off the coast of Miami. Coral reefs replace skyscrapers, and schools of colorful fish replace the bustling city traffic. Only 30 miles away from Florida's largest city is one of the world's largest coral reef systems, home to multitudes of aquatic life. Forty islets bask in the Florida sunlight at Biscayne National Park. Land represents only a small fraction of the Park's protected area; if you want to truly experience Biscayne, you'll need to grab a paddle and a snorkel.

The islands of Biscayne, with their strategic location off the southeast corner of Florida, hosted pirates and mutineers for over three centuries. Spanish galleys, stuffed with gold from the New World, were prime targets for the Caribbean's fierce privateers. Memories of the area's violent past remain intact at **Caesar Creek**, named after the legendary African pirate Black Caesar, who supposedly buried 26 bars of solid gold on one of Biscayne's islands (yet to be found).

The Park was also home to a little-known African-American entrepreneur named Israel Jones. Jones moved to South Florida in 1892, taking a variety of odd jobs as a handyman and lime farmer. Jones learned quickly and was shrewd with his savings. In 1898, Jones purchased **Old Rhodes Key**. He immediately went to work, clearing the thick gumbo limbo trees and thorny underbrush, and uncovered a rich soil base perfect for growing key limes. The family lime business boomed, and Jones soon purchased neighboring **Totten Key** to grow pineapples with his two sons, Lancelot and Arthur. As Jones grew older, his sons acquired the fruit business. Lancelot was also an expert fisherman, and his services were sought after by patrons such as President Herbert Hoover and Richard Nixon. Lancelot was keenly aware of the unique natural splendor of his island home. As developers threatened to build roadways across the Keys, Jones eventually decided to sell his land to the National Park Service, who in turn allowed him to continue living in Biscayne and teach visitors about the ocean's wonders for the rest of his life.

As you walk along the coast, you may encounter a green sea turtle waddling down from the shoreline before gliding into the reef, where over 500 species of fish, crab, clam, and lobster (not to mention dolphin and manatee) reside. This National Park is a safe-haven for these creatures, whose home has been greatly disturbed by coastal development. Witness the wild coral on a **ranger-guided snorkeling trip**. Watch South Florida's top windsurfers work the waves at **Convoy Point**. Learn about the reef's infamous shipwreck history on the underwater **Maritime Heritage Trail** where divers can explore the wreckage of six unlucky vessels from as early as 1878. Or you can just spend a lazy day paddling in Lancelot's backyard at **Jones Lagoon**, grateful that a place like this still exists.

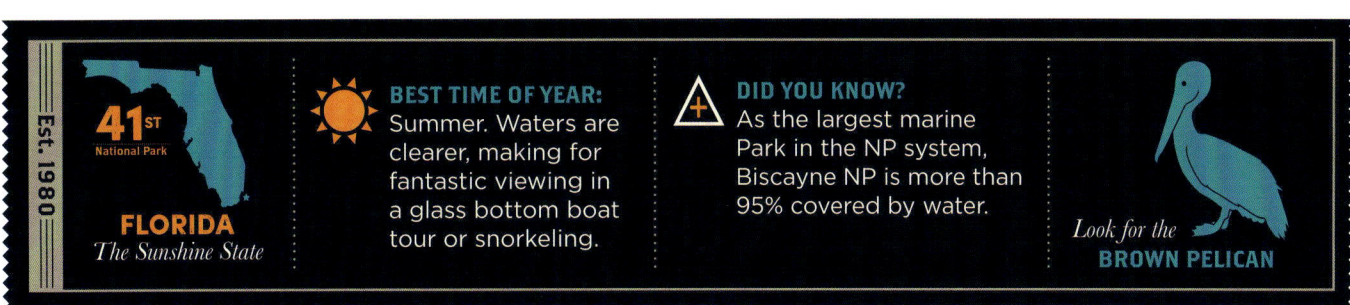

41ST National Park Est. 1980 — **FLORIDA** *The Sunshine State*

BEST TIME OF YEAR: Summer. Waters are clearer, making for fantastic viewing in a glass bottom boat tour or snorkeling.

DID YOU KNOW? As the largest marine Park in the NP system, Biscayne NP is more than 95% covered by water.

Look for the **BROWN PELICAN**

<BISCAYNE 18" X 24" Poster art created in 2013 by Michael Korfhage & Joel Anderson

BLACK CANYON OF THE GUNNISON

YOU STEP INTO THE darkest of canyons, the sun blacked out by the narrow granite cliffs. The charcoal stone looks even darker in the cold shadows. The rapids' deafening sound pounds into your skull and echoes off the walls. Your descent was treacherous to say the least; pebbles and scree had you sliding down the steep, 2,000-foot slope to the riverbank. You and one other person, an electrician and photographer named William F. Torrence, are convinced that an irrigation tunnel can be drilled into this gloomy canyon, providing desperately needed water to the nearby Uncompahgre Valley. Hundreds of people are pinning their hopes of survival in the valley on your success. As a seasoned irrigation engineer and adventurer, you are willing to risk life and limb to divert water out of this hellish ravine. Having studied the Gunnison River for months, you've noted the rapids' steady descent of 95 feet per mile. The water seethes in confined fury. You've learned from the fatal journeys of previous Gunnison River runners that this is no simple task. You've packed lightly. Instead of a boat, you and Torrence climb aboard an air mattress. Your supplies, notebooks, and Torrence's camera equipment are stowed in rubber

> *"Eventually, all things merge into one, and a river runs through it."*
> *-Norman Maclean*

bags. With a hefty kick, you push off the bank and enter the wildest ride of your life on the bone-chilling rapids through the Black Canyon of the Gunnison....

Abraham Lincoln Fellows and William F. Torrence were the first people in history to run the entirety of the Black Canyon, traveling a sopping 33 miles in 9 days. The men hiked, bouldered, swam, and rafted down the river on an air mattress. Though an equally miserable and hair-raising experience, their 1901 journey proved that an irrigation tunnel could be built. A 6 mile, 11 by 12-foot diversion tunnel was completed in 1909 thanks to the fearless efforts of these two men. The Gunnison River is now tamer than ever due to 3 dams built upstream from the National Park. And yet the rapids are still formidable, challenging even the most experienced rafters and kayakers to navigate their frothy fury.

For those who prefer to stay dry, Black Canyon of the Gunnison National Park offers plenty of opportunities to hike or drive along the canyon's north and south rims. The southern rim is more popular (and accessible) for tourists, and you will find plenty of pull-offs along the **South Rim Road** to stretch your legs and stare down into the chasm, 2,250 feet deep. **Painted Wall View** is one favorite stop as the dark granite wall face is streaked with wispy strips of pink and white crystal. An 80-mile drive will bring you to the far less visited northern rim. Explore the cliff forests along **North Vista Trail** for a concealed communion with Colorado wilderness. There are even a few trails into the canyon itself, though they are incredibly strenuous. Apply for a permit to experience the heart-pounding descent like Fellows and Torrence from the **Red Rock Canyon Route** into the depths of the Black Canyon.

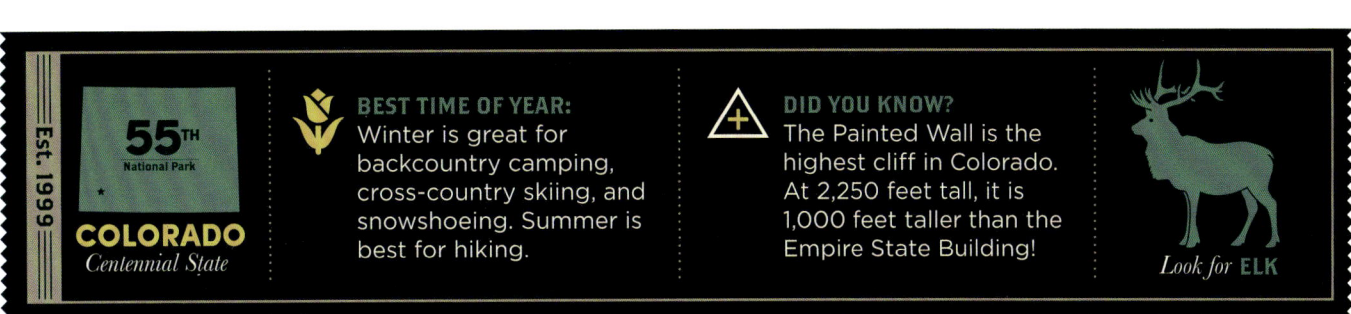

BEST TIME OF YEAR: Winter is great for backcountry camping, cross-country skiing, and snowshoeing. Summer is best for hiking.

DID YOU KNOW? The Painted Wall is the highest cliff in Colorado. At 2,250 feet tall, it is 1,000 feet taller than the Empire State Building!

Est. 1999 — 55TH National Park — COLORADO *Centennial State* — *Look for* ELK

<BLACK CANYON OF THE GUNNISON 18" X 24" Poster art created in 2019 by Aaron Johnson & Joel Anderson

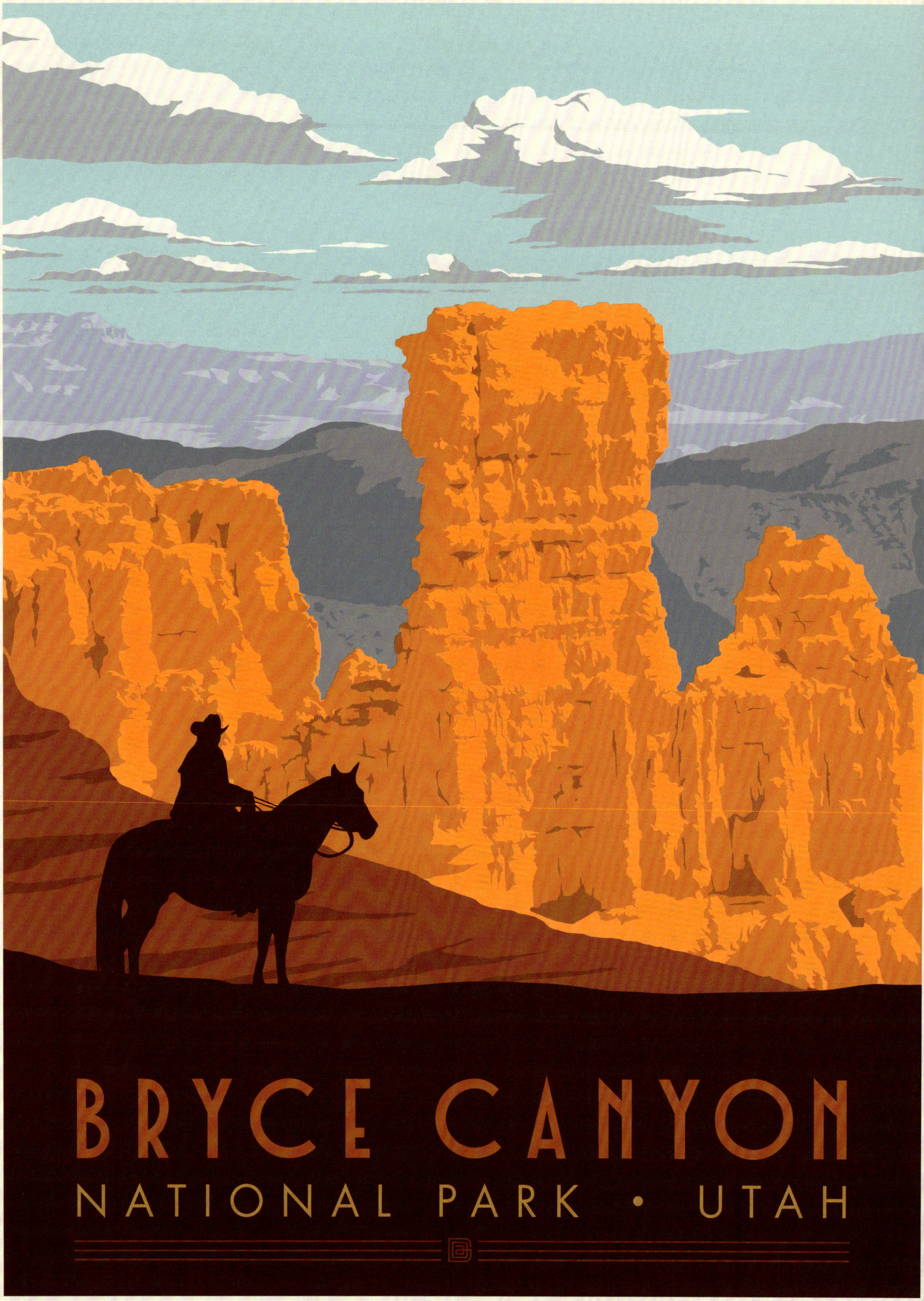

BRYCE CANYON

Photo by Joel Anderson

STEPPING out of a dry pinewood forest, you find yourself on a gusty alien planet. A congregation of castles bake red in the sun, their pointed turret heads all turned in your direction. You feel like an intruder, but you cannot help wandering further into their presence. A single, slippery pathway switchbacks down into the limestone unknown like a winding desert snake. Dust cakes your shoes as you try not to make too much noise, slipping and sliding down the crushed-pottery-like road. You are being watched. You glance up at the spindly spire faces that adorn the castle escarpments. Their ruddy rock eyes stare blankly back at you. Cold. Mute. Like the frost that so incessantly whittles away their stone bodies each night. The solemn wind courses through their conical colonies. You step out of the shadows and into their world.

Bryce Canyon National Park is home to the hoodoos. Piled like drips of wet beach sand, these hobgoblins invite you to explore their fairyland, crafted by the impartial hands of water, wind, and time. The hoodoos gather like a silent congregation, standing just wide enough apart for you to climb between their knobby knees. Wander along the serpentine **Navajo Trail** for an intimate glimpse of this multi-lithic wonderworld. Each twist and turn in **Queen's Garden** brings hikers into the presence of another gangling giant, painted rusty red in the sun. Secret passageways burrow into the castle walls. Bands of wide-eyed travelers on horseback gaze into the valley. Of all National Parks, this one stretches the limits of imagination, blending geology with myth, concrete with the surreal.

A farmer named Ebenezer Bryce first wandered into this soundless city in 1875. Pursuing wayward livestock through the area, he exclaimed that this was "one hell of a place to lose a cow." The Mormon Church had sent Bryce into this remote region of southwestern Utah, and he took it upon himself to live peacefully amongst the hoodoos. He built a cabin for his family just below

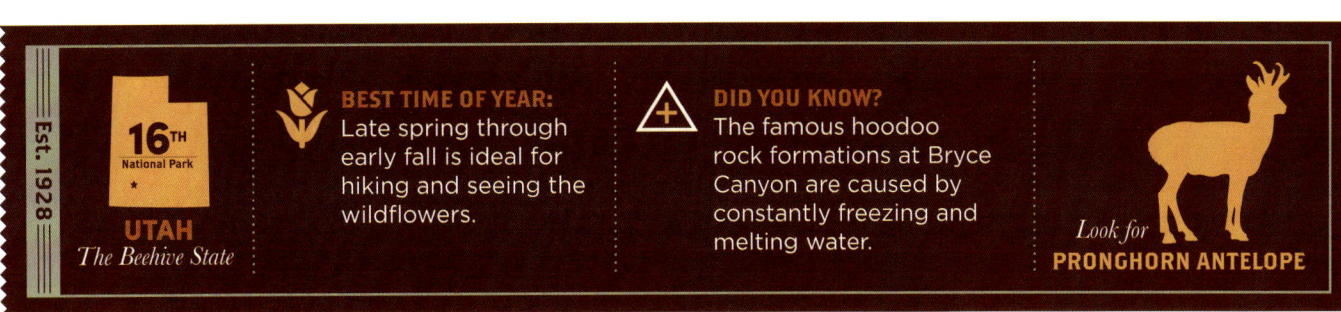

Est. 1928 | 16TH National Park | **UTAH** *The Beehive State*

BEST TIME OF YEAR: Late spring through early fall is ideal for hiking and seeing the wildflowers.

DID YOU KNOW? The famous hoodoo rock formations at Bryce Canyon are caused by constantly freezing and melting water.

Look for **PRONGHORN ANTELOPE**

<BRYCE CANYON 18" X 24" Poster art created in 2013 by Michael Korfhage & Joel Anderson

the massive hoodoo amphitheater, a gathering place for thousands of red and cream turrets. The farmer and his family would wake each morning in the presence of this stoic congregation and attempt to scrape out a living. Life among the rocks was hard and winters were harder for the Bryce family, but they persisted to till the soil and graze their livestock on the scrubby dirt mounds. Locals began calling the area "Bryce's Canyon." The Bryce family eventually moved on to a more pliant landscape, and the secret gatherings of the stone bogies carried on undisturbed.

Decades later, murmurs of the mythic Bryce Canyon reached the ears of Stephen Mather and the National Park Service. Alongside his colleague and friend Horace Albright, Mather entered the vast stronghold of the hoodoo nation in 1918. They sat upon the sloping hillside at **Inspiration Point** and pondered for hours the strange beauty of this eccentric community. The spires greeted them without a word as the whistling wind punctured the deep silence. "Marvelous; exquisite; nothing like it anywhere," Mather laughed with glee. The two friends agreed this unearthly landscape was worth savoring and made a point to share it with the outside world. In 1928, Congress established Bryce Canyon National Park, a protected playground for Americans of all ages. Work crews built roadways and blazed trails into the minaret metropolis during the Great Depression, and today the limestone kingdom of the hoodoos hosts millions of awe-struck visitors each year.

"It was wonderful to work at Bryce Canyon, where my father started his NPS career and my parents 1934 honeymoon cabin is still used as employee housing. Even now when asked to describe Bryce Canyon and its unique hoodoos, I share the feelings of a 1920's visitor to Zion, Grand Canyon and Bryce Canyon National Parks. He wrote of his feelings of majesty and wonder looking upward in Zion and feeling that he was looking down into the red infernos of hell as he stood on the Grand's rim. He acknowledged however that the enchanting and delicate beauty of Bryce Canyon could not be described. Like him, I note: there are not words, you must go and see for yourself."
— Fred J. Fagergren, Superintendent of Bryce from 1991 – 2002 (total years of NPS service: 34)

BRYCE CANYON: STAR GAZING 18" X 24" Poster art created in 2020 by Derek Anderson & Joel Anderson ʌ
BRYCE CANYON: HOODOO HEAVEN 18" X 24" Poster art based on an oil painting created in 2015 by Kai Carpenter >

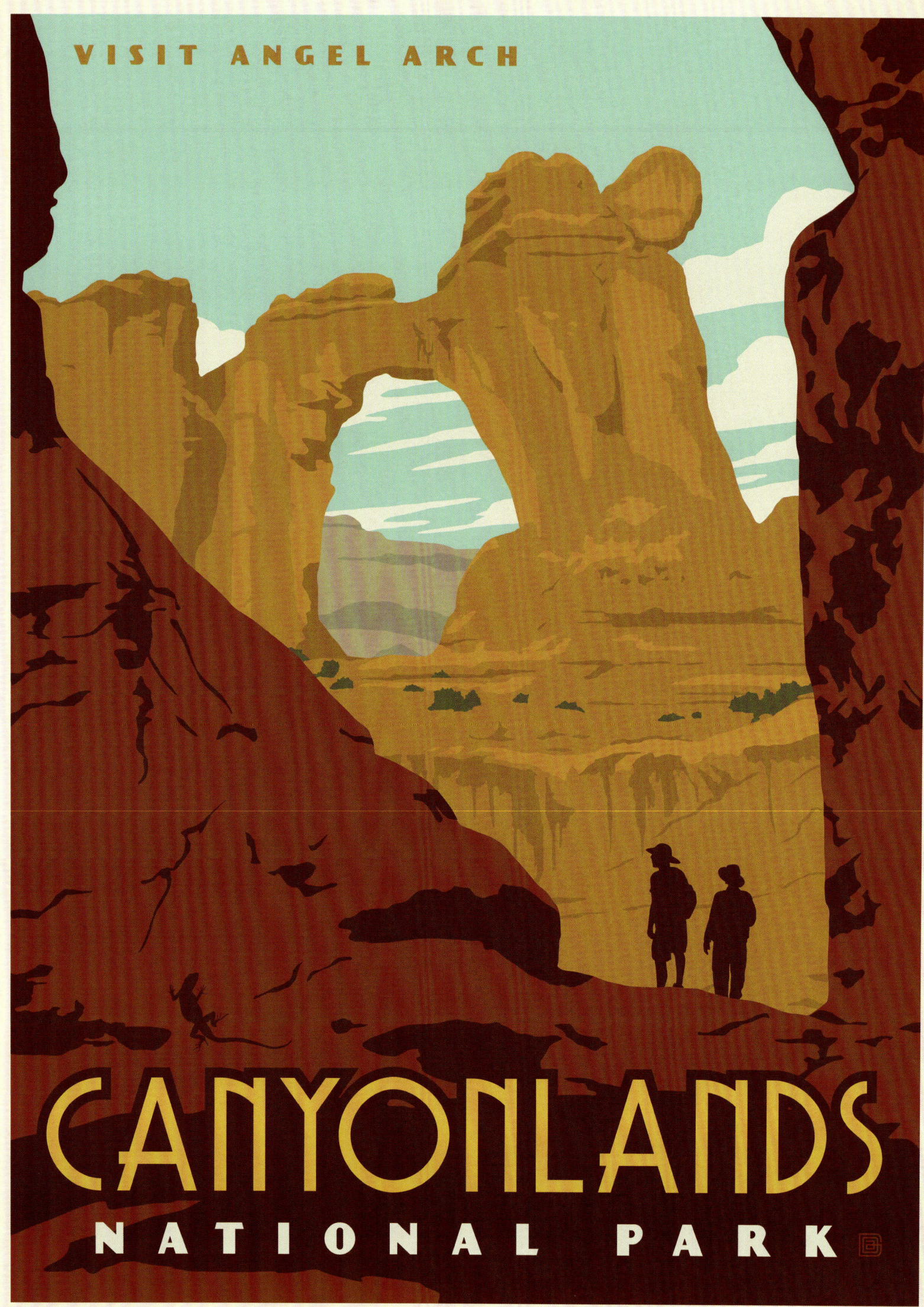

CANYONLANDS

DESERT and water intertwine to create art upon the southeastern Utah canvas of Canyonlands National Park. Two roaring rivers have slowly devoured the landscape for millennia, carving and carrying away ancient sediment from the many-layered canyon walls. The **Colorado** and **Green Rivers** collide in the center of this Park, dividing the region into three separate areas: **Island in the Sky, Needles,** and the **Maze District**. The Park's variety of pinnacles, mesas, arches, and alien-like fins and spires is immense and often overlooked; though Canyonlands is Utah's largest National Park, it is also the least visited.

Canyonlands is a prime example of rocky Utahn backcountry. Life is sparse, difficult, persistent. Junipers grip the earth with their gnarled roots, squeezing out an existence on a few drops of water. Lizards bake in the sun as the shadows of massive buttes stretch out across the sandstone valley. It is rich in its barrenness. Prehistoric natives left a masterpiece of petroglyph artwork upon the walls at **Horseshoe Canyon**. This region has been explored by miners, missionaries, cowboys, Indians, geologists: people all searching for life among the rocks.

Weapons were sought out here, too. During the Cold War, government-hired prospectors scoured Canyonlands for uranium. Miles and miles of roadways were built for discovering and transporting the ore. Little uranium was found, however, and the initial ravaging for ammo in fact brought about the Park's permanent protection. Bates Wilson, the then-superintendent of Arches National Monument, advocated for preservation of Canyonlands and led backcountry jeep tours to prove his point. A vacationing Secretary of the Interior Stewart Udall took one of these tours and brought tales of Utah's beauty back to Washington. President Lyndon B. Johnson would sign Canyonlands officially into the National Park fold in 1964.

Rivers forged a path through the high desert of Utah, and Canyonlands now features two outstanding waterways from which you can experience this National Park. Boat access to both the Green and Colorado Rivers is available outside of the Park, and local outfitters offer all you'll need for a quiet day on the water. Things get dicey past the confluence, where the combined rivers blast through **Cataract Canyon,** a 14-mile stretch of white water rapids that will challenge and reward rafters with the adventure of a lifetime.

Island in the Sky, a 43-square mile mesa "island", floats over 1,000 feet above the surrounding landscape. Located only

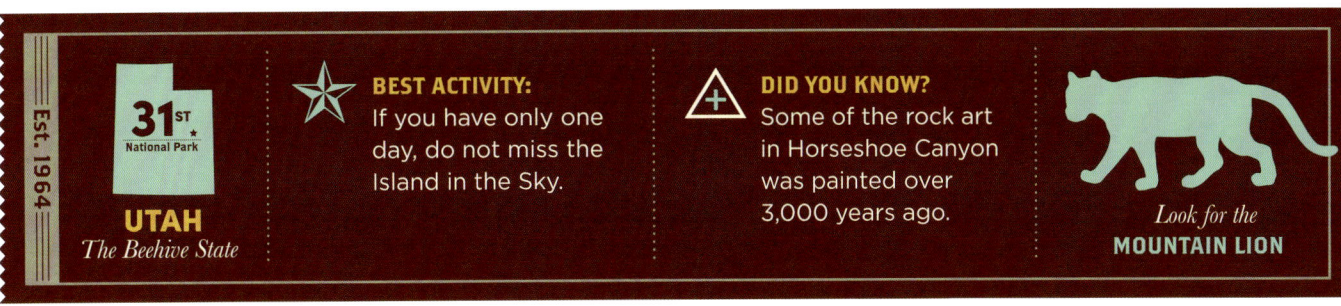

<CANYONLANDS 18" X 24" Poster art created in 2014 by Michael Korfhage & Joel Anderson

35 miles from Moab, it is the easiest section of the Park to access and the most visited. Overlooks and short hikes from a developed roadway abound here. **Mesa Arch** tops the list as the most photographed rock formation in Canyonlands as the ruddy colors of the stone bridge glow bright red and orange in the morning sunlight. An easy one-mile hike will bring you to the edge of an ocean of stone at **Grand View Point. White Rim Trail** is a favorite among hardy mountain bikers and 4WD enthusiasts. A 100-mile dirt road built by uranium prospectors, White Rim begins at the top of the mesa and winds all the way down in an exhilarating rush to the canyon floor. It is a three-to-four day trek with campsites available as rest stops along the way.

South of the Colorado and Green River confluence lies the Needles district. The Needles' skyline is populated by thousands of sandstone fingers painted red, orange, and pink. This region invites those with a little more time on their hands to explore the trails less traveled, to slide into slot canyons, and encounter sublime solitude in the Utah desert. **Chesler Park / Joint Trail Loop** is a thought-provoking 11-mile journey through the lustrous terrain of Canyon-

lands. Cowboys and Native Americans once occupied this region and the remains of their separate civilizations can be viewed together at **Cave Springs** (look for the prehistoric petroglyphs etched into the cave walls). Backpackers lodging at the **Squaw Flat Campground** can enjoy a rugged pilgrimage to the canyon floor for a neck-craning encounter with **Druid Arch.**

Backpacking in the Maze District is only for the bold and well-prepared. There are no designated hiking trails, and as the name suggests, it is easy to get lost. Jeeps and high clearance vehicles clamber up **Flint Trail** for an intense off-road expedition to secluded, farflung campsites such as **The Dollhouse** and **Maze Overlook.** Permits are required for overnight backpacking, and drivers must carry a topographical map and be ready for wretched road conditions. Thirty-two miles of gravel roads and a steep seven-mile round-trip hike will bring you to a secret art museum west of the Maze district. The **Horseshoe Canyon Unit** contains one of the most significant collections of Native American rock art in North America. The canyon walls form a ruddy canvas for **The Great Gallery,** a dazzling display of ghostly figures and mysterious symbols painted long ago.

CANYONLANDS: WONDERLAND 18" X 24" Poster art based on an oil painting created in 2017 by Kai Carpenter >

CAPITOL REEF

A PANOPLY of crafted stone beauty awaits you at Capitol Reef National Park. Best to leave your snorkel at home for this Park; Utah's Capitol Reef is actually named after a unique geological phenomenon called **the Waterpocket Fold**. This dramatic spine of tilted rock traverses the length of the Park from north to south. Geologists call this structure a monocline, a "wrinkle" in the Earth's crust pocketed with water-catching basins. Shifting tectonic plates, water, and time would create the rolling "waves" of the reef, as well as a vast portfolio of sculpted domes, cliffs, canyons, arches, and monoliths. Though no doubt an impressive collection, this lengthy museum of eroded art gave early Mormon pioneers and railway planners a colossal headache, preventing passage much like an ocean reef would to a ship. Though this area would always remain remote, appreciation would someday replace agitation, and life would be cultivated beneath the winding shadows of Capitol Reef.

The **Fremont River** flows across the north end of the reef, slipping a lush lifeline into this thirsty wilderness. For centuries, the small river valley would serve as a desert oasis, a safe haven for Native Americans and weary explorers, seeking a route across the Utah desert. By the 1800s, Mormons had settled in the valley, building villages, fertilizing the fields, and planting an orchard of fruit trees along the river banks. One enthusiastic Mormon bishop named Ephraim Pectol convinced his brother-in-law that their slice of arid paradise would make a prime tourist destination. In 1921, they began promoting the region as Wayne Wonderland, named after their nearby home in Wayne County. Pectol was elected to the state legislature a few years later and immediately reached out to President Franklin D. Roosevelt about commissioning Wayne Wonderland National Monument. Though stipulating a name change, Roosevelt agreed and set aside 37,711 acres of Utah canyonlands for the creation of Capitol Reef National Monument. Under the (unpaid) care of first custodian Charles Kelley, the Park would grow and withstand a ravaging for uranium during the Cold War. A Park-friendly government program called Mission 66 brought substantial development and paved roadways to this remote area, dramatically increasing tourism. In 1971, Congress passed a bill to protect the entirety of the Waterpocket Fold along with the surrounding territory. President Nixon signed it, and Capitol Reef National Park was born on December 18, 1971.

Over 3,000 fruit trees still fill the fragrant orchard campground of **Fruita**, and Park guests may pick a snack there before heading into the canyons. Trails lace the northern regions of the Waterpocket Fold, allowing hikers to witness a wide variety of the Reef's gloriously eroded stonework. Take in panoramic views of the wavy gorge from **Goosenecks** and **Sunset Point**. Grab a few apricots before setting out on a 3.5-mile hike to hidden **Cohab Canyon**. Follow the scenic trail to a lofty natural archway at **Hickman Bridge** and continue on up the **Rim Overlook Trail**. Bring plenty of water and time when exploring this vast landscape of sloping stone. Those who enter with patience and preparedness will be greatly rewarded.

<CAPITOL REEF: CATHEDRAL VALLEY 18" X 24" Poster art created in 2017 by Michael Korfhage & Joel Anderson

CARLSBAD CAVERNS

A SHRIEKING swarm of bats rushes out into the New Mexican twilight. Beneath the Chihuahuan Desert is a vast series of chambers, summer home to over 400,000 Brazilian free-tailed bats as well as some of the most ethereal stone architecture you will ever encounter. Dripping from the limestone ceiling are ghoulish cave features: sharp stalactite and stalagmite fingers reach out to touch one another, while swirling helictites and gypsum chandeliers look like they could reach down and wrap their wraith-white arms around you. Carlsbad Caverns National Park hosts a hive of cave systems beneath the Guadalupe Mountains. Sulfuric acid and mineral-bearing rainwater honeycombed these tunnels into the Earth, and the startling cave formations give testament to this wondrous work of persistence. The overarching theme of this Park was stated succinctly when the Department of the Interior sent photographer Robert Holley to investigate. Holley was brought to his knees by the "deep conflicting emotions of fear and awe" that emanated from the caves like summer bat clouds pouring out into the desert night.

Bats lured the first known explorers into Carlsbad. Intrigued by their nightly feeding frenzies, a young Jim White climbed down into their subterranean home in the late 1890s. He took a liking to their dank and strange living quarters, delving deeper into Carlsbad's depths by candlelight. He familiarized himself with the bats' home, naming the eerie landmarks and chambers. He began to seek out customers for spelunking trips, with little success. Of the few brave souls that showed interest in Jim's caving adventure, one would be invaluable to the Park's future. Photographer Ray V. Davis would enter Carlsbad Caverns in 1915 and capture the ghastly underworld on film. The New York Times published his photographs in 1923, producing a surge in tourism to see this supernatural landscape. President Calvin Coolidge set the cave aside as a National Monument in 1928, and Congress would declare Carlsbad Caverns a National Park two years later.

Carlsbad Caverns may still host an enormous bat population, but that shouldn't scare you away from exploring their illustrious abode. The bats leave guests alone, sleeping during the day and feasting on tasty mosquitos and other flying pests by night. Self-guided and

> "The Grand Canyon with a roof on it."
> *-Will Rogers*

ranger-led trails are both available at Carlsbad. Peer into the **Bat Cave** and sneak past **Witch's Finger** on the **Natural Entrance Tour.** See the dramatic candelabras and limestone draperies of **Queen's Chamber** on the **King's Palace Tour.** Enter a world untouched by the sun in the mystic tunnels of Carlsbad Caverns National Park.

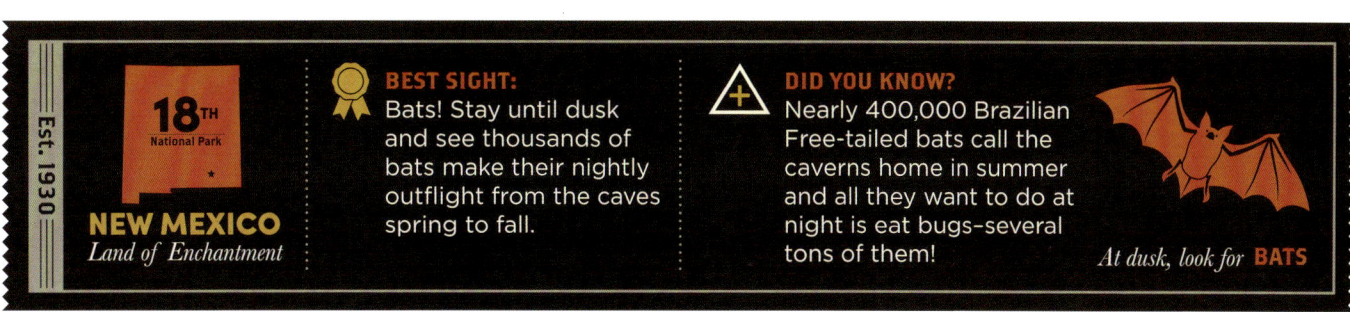

BEST SIGHT: Bats! Stay until dusk and see thousands of bats make their nightly outflight from the caves spring to fall.

DID YOU KNOW? Nearly 400,000 Brazilian Free-tailed bats call the caverns home in summer and all they want to do at night is eat bugs-several tons of them!

Est. 1930 · 18TH National Park · NEW MEXICO *Land of Enchantment* · *At dusk, look for* **BATS**

<CARLSBAD CAVERNS 18" X 24" Poster art created in 2013 by Michael Korfhage & Joel Anderson

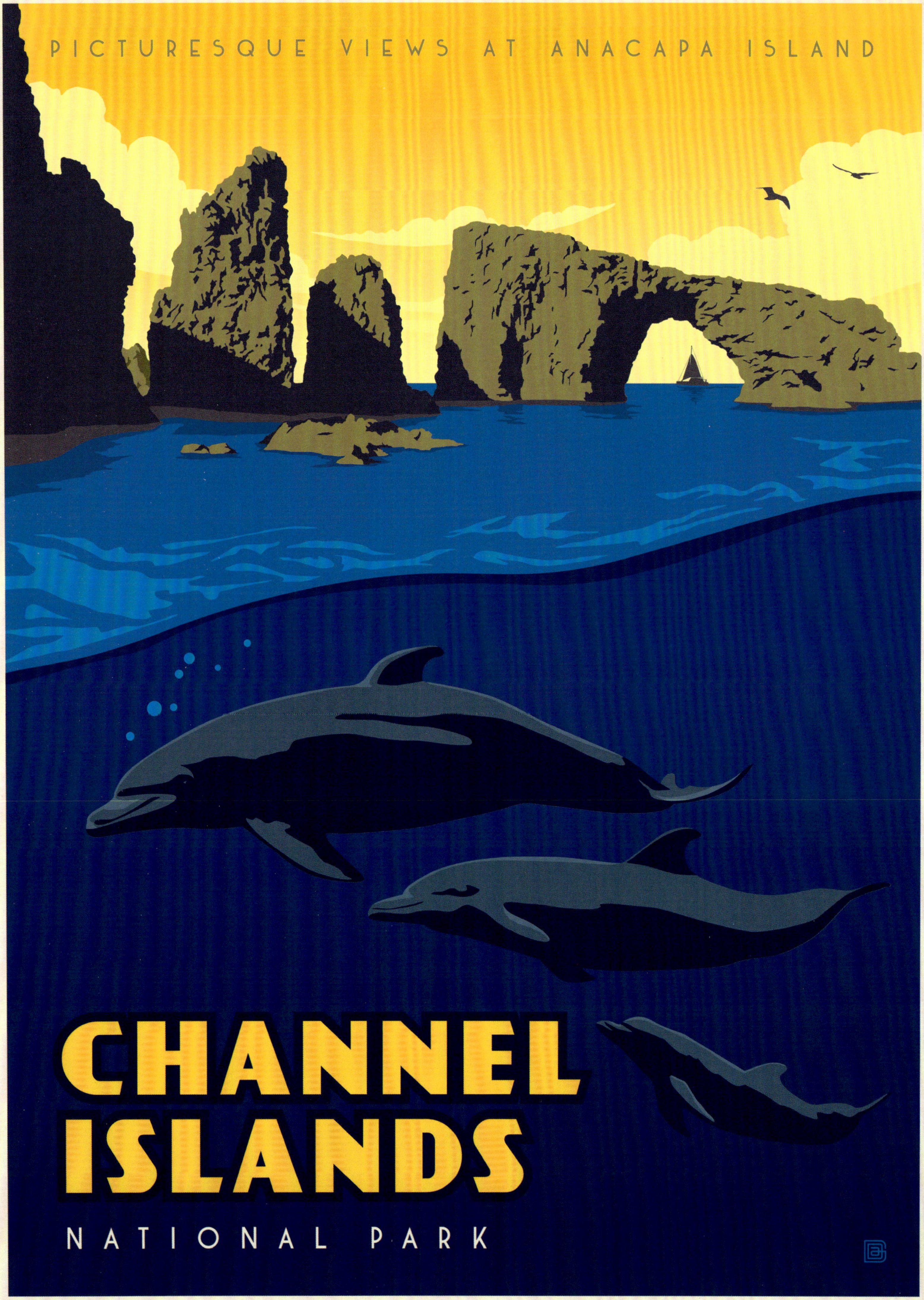

CHANNEL ISLANDS

THE PACIFIC OCEAN dashes against a chain of rocky isles off the coast of Southern California. It's hard to believe there's still undeveloped land so close to one of our nation's largest cities. Flocks of brown pelicans, seagulls, and puffins glide on the salty gales to their cliff-side nests. Pods of dolphin chase after anchovies as blue whales trundle through underwater forests of sea kelp. Boisterous colonies of sea lions bicker and bark on the pebbled beaches. Bright yellow kayaks dot the rugged coasts, wandering in and out of the islands' many sea caves. This is Channel Islands National Park, an island refuge sanctified from the smog of Los Angeles. Often referred to as the "Galapagos of the North," this wilderness archipelago presents a living snapshot of Southern California before modern-day America moved in.

The Chumash lived on the Channel Islands for thousands of years, sailing back and forth from present-day L.A. in redwood canoes while hunting for seals. Their quiet way of life was forever altered when Spanish explorers discovered their island villages in the mid-16th century. Though friendly trade partners at first, the Europeans soon over-hunted and exploited the islands' natural resources, and their foreign diseases decimated the Chumash. Mexico later claimed the islands as a prison and sheep ranch before the U.S. military took possession in the early 1900s. Today, Channel Islands National Park and Marine Sanctuary still protects the original wildlife of these coastal islets and the wonders that live below the surface of the azure Pacific.

Your island adventure begins on the mainland at **Ventura Harbor's visitor center**. Here, Park Rangers have developed a unique interactive program to teach visitors about the Channel Islands' exquisite sealife. Donning microphone-equipped SCUBA gear and handheld cameras, Rangers dive into the Park's thick kelp forests off the coast of nearby **Anacapa Island**. Standing dry in the visitor center, Park guests have the opportunity to see what the divers see and ask questions about the aquatic ecosystems on-screen. Waiting in the harbor is a fleet of ferry boats, ready to carry passengers across the rough coastal channel to the Park's five islands: Anacapa, **Santa Cruz, Santa Rosa, San Miguel**, and **Santa Barbara**. Visitors must bring their own food and water before making the trek out. The remoteness of these islands generates its own special appeal; out here you feel thousands of miles away from any trace of urban sprawl. Watch the rowdy mob of sea lions congregate at **Point Bennett** on San Miguel. Climb up to a dramatic 150-foot cliff above the roaring Pacific at **Inspiration Point** on Anacapa or paddle into a chilly sea cave at **Scorpion Beach** on Santa Cruz Island. Take a trip to these rustic Californian islands and discover a world where the ocean still reigns supreme.

40TH National Park · Est. 1980 · **CALIFORNIA** *The Golden State*

BEST TIME OF YEAR: Summer is the best time for diving, snorkeling, swimming, kayaking, and sailing.

DID YOU KNOW? Channel Islands National Park consists of 249,354 acres, half of which are under the ocean.

Look for the **ISLAND FOX**

<CHANNEL ISLANDS 18" X 24" Poster art created in 2015 by Michael Korfhage & Joel Anderson

CONGAREE

OLD GROWTH forest thrives on the banks of the Congaree River. Over 75 species of trees vie for the sun's rays in the lofty canopy. Loblolly pines, some as tall as skyscrapers, mingle with the oak, bald cypress, water tupelo, and holly populations. Ferns and fungi coat the lush forest floor where the bizarre "knees" of cypress roots pop out of the ground. Gauzy veils of Spanish moss and sweltering humidity remind you you're in the American South. Congaree is a land outside of time, where birds, fish, insects, and reptiles revel on the floodplain. Humans are invited to observe this teeming ecosystem from the **Boardwalk Trail**, a 2-mile elevated pathway coursing into the watery woodlands of Congaree National Park.

The Congaree region was named after the Congaree tribe native to South Carolina some 500 years ago. Hunting and fishing along the lowlands, the Congaree may well be the last successful human residents to have ever lived here. Most European settlers were repelled by the mosquito-thick floodplain, but their brief visits still corrupted the natives: smallpox wiped out the tribe in the late 1600s. After the Indians passed away, settlers had great difficulties planting and grazing their cattle along the river. With massive flooding up to 10 times each year, the soil was always soggy and often rinsed away. Loggers thought they might fare better and entered the dense woodlands with axes and saws. They too would be disappointed as access roads were next to impossible to build and heavy logging equipment sank into the mire. Further frustration arose when loggers tried to float the few cut trees downriver. Too green to float, the leveled giants sank straight to the bottom while the woodpeckers laughed in their canopies.

It wouldn't be until the 1970s when the Congaree trees were threatened again. This time, loggers armed with lighter equipment took down the elderly trees with a vengeance. The Sierra Club soon learned of this scourge on the East Coast. Their pleas for one of America's last and largest remaining bottomland hardwood forests resulted in the establishment of a National Monument in 1976. Though Hurricane Hugo would ravage Congaree in 1989, the trees continue to command this South Carolina jungle. Congress designated the Congaree floodplain a National Park in 2003.

Congaree is small, about 24,000 acres in size with only 20 miles of trailways. However, Rangers offer guests a unique opportunity to explore the Park on a **free canoe trek** down the Congaree River each weekend. Paddling and bird watching are the primary activities here. Over 170 bird species flutter through the gloomy treetops. The ranger-led **"Owl Prowl"** is a popular nocturnal activity where guests are invited to seek out the forest's array of hooting inhabitants. Though miniscule, Congaree is an animal kingdom that has always protected its own. Wander into this floodplain forest of the Old South and see for yourself.

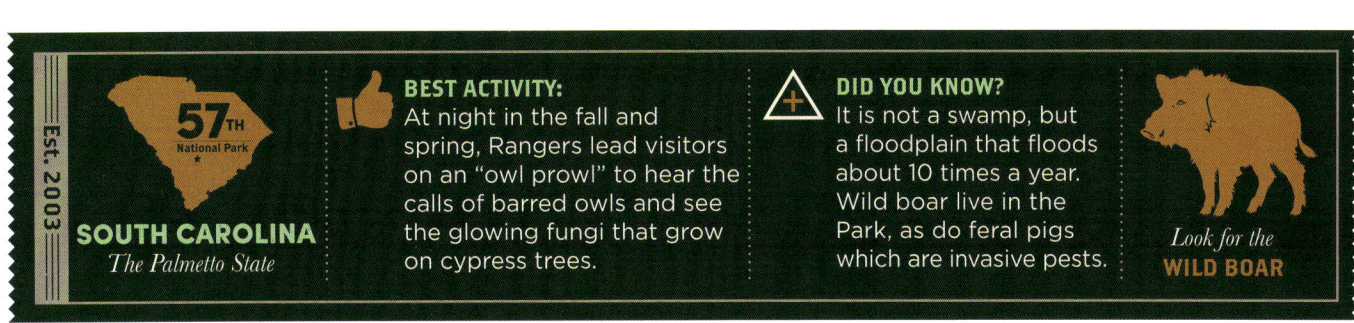

57TH National Park • Est. 2003 • **SOUTH CAROLINA** *The Palmetto State*

BEST ACTIVITY: At night in the fall and spring, Rangers lead visitors on an "owl prowl" to hear the calls of barred owls and see the glowing fungi that grow on cypress trees.

DID YOU KNOW? It is not a swamp, but a floodplain that floods about 10 times a year. Wild boar live in the Park, as do feral pigs which are invasive pests.

Look for the **WILD BOAR**

<CONGAREE 18" X 24" Poster art created in 2015 by Aaron Johnson & David Anderson

CRATER LAKE

A POOL of blue perfection glitters before you at Crater Lake National Park. As with many National Parks, the now tranquil Crater Lake has a violent geological past. A volcano named Mt. Mazama erupted here about 7,700 years ago. Steam pressure from Mazama's magma blew the top off, leaving a five-mile wide, 1,943-foot deep crater (or caldera). The walls of the caldera were sealed watertight by Mazama's lava and left to cool high up in the Cascade Mountains. With the Park's average annual snowfall of 44 feet per year, it wasn't long before the spacious caldera was filled with the purest, cleanest mountain water. Now it is the deepest lake in the United States and enjoyed by about half a million people each year.

William Gladstone Steel was an early champion of preserving the lake. As a Kansas teenager in 1870, Steel read about Oregon's "sunken lake" from a newspaper he had wrapped his lunch in. The description captured his imagination and he vowed to visit someday. Fifteen years later, Steel got his chance. He was astounded: "Imagine a vast mountain six by seven miles through, at an elevation of eight thousand feet, with the top removed and the inside hollowed out, then filled with the clearest water in the world, to within two thousand feet to the top ... and you have a perfect representation of Crater Lake." Steel kept this "hollowed out" mountain in the forefront of his mind for the next seventeen years as he lobbied, campaigned, and promoted Crater Lake as America's next National Park. In 1902, Crater Lake became a Park and Steel's newspaper dream had been saved for the pure enjoyment of future generations.

As expected, the lake is the centerpiece of this sublime Park. Trails wind up into the surrounding mountains, offering hikers rousing views into the crystalline waters below. Hike up **Mount Scott** to the highest point in the Park and take in the unblemished landscape of Crater Lake. Down by the shore, ferries carry the curious to **Wizard Island**. The **Rim Drive** is an incredible 33-mile round trip speckled with scenic overlooks and picnic areas around the lake. The road is open only in the summer and early fall before snow envelops the area once more.

Est. 1902 — 5TH National Park — OREGON *The Beaver State*

WINTER ACTIVITIES: In the winter, Ranger-led snowshoe hikes are offered on weekends, usually beginning in late November and running through late April.

DID YOU KNOW? Its depth of 1,943 feet (592 meters) makes it the deepest lake in the United States and the ninth deepest lake worldwide.

Look for **PRONGHORN ANTELOPE**

<CRATER LAKE 18" X 24" Poster art created in 2015 by David Anderson & Joel Anderson
^CRATER LAKE: FOX 18" X 24" Poster art created in 2017 by Michael Korfhage & Joel Anderson

CUYAHOGA VALLEY

A SPARKLING RIVER

weaves through the Cuyahoga Valley in northeastern Ohio. Verdant forest, bubbling waterfalls, mossy boulders, and a wide array of wildlife furnish the valley in splendor. Most Americans probably don't realize there's a National Park just outside Cleveland, but locals flock to this hidden gem of natural beauty. Gently winding out of Lake Erie, the Cuyahoga (Iroquois for "crooked") River was once a primary trade route for ships heading towards the Gulf Coast via the Ohio & Erie Canal. Engineers constructed a 101-mile long **Towpath Trail** for donkeys and horses to tow ships through the canal's various locks. The north to south riverside pathway is now a go-to attraction for Park visitors seeking a quiet stroll or bike ride.

Though serene today, Cuyahoga Valley National Park is a living reminder that unbridled production has consequences. Throughout the latter half of the 1800s, Cleveland's shipping industry boomed, choking the river with boat traffic and sewage. Wildlife soon fled from the toxic waters oozing with chemicals and waste. Several times the Cuyahoga even caught fire, earning it the odious title "the river that burned." In 1969, after a scathing article by Time Magazine about Cuyahoga's pollution, local residents and environmentalists responded in what would be one of the most dramatic environmental turnarounds in American history. Washington passed clean water laws, and Congress set Cuyahoga Valley aside as a National Recreation Area in 1974. Mass cleanup projects began all across the valley, and Ohioans worked tirelessly to bring the land back to life. Their rehabilitation efforts paid off: Cuyahoga Valley became a National Park in 2000, and a wide variety of plants and animals now occupy the landscape once more. River otters, tundra swans, turtles, white-tailed deer, blue herons, even bald eagles all dwell along the crooked river. As a Park, Cuyahoga Valley represents Americans at our worst and our best, failure and redemption. It is a landscape rescued from America, for America.

Not only is Cuyahoga Valley National Park veined by roadway and river but by rail as well. Park visitors can gaze out over Ohio's rolling hills and floodplain on board the **Cuyahoga Valley Scenic Railroad.** This charmingly vintage railway courses through the entire Park, picking up and dropping off guests at various stations along the way. Hiking is also a beloved pastime here in a Park with over 70 waterfalls. **Brandywine Falls** tops them all, a 60-foot display of foaming waterworks that draws a large crowd each year. The **Ledges Trail** is another prime hiking destination. It's hard to imagine you're still in suburban Ohio as you wander past mossy sandstone through a deciduous forest chiming with songbirds. Find refreshment and renewal in Cuyahoga Valley, where a river of life flows once more.

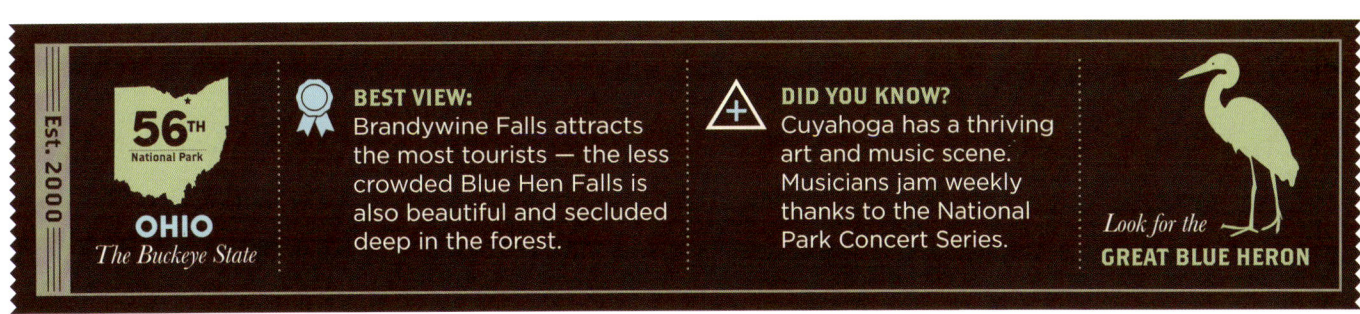

Est. 2000 — 56TH National Park — OHIO The Buckeye State

BEST VIEW: Brandywine Falls attracts the most tourists — the less crowded Blue Hen Falls is also beautiful and secluded deep in the forest.

DID YOU KNOW? Cuyahoga has a thriving art and music scene. Musicians jam weekly thanks to the National Park Concert Series.

Look for the **GREAT BLUE HERON**

<CUYAHOGA VALLEY 18" X 24" Poster art created in 2013 by Michael Korfhage & Joel Anderson

DEATH VALLEY

BLEACHED BOULDERS lie still on the flatlands, baking beneath a torrid sun. The land is barren. The empty lake basin looks like a monotone mosaic, countless dirt patches held together by a raw web of cracks. Across this vast mesa race the immobile rocks, their pathways marked by the dusty trails they've left in their wake. They are the **Sailing Stones** of Death Valley National Park. Though no one knows for sure, scientists believe these stones travel by atypical rainstorms or by strong winter winds slowly pushing the stones across the frozen flats. But rain seems nonexistent here. Averaging right around 2 inches of rainfall per year, Death Valley is without a doubt one of the driest regions in America. Any moisture is a gift for this parched landscape, and the sun seems to blaze hotter here than anywhere else. Average highs in August are 115 degrees Fahrenheit. You can descend into the lowest point on the continent at **Badwater Basin,** 282 feet below sea level. Death Valley is dry, deep, and vast: it is the largest National Park south of Alaska, 3.4 million acres of chapped mudflats and desolate mountain ranges. And yet this forsaken wilderness has learned to blossom with very little. The valley needs only a few raindrops in the cooler winter months to clothe the naked earth in spring wildflowers, some of the most spectacular you will see anywhere. The night skies glisten all the brighter when you're standing on the valley floor cloaked in soft white starlight. Despite the harsh environment, Death Valley National Park welcomes over a million guests each year who discover enchantment in the heat.

Imagine getting lost in a place like this. A team of Midwestern '49ers, drawn to California by rumors of gold, hitched together 100 wagons and wandered into this remote region on their way to the coast. Two months later, they were still in Death Valley, unable to find a way out. The Panamint and Amargosa mountain ranges had the travelers completely hemmed in. The men were haunted by "hunger and thirst and an awful silence." Having to abandon their wagons and eat their own oxen, the parched pilgrims finally escaped the basin on foot via **Emigrant Pass,** wishing good-bye and good riddance to this "Death Valley". Other visitors to the valley were far more fortunate. Before signing on as the National Park Service's first director, Stephen Mather made millions of dollars raking up borax from the valley floor. Mather named his company 20 Mule Team Borax after the long mule trains that would tramp across Death Valley and lug out 10 tons of borax a haul.

Visit **Furnace Creek** to learn about the Park's rich mineral history and ascend one of the valley's most scenic vistas at sun-drenched **Zabriskie Point.** Enter the off-road void at the **Racetrack,** where a four-wheeler or high-clearance vehicle grants you access into a waterless sea skimmed by Sailing Stones. Arid mystery and promising potential simmer down here on the desert flats.

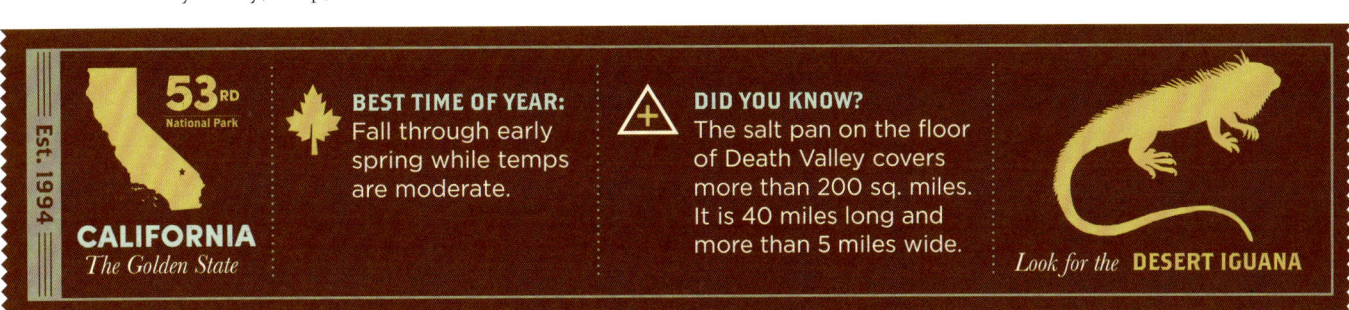

53RD National Park — Est. 1994 — **CALIFORNIA** *The Golden State*

BEST TIME OF YEAR: Fall through early spring while temps are moderate.

DID YOU KNOW? The salt pan on the floor of Death Valley covers more than 200 sq. miles. It is 40 miles long and more than 5 miles wide.

Look for the **DESERT IGUANA**

<DEATH VALLEY 18" X 24" Poster art created in 2013 by Michael Korfhage & Joel Anderson

DENALI

SIX MILLION acres of sweeping Alaskan wilderness fill the borders of Denali National Park. The Park feels almost as wide as it does tall: Denali's central feature is the mighty **Mount Denali**, North America's tallest mountain. Reaching at well over 20,000 feet, Mount Denali is a colossus that beckons only the bravest to scale its icy slopes. For over a century, climbers from all over the world have dreamed of ascending the "The High One," formerly known as Mount McKinley. Early mountaineers, along with an influential bohemian naturalist named Charles Sheldon, put this Alaskan wilderness on the map as America's Last Frontier. A 92-mile **Park Road** now winds through the foothills of Mount Denali, allowing guests to see the wild Dall goats Sheldon studied with such devotion as they clambered over the foot of the great mountain.

Denali, like Alaska, is a land of extremes, a brand of wildness that far exceeds man's ability to control it. A grizzly bear carries food back to her den at **Sable Pass**, while hungry wolves stalk a large herd of caribou on the **Plains of Murie**. Summer wildflowers carpet the valley, dancing golden beneath a cloud-cloaked Mount Denali. It was here, in a cabin beside the **Toklat River,** that Charles Sheldon lived and observed the unadulterated wilderness around him for an entire year. Much of Alaska was still unknown territory to most Americans in 1915, but Sheldon believed this land was sacred, a place that represented the idea of freedom like nowhere else. Sheldon and his mountaineer guide Harry Karstens spent a long, sunless winter discussing the possibility of a Park here, of an organized American effort to guard Alaska's enormous wildlife population from prospectors and over-eager sportsmen. While the tundra was vast, more and more people were beginning to flock to Denali. A railroad from Anchorage to nearby Fairbanks was almost complete, and miners were already tramping into the area. Sheldon knew Congress would need to act fast, so he moved to Washington full-time to campaign for his beloved mountain and the wildlife that surrounded it. In 1917, Mount McKinley National Park was established. The Park would be expanded and renamed Denali in 1980.

Harry Karstens knew the power of Mount Denali firsthand. Karstens, along with two others, climbed the mountain's South Peak in 1913, the first group to reach the ceiling of the continent. Karsten's ascent is imitated today, as climbers from all over the world still attempt to reach the lofty summit. Park visitors can also savor Denali's grandeur from a campsite at **Wonder Lake** or soar above the glacial mountains on an unforgettable **flightseeing tour.** Whether from the sky above or the valley below, Denali National Park is a rare glimpse of untamed America.

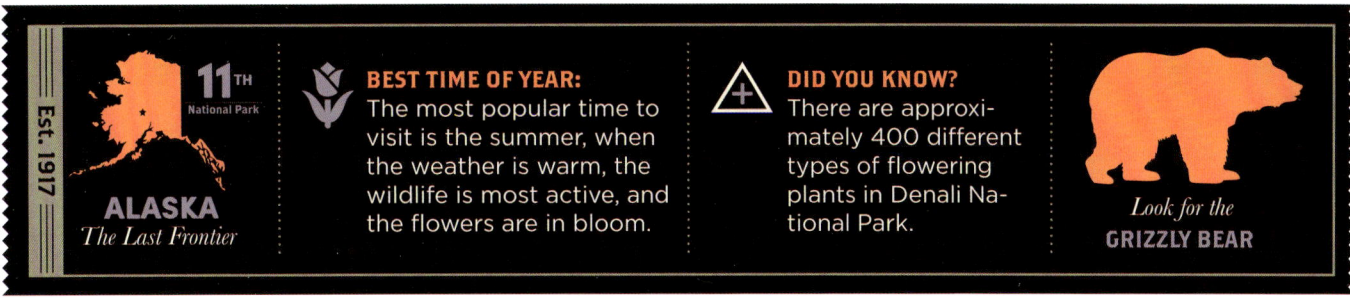

11TH National Park · Est. 1917 · **ALASKA** *The Last Frontier*

BEST TIME OF YEAR: The most popular time to visit is the summer, when the weather is warm, the wildlife is most active, and the flowers are in bloom.

DID YOU KNOW? There are approximately 400 different types of flowering plants in Denali National Park.

Look for the **GRIZZLY BEAR**

<**DENALI: DALL SHEEP** 18" X 24" Poster art created in 2018 by Derek Anderson & Joel Anderson

DRY TORTUGAS

WHITE SEAPLANES bob gently on the shores of a 19th century fortress. Seventy miles southwest of Key West, an imposing stronghold lined with arches and cannon punctuates the Gulf's crystal teal waters. Though the U.S. Navy no longer utilizes the fortress at Dry Tortugas National Park, the historical significance of **Fort Jefferson** makes this tropical site indispensable. Less than 500 feet away from this citadel of warfare is a natural bird sanctuary. **Bush Key** swarms with black-capped sooty terns and other seabirds finding respite and a meal on the shores of this desert island. Park visitors may bird-watch from the fort's ramparts, or take a stroll along the **seawall** and moat where stingray, starfish, and gray snapper loiter in the still waters. Once loaded with ammunition, the fortress and surrounding keys at Dry Tortugas National Park now exist as an aquatic playground.

Spanish explorer Juan Ponce de León supposedly moored on these islands in the early 1500s. He and his men feasted on the region's prolific turtle population, inspiring a full-bellied de León to name the region "Las Tortugas" or "The Turtles." Spanish ships made these islands a regular stop on their route to the Americas, producing a spike in piracy and shipwrecks along the isles' hidden reefs. Divers today can explore the 260-foot remains of a Norwegian sailboat called *Avanti* or "The Windjammer," just south of **Loggerhead Key**. As the turtle population waned and the United States rose to power, Las Tortugas became more than just an idyllic spot for turtle soup. American military strategists chose the island's **Garden Key** as a premier location for a coastal fortress.

Dry Tortugas National Park now protects the stout brick hexagon of Fort Jefferson. Standing at 45 feet tall with a circumference of nearly half a mile, this bulwark guarded America's trade ships from pirates in the Gulf of Mexico through the latter half of the 1800s. During the Civil War, Union forces also used the isolated location of this Florida Key as a prison for deserters. One famous inmate was Dr. Samuel Mudd, who had bandaged and splinted the leg of John Wilkes Booth immediately after Booth had assassinated President Lincoln at Ford's Theater. As a prison, Fort Jefferson was difficult to maintain as no fresh water was available on the island, and tropical storms wreaked havoc on the fort's exterior (the islands' utter lack of fresh water earned them the unfavorable description "dry"). President Franklin D. Roosevelt designated Dry Tortugas as a National Monument to protect the birds and sealife in 1935. The islands would become a National Park in 1992.

Strap on some flippers and snorkel in the shallows around Garden Key, where coral reef and forests of sea grass await your inspection. Venture further out on a SCUBA tour into **Sherwood Forest,** a lively community of coral, crustaceans, turtles, and fish of many hues. Kayaking opportunities also abound in the glittery waters of the Gulf. Experience the historical and natural splendor of this National Park in the sunny Florida Keys.

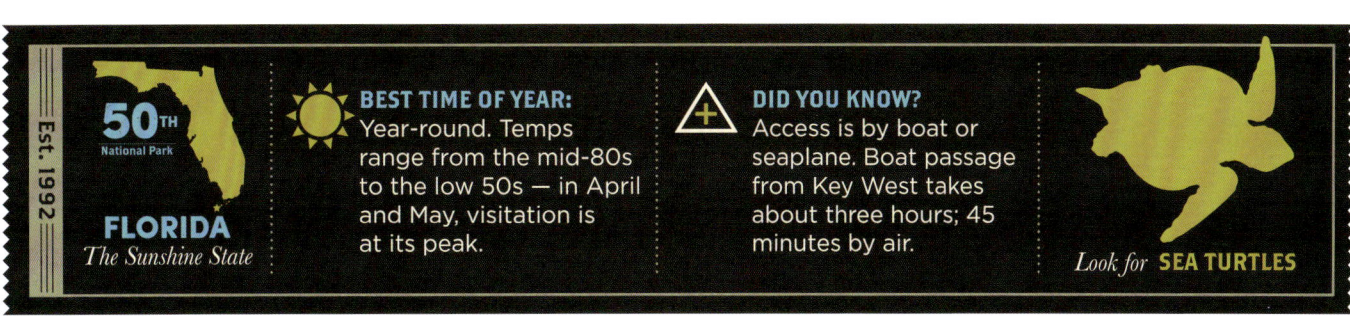

<DRY TORTUGAS 18" X 24" Poster art created in 2015 by Michael Korfhage & Joel Anderson

EVERGLADES

A TRANSITIONAL landscape blurring the lines between water and earth, the Everglades wetlands soak up over 1.5 million acres of southwestern Florida. Park visitors can experience one of the most unique ecosystems in the country from a canoe, gliding along the shallow waters of the **Wilderness Waterway** where alligators and manatees, ibises and egrets, cypresses and mangroves all thrive in the balmy coastal marsh. Over 350 species of birds live within the watery confines of the Park, making for a grand bird-watching getaway. Despite developers' repeated attempts to stem their slow tide, the mighty waters of the Everglades continue to roll on towards the sea. Life, though threatened, flourishes in the swamplands.

The Everglades' past is a troubling one. In the early 1900s, thousands upon thousands of Floridian birds were killed and plucked to decorate women's hats. Local politicians and big businessmen saw the Everglades as a site to be drained and developed. Dikes, dams, and levees were built just outside the present-day Park's boundaries, diverting essential freshwater flow from Lake Okeechobee and the Kissimmee River. Everglades National Park, unlike its western counterparts, is an area set aside primarily for the protection of a threatened ecosystem rather than breathtaking scenery. In a part of the country that's so thickly populated and developed, the Everglades continue to survive. Still, more than 50% of the original Everglades region has already been destroyed and reclaimed for human use. The Park today protects a portion of what remains. Only time will tell how much longer these teeming Florida wetlands will exist.

The Everglades have lived in a state of contention for almost a century. Due to their lack of stunning vistas or obvious natural beauty, the region is often written off by many as a mosquito-infested wasteland. But a few people believed this was a place worth saving. A journalist named Marjory Stoneman Douglas along with a visionary conservationist named Ernest F. Coe would stand toe-to-toe with South Florida's land-hungry investors and commercial developers to defend the swamp.

A former land developer himself, Coe was drawn to the Everglades and soon treasured the slow-moving rivers of life that flowed into the Gulf. He was shocked that people were so quick to destroy such a unique ecosystem, where rare wildlife, orchids, and tropical trees depended on the shallow flooding. He called for the creation of a National Park that included not only the Everglades, but the Big Cypress Forest to the north and Key Largo to the southeast as well. The feisty Marjory Stoneman Douglas, journalist for the

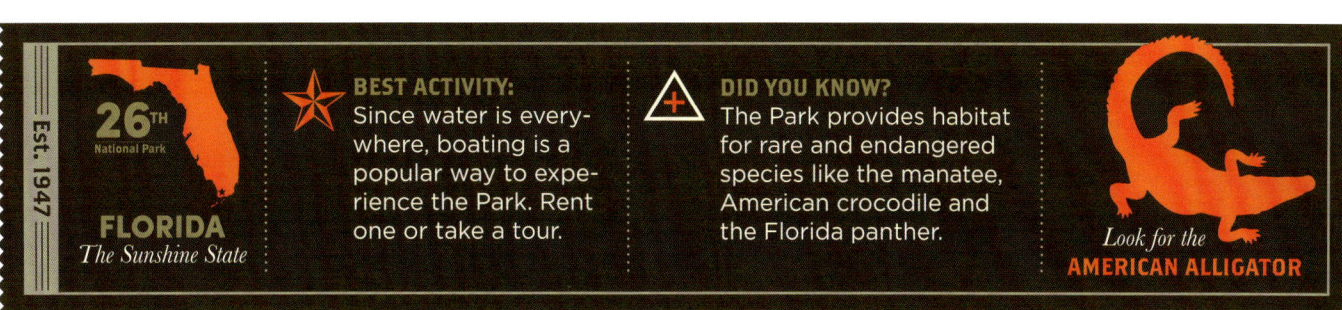

<EVERGLADES 18" X 24" Poster art created in 2010 by Andy Gregg & Joel Anderson

Miami Herald, supported his vision. Douglas spent five whole years studying the Everglades before publishing her perspective in 1947. Her poetic commentary, matched with her witty barbs against good-old-boy politics, gave a major boost to society's outlook on the wetlands. She wrote:

"There are no other Everglades in the world.... Nothing anywhere else is like them; their vast glittering openness, wider than the enormous visible round of the horizon, the ... sweetness of their massive winds, under the dazzling blue heights of space.... The miracle of the light pours over the green and brown expanse of sawgrass and water, shining and slow-moving below, the grass and the water that is the meaning and central face of the Everglades of Florida. It is a river of grass."

In December 1947, Coe and Douglas's struggle for the Everglades finally paid off. Florida legislature raised the $2 million necessary to purchase the remaining private swampland, and Congress designated the Everglades as a National Park.

Though this Park is more accessible by canoe than foot, the Park Service has built a few excellent trailways from which to experience the incredible Everglades ecosystem without getting wet. An easy, highly rewarding nature walk along **Anhinga Trail** provides up-close opportunities to (safely) meet an alligator, while birds of many shapes and sizes can be watched at **Eco Pond.** Take the 15-mile **Tram Road** to a 45-foot tall observation tower that overlooks the glistening wetlands. You'll also be standing at the highest point in the Park, as the Everglades' elevation never exceeds 8 feet above sea level. Be sure to plan your visit for the wintertime as heavy rain, hurricanes, and swarms of mosquitoes make a summer trip to the Everglades much less enjoyable. The Park is a reminder to us that nature is fragile, that water is life. May it continue to flow through the complex biosphere of the Everglades.

"The Everglades is all about water. It is difficult to truly understand the fragile nature of the Park without being on the water or in the water. My favorite memories were canoeing or slogging through the sloughs, and looking for rookeries in Florida Bay—only the sounds of birds broke the silence."
— Maureen Finnerty, Former Superintendent of Everglades from 2000-2004 (total years of NPS service: 32)

SILENT EVERGLADES 18" X 24" Limited Edition Print based on an oil painting created in 2015 by Kai Carpenter >

GATES OF THE ARCTIC

IN THE FAR REACHES of America's Last Frontier is a National Park the size of Switzerland. Northern Alaska is the purest form of desolation. Formidable mountain crags cast their shadows over the dark rivers, ribboning across the treeless tundra. A lonesome caribou herd calls out into the gloom. Aurora glow sweeps across the night sky. The Rocky Mountain range ends here, at the northernmost National Park in the United States. Gates of the Arctic National Park lies completely above the Earth's Arctic Circle, where the sun never seems to set throughout the short summer and refuses to rise in a long and brutal winter. Much like the landscape, the weather is tempestuous and fickle. A snowstorm can occur any time of the year. Only the stoutest adventurers would even consider visiting a place like this. There are no trails or campgrounds. There are no roads in or out of the Park. Access into the Gates is possible only by air taxi or on foot. But the harsh Alaskan landscape is nonetheless incomparable for its unspoiled backcountry and poetic simplicity.

> *In the early morning when the first faint light*
> *Cuts the murky blackness of the cool calm night,*
> *While the gloomy forest, dismal, dark, and wild,*
> *Seems to slowly soften and become more mild,*
>
> *When the mists hang heavy, where the streams flow by*
> *And reflect the rose-tints in the eastern sky,*
> *When the brook trout leaps and the deer drinks slow,*
> *While the distant mountains blend in one soft glow,*
>
> *'Tis the precious moment, given once a day,*
> *When the present fades to the far-away,*
> *When the busy this-time for a moment's gone,*
> *And the Earth turns backward into Nature's dawn.*
> *-- Bob Marshall*

In the 1930s, writer and forest conservationist Bob Marshall journeyed up Alaska's **Koyukuk River** to the North Fork. There he encountered two lofty sentinels, **Frigid Crags** and **Boreal Mountain**. Following the river between these two behemoths, Marshall entered a vast glacial wilderness, void of human development. He had crossed a threshold into what is today known as the Gates of the Arctic. His documented journey would inspire Congress to set aside this region as a National Park in 1980.

Grizzly bear, wolf, caribou, and fox continue to scratch out a meager living on the boggy taiga. Six rivers flow through the Park, providing a wild rafting adventure for those daring enough to enter the frigid rapids. The **Kobuk** and Koyukuk rivers are two of the more popular routes to float through the boundless Alaskan backcountry. The Gates welcome the bold. Enter and be amazed.

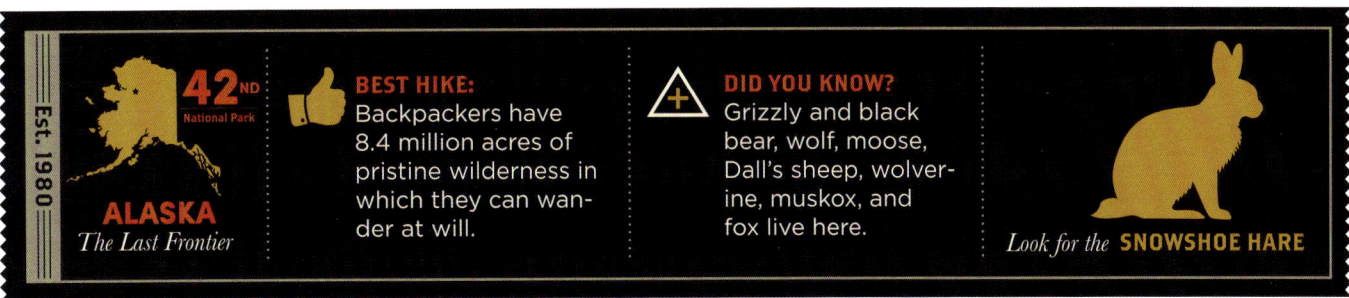

<GATES OF THE ARCTIC 18" X 24" Poster art created in 2015 by David Anderson, Aaron Johnson & Joel Anderson

GATEWAY ARCH

THE MIGHTY MISSISSIPPI

River rolls down from its headwaters at Lake Itasca, Minnesota, 2,340 miles to the Gulf of Mexico. It is the second-longest river in the United States and perhaps one of the most historically and geographically significant—serving as a modern day marker between the eastern and western states of America. Before the spread of railroads, the Mississippi was the lifeblood of American trade and commerce. One of the most prominent cities along the shores of the Mississippi River is St. Louis: a bustling hub for industry, culture, and Midwestern society throughout the 1800s. It was here that many families began their great migration into the newly opened West, symbolized by the city's iconic **Gateway Arch**. The nearby **Old Courthouse** is home to some of the most defining court cases in our young nation's history. First established as the Jefferson National Expansion Memorial in 1935 by Franklin D. Roosevelt, Gateway Arch National Park now protects these two American-built structures which testify to the spirit of freedom and self-determination that is so precious to this country.

Looming above the city of St. Louis is the 630-foot steel parabola known as the Gateway Arch. Designed by Finnish-American architect Eero Saarinen and completed in 1965, the Arch not only serves as a symbolic gateway to the West but as a memorial to the Americans who helped shape this country into what it is today. It was here that marked the eastern border of Thomas Jefferson's Louisiana Purchase, an 827,000 square-mile region which includes a host of natural wonders that would someday become National Parks. Without the Louisiana Purchase, Lewis and Clark would likely have never set out from the St. Louis area in 1803 on their 8,000-mile trip to the Pacific Ocean and back, revealing now-cherished regions such as the Grand Tetons, the Rocky Mountains, and the Columbia Basin.

At the foot of the Arch, across the lawn, rests the stoic Old Courthouse. Built in 1839, this recently-restored building preserves the memory of those who fought to give all Americans what we now enjoy. It was here that the enslaved Dred and Harriet Scott sued for their freedom, showing the world that they too had intrinsic worth and deserved a rightful place in the American experience. Though they would eventually lose their case in the Supreme Court, their struggle would inspire many to battle for the abolition of slavery and culminate in Abraham Lincoln's Emancipation Proclamation.

You can learn all about the history of St. Louis and Westward Expansion at the **Park Museum**. Get some fresh air and enjoy an urban greenway as you take in the many different angles of the Arch via **Gateway Arch Trail**. Purchase your tram tickets in advance and make the 4-minute ascent to the **top of the Gateway Arch** for incredible aerial views of St. Louis and the Mississippi River. Take a Ranger-led tour of the Old Courthouse to learn more about the monumental arguments that rang off these walls. Don your seersucker linens and end your day in style with a cruise down the **Mississippi River** in an old fashioned steamboat.

- Est. 2018
- **MISSOURI** — *The Show Me State*
- America's **60TH** National Park
- **DID YOU KNOW?** The Gateway Arch is the tallest monument in the U.S. at 630 feet (192 m) tall.
- **BEST TIME OF YEAR** Visit St. Louis in April for spring blossoms, cooler temperature, and the beginning of baseball season.
- *Look for* **PEREGRINE FALCONS**

<GATEWAY ARCH 18" X 24" Poster art created in 2019 by Derek Anderson & Joel Anderson

GLACIER

NOTHING compares with the icy peaks of Glacier National Park. You feel so tiny, an insignificant speck with a backpack before such giants. The mountain air is bracing and a sense of awe-struck wonder overwhelms you as you ride along the **Going-to-the-Sun Road**. This 50-mile engineering marvel carries automobiles and red vintage tour buses deep into the Park, curling around stark vistas and tunneling into the very mountains themselves. Every bend in the road reveals something new, one wondrous detour after the next. Glacial lakes mirror jagged mountain teeth, grizzly bears and mountain goats wander the hillsides foraging for their next meal, and frantic waterfalls race hundreds of feet to the valley below. The beauty is celestial. Park advocate George Bird Grinnell put it best when he called Glacier the "Crown of the Continent."

Glacier is enormous, occupying over 1,000,000 acres of northern Montana. It is adjacent to Alberta's Waterton National Park across the Canadian border. In 1932, the two Parks partnered together to become the world's first InterNational Peace Park. The Parks are administered separately but share in the study and management of the area's unique wildlife population. Hikers can now traverse national lines on the **InterNational Peace Park Hike**, lead by Rangers from both countries. Don't forget your passport!

Way before the land was set aside as a National Park, Blackfoot Indians lived here, at the base of a lone peak they called Chief Mountain. This land was a sacred place for the Blackfeet; they would hunt for bison in the nearby valleys and climb the mountains to pray. It was a quiet and solitary region for hundreds of years until an 1890s mining boom brought greedy prospectors into the area, seeking wealth from the Northern Rocky Mountains. The Blackfeet could do little to slow the invasive gold rush and were soon forced to sell 800,000 acres of their land. George Bird Grinnell was Glacier's most passionate conservationist and a friend to the Blackfeet. Grinnell had climbed and named many of the area's glacier-formed mountains and creeks. He called for fair treatment of the Native Americans but also promoted the area as an ideal place to form a National Park. His Park fervor eventually overcame his feelings for the Blackfoot homeland. Congress added Glacier as a National Park in 1910 and would designate a reservation of 1.5 million acres to the east for the Blackfoot Nation. With the area now under

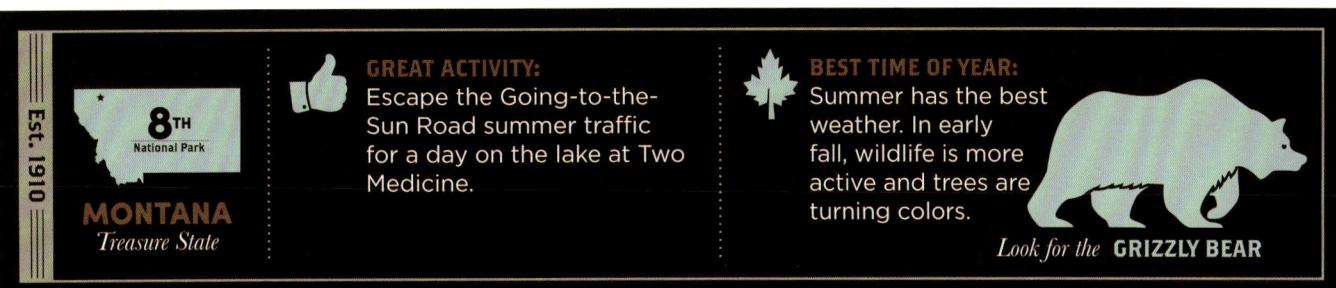

GREAT ACTIVITY: Escape the Going-to-the-Sun Road summer traffic for a day on the lake at Two Medicine.

BEST TIME OF YEAR: Summer has the best weather. In early fall, wildlife is more active and trees are turning colors.

Look for the **GRIZZLY BEAR**

Est. 1910 — 8TH National Park — **MONTANA** *Treasure State*

<**GLACIER** 18" X 24" Poster art created in 2012 by Michael Korfhage & Joel Anderson

Washington's jurisdiction, the next question was how to draw people out to this Montana wilderness. Many of the wealthier American families around this time were taking summer trips to Europe. The Great Northern Railway, among other American railroad companies, saw the creation of National Parks as an excellent way to keep vacationing Americans in the States and on their luxurious railcars. They promoted the Park to Easterners with dramatic artwork of Glacier's vistas, and hired Blackfeet to perform ritual dances and songs in theater halls all across the eastern U.S. The railway's motto was "See America First." The national promotion was a major success, and train-riding tourists arrived in droves.

The Park System's first director, Stephen Mather, recognized the value of American tourism, not only from the obvious financial and patriotic standpoints, but also as someone trying to save the land. Busy Parks meant more government funding, which would help to keep private mining and logging companies away from the unmarred, now public wilderness.

Glacier National Park is a hiking epicenter, with over 700 miles of trails and hundreds of campsites scattered about the vast backcountry. **Logan Pass** and **Many Glacier** are both excellent locations to start a backpacking adventure in the central area of the Park. Twenty-five active glaciers still carve out the mountain passes of these highlands. Peering into **Hidden Lake** is worth the hike (the summer crowds thin out the higher you climb). And for an end-of-the-day respite, the lovely **Lake McDonald** and **St. Mary Lake** lie alongside each Park entrance. These are great spots for relaxing after a long drive through Glacier.

"Glacier National Park is a hikers' paradise and as a young ranger I learned the trails and the strengths of the mountains and valleys of the east side of the Park. All my stress and the problems of the sub-district in the summers would fade away and the quiet peace of the Park would revive me every time I hit the trails. Once you have experienced the beauty and majesty of this place you will return again and again to recharge yourself and re-create the feelings you experienced."
— Bill Pierce, Former Ranger at Glacier from 1972-1975
(total years of NPS service: 38)

GLACIER: A VIEW TO REMEMBER 18" X 24" Poster art based on an oil painting created in 2015 by Kai Carpenter ʌ
GLACIER: GOING TO THE SUN ROAD 18" X 24" Poster art created in 2013 by Joel Anderson ʌ
GLACIER: MOUNTAIN GOAT 18" X 24" Poster art based on an oil painting created in 2017 by Kai Carpenter >

GLACIER BAY

A GREAT THUNDERING world of ice envelops the southeastern Alaska coast. Dark peaks poke up through their shawls of snow. The 3 million-plus acres of Glacier Bay National Park may be a bundled world of frost, but nature has recently provided a pathway for humans to enter this icy chamber. Less than 300 years ago, Glacier Bay did not exist. What is now a cruise ship-welcoming inlet was once a glacier-choked frozen mass. Since 1794, the region's glaciers have shrunk back more than 60 miles, unveiling a pristine fjord flanked with rainforest and lichen-coated hillsides. Otters feast on fresh crab legs while a colony of sea lions basks out on the sunlit shores. Humpback and killer whales breach further out in the thawing estuaries. Glacier fragments break off and crash into the sea (called "calving"). Glacier Bay National Park is an ever-transforming terrain that invites you to peek beneath the icy armor of Alaska and find a vibrant body of new life.

Accompanied by a group of Tlingit warriors, John Muir once canoed the 800 miles from Fort Wrangell to Glacier Bay in 1879. Glaciers had fascinated Muir for years, inspiring him to write dozens of essays on their extensive sculpting of his beloved Sierra Nevada Mountains in California. In Alaska, Muir felt he had returned to the Earth's Ice Age. He gasped in awe as icebergs cracked off the frozen slopes and exploded into the water. He pondered the paradox of creation by destruction: "... Nature is ever at work building and pulling down, creating and destroying, keeping everything whirling and flowing, allowing no rest but in rhythmical motion, chasing everything in endless song out of one beautiful form into another." Muir's arduous initiation to the Alaskan wilderness stoked in him a passion for Glacier Bay.

Eleven years later, at the age of 52, Muir returned for a 9-day solo excursion despite a chronic cough. Ever the optimist in nature's healing powers, a drenched and sunblind Muir decided to camp atop a tidewater glacier. He awoke to find his cough gone and his health restored. "No lowland microbe can survive on a glacier," he said. Baffled by this eccentric adventurer, the local Tlingits began calling him "Great Ice Chief." The Ice Chief would later have an imposing glacier named after him. Since then, Muir's glacier has melted back into the valley where it remains to this day. **Muir Inlet** invites kayaks and canoes to explore the freshly melted waterway left in the glacier's wake.

Adventure awaits on land as well. Delve into a newly established forest on the **Bartlett River Trail**, where a wide variety of wildlife play and feed on the banks of the estuary. Be sure to bring a rain jacket and wear layers. Even in the summer the climate is cool and wet. Take a boat tour of the bay's interior fjords, where dramatic glacial splash-shows rock the walls of **Tarr** and **Johns Hopkins Inlets.** An unforgettable adventure awaits you in this Alaskan cocoon of water and ice.

"Glacier Bay is a time machine. To travel its waters from Icy Strait to Marjorie Glacier is to leap—in just a few hours—from a mature rain forest to the Little Ice Age. It is a dynamic, ice-carved world where rising land seems to expand in relief, eased of its glacial burdens. It is the homeland of the Tlingit peoples. And as a National Park, it belongs to all Americans, its citizen-owners, in perpetuity." — Cherry Payne, Retired Park Superintendent at Glacier Bay from 2007-2010 (total years of NPS service: 34)

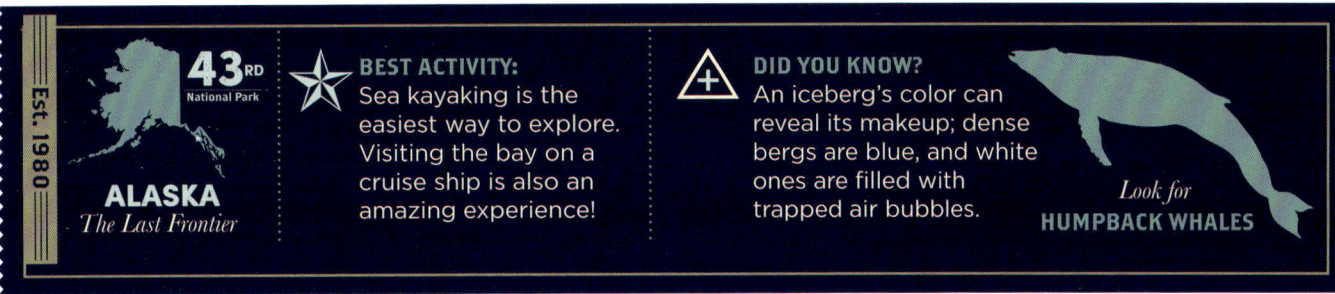

43RD National Park — Est. 1980 — **ALASKA** *The Last Frontier*

BEST ACTIVITY: Sea kayaking is the easiest way to explore. Visiting the bay on a cruise ship is also an amazing experience!

DID YOU KNOW? An iceberg's color can reveal its makeup; dense bergs are blue, and white ones are filled with trapped air bubbles.

Look for **HUMPBACK WHALES**

<GLACIER BAY 18" X 24" Poster art created in 2012 by Michael Korfhage & Joel Anderson

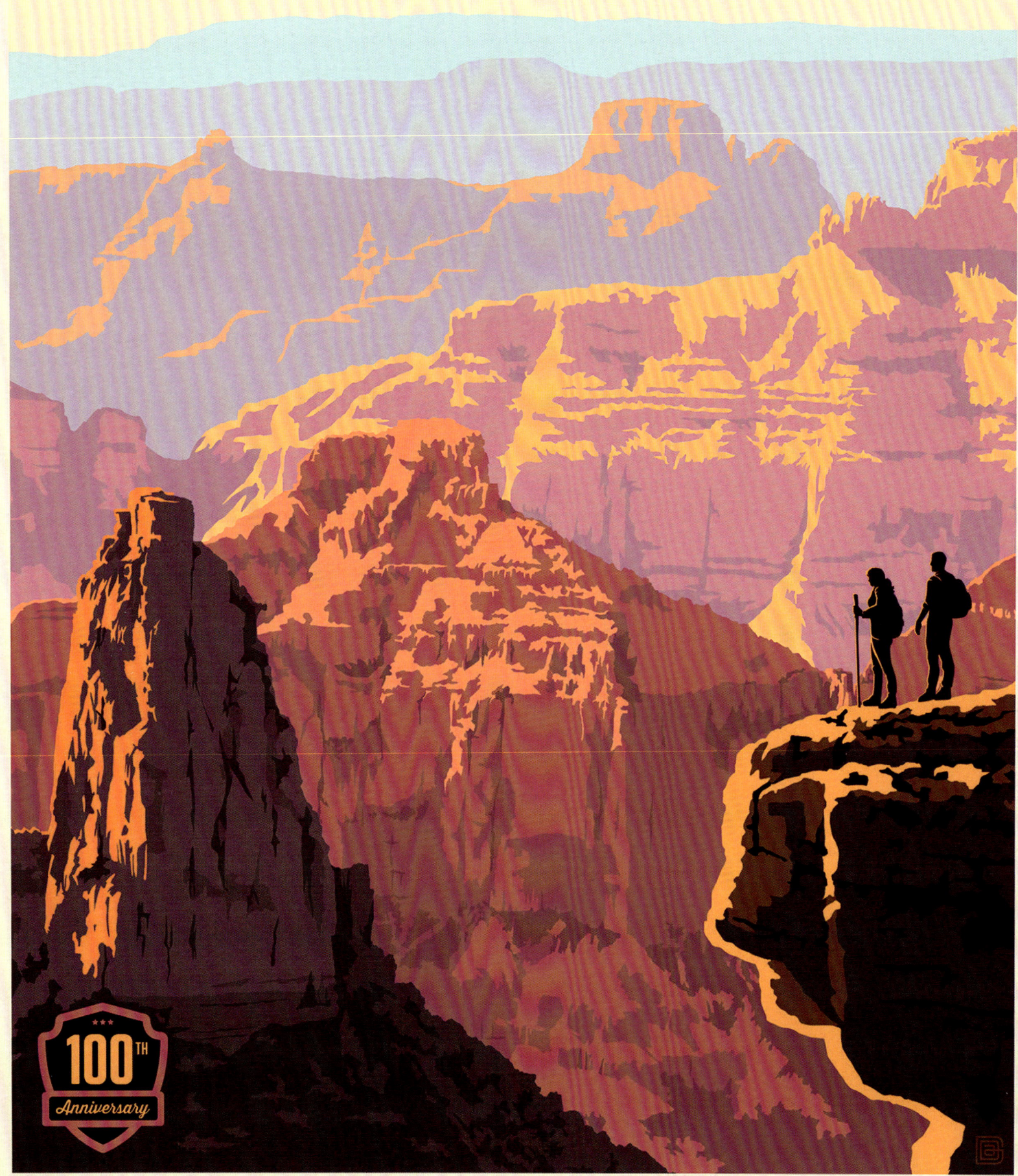

GRAND CANYON

STANDING ON THE EDGE of the Grand Canyon, a zealous President Theodore Roosevelt beseeched Americans to recognize what a wonder we possessed within our borders: "In the Grand Canyon, Arizona has a natural wonder which is in kind absolutely unparalleled throughout the rest of the world. I want to ask you to keep this great wonder of nature as it now is. I hope you will not have a building of any kind, not a summer cottage, a hotel or anything else, to mar the wonderful grandeur, the sublimity, the great loneliness and beauty of the canyon. Leave it as it is. You cannot improve on it. The ages have been at work on it, and man can only mar it."

The beauty of the National Park System is that the Parks were specifically created as a "democratic inheritance" for all Americans to enjoy. If you are an American, the Parks are yours. They belong to you. They belong to your children and your children's children. They are not meant for just a wealthy few, but for all to enjoy. You go to the Parks to see outside of yourself, to suddenly become small in the midst of such majesty. In no place does this sensation feel more apparent than at Grand Canyon National Park. Songs have been written, photographs taken, and conversations stalled in the attempt to describe it. The Grand Canyon is just as fitting for poetry as science. It is vast: 277 river miles long, up to 18 miles wide, and over a mile deep. It is pure: visibility on a clear day averages between 90 and 110 miles. It is old: rock dating back almost 2 billion years lies on the canyon floor.

Spread over 1,218,375 acres of protected land, the Grand Canyon is unspeakably glorious, transcending any human attempt to imagine or explain it. Light and shadow playfully splash their hues across a rippling canvas of stone. As with all great architecture, each view of the Grand Canyon uniquely depends on the weather and time of day. Though there are a large variety of ways to encounter it, almost any angle will give you the same experience: a reverent sense of smallness. And while it can never be fully understood, the Grand Canyon beckons to be explored, whether from its two rim regions or down on the canyon floor.

The **South Rim** is a popular destination for 90% of the Park's 5 million annual visitors. Though crowded in the summer, especially around **Bright Angel Lodge**, with a little hiking you can escape the crowds for a quiet overlook along the **Rim Trail**. Trails into the Canyon such as **Bright Angel** and **South Kaibab** are accessible from the South Rim as well.

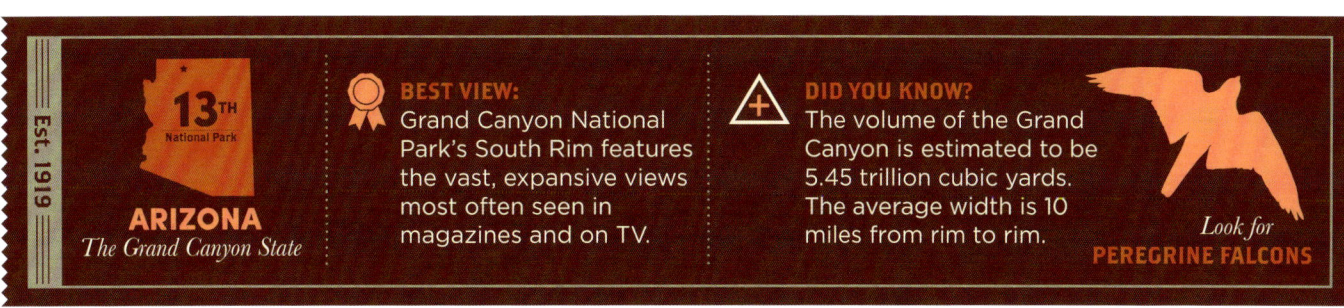

BEST VIEW: Grand Canyon National Park's South Rim features the vast, expansive views most often seen in magazines and on TV.

DID YOU KNOW? The volume of the Grand Canyon is estimated to be 5.45 trillion cubic yards. The average width is 10 miles from rim to rim.

Look for **PEREGRINE FALCONS**

13TH National Park
ARIZONA *The Grand Canyon State*
Est. 1919

<GRAND CANYON: 100th ANNIVERSARY 18" X 24" Poster art created in 2018 by Aaron Johnson & Joel Anderson

Reaching the **North Rim** requires a 220-mile journey by car, but visitors savor the North Rim's less congested, alpine-forested area. The North Rim is 1,000 feet higher than the South and provides the highest vista in the Park from **Point Imperial** (8,803 feet above sea level).

Rafting on the **Colorado River** through the Grand Canyon, as described by Eric Henze in his book *RVing With Monsters,* is "truly a defining moment in anyone's life. It is an experience that moves beyond words, resets your definitions of awe and wonder, brings a restful peace to the soul and at times puts you in moments of unholy terror that — on getting to the other side of — help remind you just how awesome it is to be alive." Though it will require a reservation up to a year in advance (and nerves of steel), rafting the Colorado is yet another unforgettable way to experience one of America's greatest treasures.

"The Canyon is more than a National Park or a global icon. It is more than what can be revealed through a photograph or the turn of words. For some, it is just a deep hole in the landscape. For others, it is a spiritual connection with creation. For me, it is all of that and more. I was born in a small two room clinic on the South Rim because my father was just starting his career with the National Park Service and my mother, with clear intention, chose that place to have her first born. When I returned to Grand Canyon as Superintendent, my connection was very special because of this. It was a place of beginnings; a place that transcended origins and endings. I knew of the importance to care for it, to protect it and to preserve it, which is what my job required. But, I also knew it was my birthplace and represented the start of a three generation family history protecting National Parks which made my job even more important to me. Both of my parents now lie in the Pioneers Cemetery on the South Rim having returned to the Canyon for their final journey. And, the power of the Canyon continues, always greater than the visitors who experience it and the people who have lived with it and cared for it over the years."

— Robert Arnberger, Superintendent of Grand Canyon 1994-2000 (total years of NPS service: 34)

GRAND CANYON ILLUSTRATED MAP 18" X 24" Poster art created in 2019 by Aaron Johnson & Joel Anderson ∧
GRAND CANYON RIVER RAFTING 18" X 24" Poster art created in 2020 by Aaron Johnson & Joel Anderson >

GRAND TETON

JUST south of Yellowstone National Park, a lofty mountain range rises from the flat Wyoming plains. No foothills impede the view; the lonely granite-gray peaks of the Tetons dominate the skyline, mirrored by glacial lakes at their exposed base. Many rugged outdoor adventures have begun with these snow-capped peaks looming in the distance. An invigorating desire for discovery takes hold of the young and old, all those who are willing to climb up one of the Park's spectacular vistas or wash themselves with glorious scenery at the **Snake River**. Grand Teton National Park is a place both distinct from and intertwined with its older sister Yellowstone. Large elk herds winter beneath the shadows of the Tetons, while a wide variety of waterfowl swim and nest in the glittery waters of **Jackson Lake**. A Park that was originally formed from struggle and well-intended deception is now one of the finest natural wonderlands in the West.

French fur trappers first christened the "Grand Tetons" in the 17th century and spent much time in the area exploring and hunting the area's prolific beavers. Winters were harsh but a few hardy frontier families and trappers, such as David Jackson, persisted to live in the valley beneath the mountains. The town became known as Jackson Hole.

An enthusiastic Yellowstone superintendent named Horace Albright united with billionaire John D. Rockefeller, Jr., to set aside the region as a National Park in the mid-1920s. Rockefeller's sincere devotion to the Park idea led him to quietly purchase large parcels of private Jackson Hole land around the mountains. Disguised as a Utah land company, the scheme worked at first. But when locals discovered Rockefeller's deceit, they refused to give him another inch, outraged by his sly attempt to 'steal' their land for Washington's use. Though the Teton Mountains themselves would be designated a Park in 1929, Congress would not accept Rockefeller's land donation, and the valley's resplendent meadows and wetlands would remain in limbo until 1943. That year, despite Wyoming's furious refusal to comply, President Roosevelt invoked the Antiquities Act, officially grafting Jackson Hole's valley into Grand Teton National Park. Rockefeller's land would be added to the Park in 1950. Anti-Park sentiment was strong throughout the state for a few more years but would eventually fade as tourism increased. Now, the majestic Tetons are enjoyed by 3 million people each year and the mountains take center stage at this beloved National Park.

Glaciers carved out the mountains in northwest Wyoming, leaving behind a 40-mile long chain of jagged peaks known today as the Grand Tetons. These mountains appear more imposing than usual because of their lack of foothills. Adorning the feet of these giants is a pristine collection of meadows, glacial lakes, and river beds.

Jenny Lake is one of the most popular spots in the Park, and for good reason. The Park's second largest lake offers stunning views of the Tetons as well as a gateway into a Wyoming backpacker's paradise. From the Jenny Lake

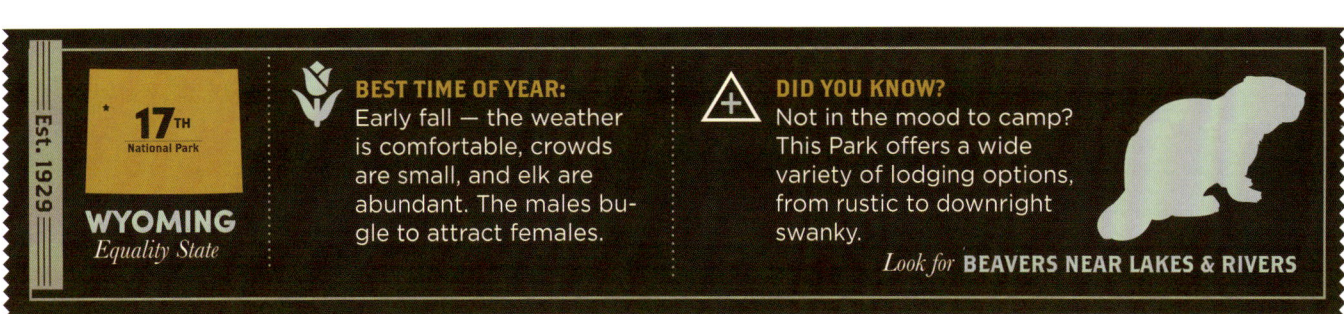

BEST TIME OF YEAR: Early fall — the weather is comfortable, crowds are small, and elk are abundant. The males bugle to attract females.

DID YOU KNOW? Not in the mood to camp? This Park offers a wide variety of lodging options, from rustic to downright swanky.

Est. 1929 · 17TH National Park · **WYOMING** *Equality State*

Look for **BEAVERS NEAR LAKES & RIVERS**

<**GRAND TETON** 18" X 24" Poster art created in 2010 by Andy Gregg & Joel Anderson

Visitor Center, hikers can indulge in the scenery from the flat trails around the lake or get straight to the point and ride the ferry across for a small fee. For shorter family hikes (most crowded in peak season), try the half-mile jaunt up to **Hidden Falls.** Continue up the Hidden Fall trail for a spectacular overlook of Jenny Lake from **Inspiration Point.** If you're physically prepared for a full-day excursion, continue on this same route to the Cascade - Paintbrush Loop, leading to an unforgettable finish at **Lake Solitude.** Stouthearted backpackers can test their lung capacities on the way up to **Amphitheater Lake** from the Lupine Meadows Trailhead.

The 42-mile scenic loop drive from Moose Junction to Jackson Lake is a veritable feast for the eyes as you wind your way through the Park with the Tetons always in view. It's hard not to find a picturesque photo-op along this route. Some of the most breathtaking spots can be found atop **Signal Mountain,** from **Schwabacher's Landing,** the **Oxbow Bend Turnout,** and by taking a slight detour into the **Mormon Row Historic District.** Keep an eye out for wildlife while driving through the Park. Bison, elk, moose, pronghorn, and mule deer all enjoy grazing in the meadows and will sometimes venture into the roadways.

For a more rustic Tetons tour, channel your inner Teddy Roosevelt and saddle up. Horseback rides are available through Park-authorized ranches. Trot through the sagebrush at sunset and watch the shadows lengthen across the snow-covered highlands. A few of these privately run ranches offer week-long Western adventures where you can ride, eat, and sleep like a cowboy while trying your hand at cattle driving.

Paddlers will be hard-pressed to find a more gorgeous location for a float than the Snake River. It runs 50 miles through the Park, lining the base of the Teton mountain range all the way to **Jackson Lake.** This region is a popular destination for boating enthusiasts. Kayakers enjoy the whitewater rush of a swelling Snake River in the springtime. Pontoon boats and scenic cruises churn across Jackson Lake, offering a more laid-back way to bask in the alpine scenery. Fly fishermen from all over the world make the trip to this Park to catch the native cutthroat trout.

Dwarfed by its iconic neighbor to the north, the Grand Tetons can be easily overlooked by time-strapped tourists on their way to Yellowstone. But these mountains should not be missed. Visitors of all ages and interests will have no trouble finding ways to fill their day with adventure at Grand Teton National Park.

GRAND TETON: RIDERS   18" X 24" Poster art created in 2020 by Derek Anderson & Joel Anderson ∧
GRAND TETON: SAND HILL CRANE   18" X 24" Poster art based on an oil painting created in 2017 by Kai Carpenter >

GREAT BASIN

WAVES OF PARCHED sagebrush sigh in the high desert wind of central Nevada. Painted in the driest of watercolors, this landscape persists to exist in arid beauty. A lonely summit, worn ragged by the elements, looms over the tumbling basin valley. **Mount Wheeler** is a 13,000-foot sentinel for this barren wilderness, centerpiece to Great Basin National Park. The Park represents a much larger region of the American West, a vast system of bowls, or "basins" scooped into the states of Nevada, Utah, Idaho, Oregon, and California. These valleys are inland water traps, collecting scant rainfall and mountain streams in mudflats and salted lakes while providing no outlet to the ocean. The result is a bone dry, gusty environment where only tough, well-adapted wildlife survives. Gnarled, weathered roots of the world's oldest trees anchor themselves against the ruthless gales here. Great Basin's bristlecone pines are a natural phenomenon: a small grove of pinetrees older than King David cling to the rugged highlands of Mount Wheeler. Shaped and polished by the wind, these pines epitomize life in the Great Basin, a place where nature continues to stubbornly defy its harsh environment.

Great Basin National Park was once home to an industrious gold-miner-turned-rancher named Absalom Lehman. A mining failure in California but a smashing success in Australia, Lehman knew from firsthand experience how to thrive in difficult circumstances. After his wife and daughter passed away in Australia in the 1880s, Lehman moved to Nevada, where he lived his first summer "under a pine tree with Indians for neighbors." He quickly adjusted to his new surroundings, remarried, and established a ranch in the Park's northeastern corner. Friends, relatives, and newcomers all flocked to Lehman's ranch, and the homestead became a bustling village and orchard. While out on a jaunt one day, Lehman stumbled upon a small series of caves beneath the foothills of Mount Wheeler. He soon began guiding lantern tours into **Lehman Caves**. Park visitors can still enter this limestone sanctuary beneath the desert today.

Encounter the old bristlecones that watch over this National Park atop Mount Wheeler. Ascend the exposed summit via **Wheeler Peak Trail**, where winded climbers are rewarded with an incredible panoramic view of the Basin. **The Bristlecone Forest Loop** lies just below the summit and invites guests to ponder their own finite existence in the midst of such ancient life. Plunge into the subterranean world of Lehman Caves on the **Grand Palace Tour**, where dangling stone tendrils await you. Through struggle rises brilliance in Great Basin National Park.

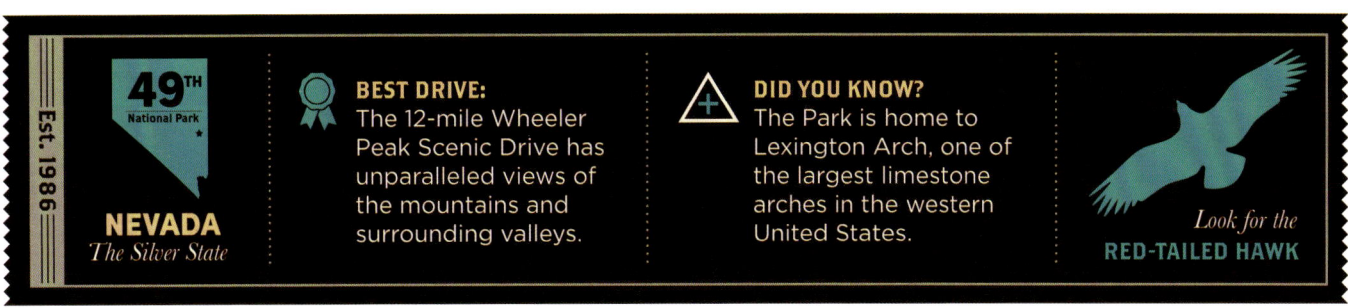

<GREAT BASIN: BIGHORN SHEEP 18" X 24" Poster art created in 2020 by Derek Anderson & Joel Anderson

SAN LUIS VALLEY · COLORADO

GREAT SAND DUNES
NATIONAL PARK

GREAT SAND DUNES

GUSTY FINGERS comb the tresses of a vast golden dune. All is in motion. All is still. A dance sways ever on in the wild silence between sand and wind at Great Sand Dunes National Park and Preserve. These playful dunes imitate their stoic thirteen thousand-foot parents, the **Sangre de Cristos Mountains**, hovering in the background. Incessant gales blow down from the mountains to craft and shape this sandscape. What now appears to be a desert scene straight out of North Africa was once a sediment-rich lake. The **San Luis Valley** is all that remains of Lake Alamosa, which rested between the Sangre de Cristos Mountains to the east and **San Juan Mountains** to the west. The Park's concealed alpine lakes attest to a time when water was abundant in southern Colorado. The Park today seems perfectly content to exist as a paradox, a sweeping scene of both constancy and change. Though the sandy patterns resemble waves on a tumultuous sea, the vast dunes themselves seem to loom immobile. A hiker's footprints along the ridgeline are soon wiped clean by the shifting breezes. Surface temperatures on the dunes can range from a scorching 150 degrees in the summer to 20 below on the coldest winter nights. The highest of these sandy mountains is **Star Dune**, a 750-foot tall giant that peers out over the entire dunefield. This Park is home to the largest dunes in North America. Atop these golden peaks you can experience the riveting silence that explorer Zebulon Pike once felt as he peered over this dry sea and pondered a way across. Most people today are more bent on enjoying the sand: hiking, sledding, sandboarding, or sprinting down these rippled hills are all favorite pastimes among Park visitors.

Though sand is the primary attraction (and there's plenty to be had), Great Sand Dunes National Park and Preserve also features a complex ecosystem of wetlands, grassy plains, mountain forests, and tundra. Camouflaged amphibians, circus beetles, and kangaroo rats make their homes in the mountains of dust. Bison, face-painted badgers, and pronghorns roam the grasslands. Pika, mountain lions, snowshoe hare, and bighorn sheep scrape out a living beneath the pines and firs of the Cristos highlands. You can explore all of these environments with the help of a sturdy pair of hiking boots and an all-terrain vehicle for traversing **Medano Pass Primitive Road.** For a more low-key escapade, build a sand castle and take a refreshing dip in **Medano Creek.** This waterway courses alongside the dunefield to rejuvenate both man and animal in the high desert. Make the journey out to the San Luis Valley and enjoy America's grandest sandbox. Don't forget to bring your sunglasses!

58TH National Park
Est. 2004
COLORADO Centennial State

👍 **BEST ACTIVITY:** Sandboarding!

⊕ **DID YOU KNOW?** The sand can heat up to 150°

⊕ **DID YOU KNOW?** Medano Pass is a popular destination for "fat" bikes, a mountain bike with extra-thick tires for riding on sand.

Look for **MOUNTAIN LIONS**

<GREAT SAND DUNES 18" X 24" Poster art created in 2014 by David Anderson & Joel Anderson

GREAT SMOKY MOUNTAINS

THE DUSKY blue hills of the Smokies roll off into the distance from the view atop **Clingmans Dome** at Great Smoky Mountains National Park. This scene is a glimpse into the old Appalachian country, a moment that could have been made a thousand years ago when the woods were young. Hemlock, oak, red spruce, fraser fir, and tulip poplar still populate the old forests today, housing one of the most diverse populations of plants, animals, and insects of any temperate climate in the U.S. The Park ranges in elevation some 6,000 feet and spreads across 800 square miles of Tennessee and North Carolina backcountry. The glory of the Appalachian Mountains is encompassed here: in a single hike from bottom to top, you'll experience a range of ecosystems equivalent to hiking from Georgia to Maine. The trees make the Smokies, but they were not always treated with such reverence; the brink of deforestation awoke local Americans to derail the seemingly inevitable. Now the Smokies are at the center of the National Park experience in the East. A third of the entire U.S. population lives within a day's drive of the Park. Add to that the Park's well-maintained road system connecting travelers to two mid-major southern cities, and it's no wonder why over ten million people visit the Smokies each year.

What is now a prime tourist destination was once a hideaway for social outcasts and the estranged: isolated farming families, moonshiners, former Confederate soldiers, convicts, and Cherokee Indians that refused to march the Trail of Tears. It was in this Appalachian melting pot that Horace Kephart found refuge in 1904. Once a brilliant Ivy League scholar and entrepreneur, Kephart was now a broken man. Having lost his family, his business, and nearly his mind, he fled to the Smokies for renewal. In the mountains, he found solitude, rest, and time to write. His books about camping and life in Appalachia were a national success, providing Kephart a platform for advocating the protection of his adopted home. Meanwhile, large Eastern logging companies ate up the Smoky Mountains with locust-like ferocity. Stripping a patch

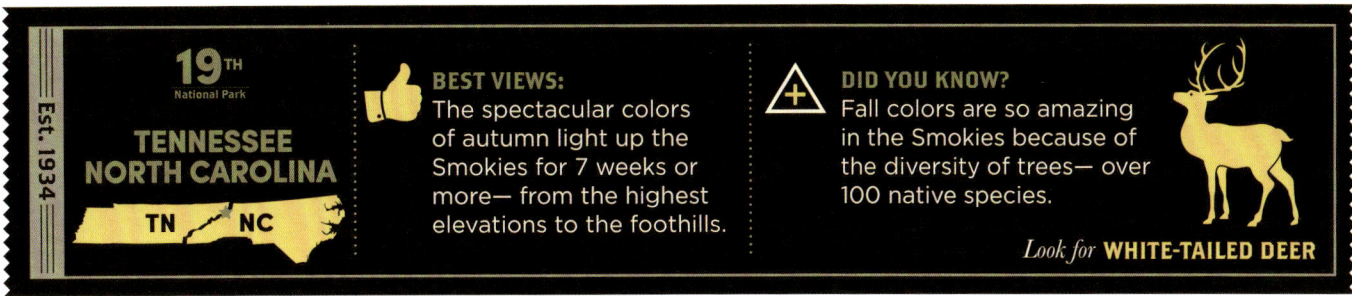

^SALAMANDER 18" X 24" Poster art created in 2017 by Derek Anderson & Joel Anderson
<GREAT SMOKY MOUNTAINS 18" X 24" Poster art created in 2013 by Michael Korfhage & Joel Anderson

of old forest clean, they'd move on to the next area, hiring local townspeople at each stop. Kephart and his new friend, a Japanese immigrant turned Asheville photographer named George Masa, set out to survey the mountains and advocate their salvation. Masa's stunning photography alongside Kephart's essays moved millions, and the state governments of Tennessee and North Carolina soon joined their rallying cry for a Park. President Calvin Coolidge would designate the Smokies as a National Park site in 1926, with the sole condition that no government funding be necessary to create or maintain it. Large tracts of private land still needed to be purchased to keep the Park from dying at birth. Local communities, rich and poor, all joined together to raise the $10 million necessary to keep the dream alive. John D. Rockefeller, Jr., son of the wealthiest man in America and a devoted lover of the Parks, would also contribute, donating $5 million to the cause. Then, in the year of the stock market crash of 1929, President Franklin D. Roosevelt completed the task, purchasing the last $1.5 million worth of private land in order to firmly establish a National Park in the

Great Smoky Mountains. This would be the first time in U.S. history that the government would purchase private land to create a National Park. The efforts of the great and the small, public and private, capitals and churches, made the Smokies what they are today. It seems only fitting that these old woodlands in the Appalachian hills are now so deeply cherished by tens of millions of American people.

Nature abounds in the Great Smoky Mountains. Over 1,500 species of wildflowers color the Park, and the vantage points from which to see them are just as numerous. Visit **Cades Cove** for chance encounters with the area's teeming wildlife. The Smokies are an opulent home for black bears, white tailed deer, wild turkey, squirrels, fox, salamanders, and (in the summer) fireflies. Waterfalls sing praises throughout the Park, especially at **Ramsay Cascades** and **Rainbow Falls**. Experience elevated elation from a hike up **Mt. Le Conte** or take in the timeless vista that inspired Kephart and Masa from Clingmans Dome. Thanks to early advocates like these two men, the Smokies remain a people's Park: an accessible yet unspoiled sanctuary for American wilderness.

"The Smokies are a wilderness crown found between Tennessee and North Carolina. You really feel the majesty of the mountains and forests as you explore the top of the Appalachian range. You also sense the history of the area as you discover the valleys where people lived for ages. Cataloochee was one of those valleys where I always experienced a journey back through time when families lived in the valley for many generations with very little contact with the rest of the world."
— Bill Pierce, Former Ranger at Great Smoky Mtns from 1977 – 1981
(total years of NPS service: 38)

APPALACHIAN TRAIL 18" X 24" Poster art based on an oil painting created in 2017 by Kai Carpenter ^
GREAT SMOKY MOMENT 18" X 24" Poster art based on an oil painting created in 2015 by Kai Carpenter >

GUADALUPE MOUNTAINS

OCEAN AND DESERT. Reefs and peaks. Sponges and pine. Guadalupe Mountains National Park, at one time or another, contained all of these. This is a relatively obscure Park with a rich geological and cultural history. The waterless landscape in west Texas was once a shallow sea, home to a 400-mile long horseshoe reef that is now a fossilized mountain range. Today, the two highest points in Texas jut out of this Park's ancient coral shoal. At 8,749 feet, **Guadalupe Peak** is the tallest mountain in Texas and its neighbor, **El Capitán**, looms 8,064 feet high and can be seen from up to 50 miles away.

Life still abounds in these mountains, a desert oasis above the harsh Chihuahuan wastelands. Where primordial fish, coral polyps, algae, and sponges once thrived is today a haven for elk, black bears, roadrunners, and, of course, backpackers. Those who make the trek out to these oft-overlooked Texas highlands will discover a landscape brimming with adventure.

The Guadalupe Mountains have never been a hospitable landscape for human life, but stone age artifacts have been found in the area dating some 12,000 years. Petroglyphs and pottery are all that remain of these ancient nomads. In more modern times, the Apache used to hide out in the mountain caves and hunt for game when not raiding nearby homesteads. They would live in isolation from white men until the mid-1800s when Texan prospectors sought out a pathway through the mountains.

American dreams of transcontinental railways and a cross-country mail road were brought into western Texas, and the era of the Apache soon came to a close. U.S. militiamen were sent in to drive out the natives and clear a safe passage for the mail coaches. In the midst of this bloody war, two brothers built a house at **Frijole Ranch** in 1876. This building would serve as the area's main community center and post office for the next 70 years until it was purchased by successful banker-turned-rancher J.C. Hunter. Along with petroleum geologist Wallace Pratt, Hunter purchased thousands of acres around the Guadalupe Mountains. Hunter and his son raised goats in the Park's mountain highlands, while Pratt built family summer homes within the stunning **McKittrick Canyon.** These men recognized the unique beauty of their backyards and, in time, donated their land to the National Park Service to create Guadalupe Mountains National Park, which opened in 1972.

Thanks to the generous donations of the Hunters and the Pratts, the Guadalupe Mountains are now accessible for all to enjoy. Witness bright fall foliage in the Texas highlands on the **McKittrick Canyon Trail** in late October. This trail is considered one of the best hikes in the Lone Star State no matter what month it is. Get personal with the state's highest point on a pebbled pathway up to Guadalupe Peak or backpack into a secluded conifer forest for a night under the stars at **Pine Top.** Streams of life still flow through the Guadalupe Mountains. Venture up and wash yourself in the hidden wonders that await you.

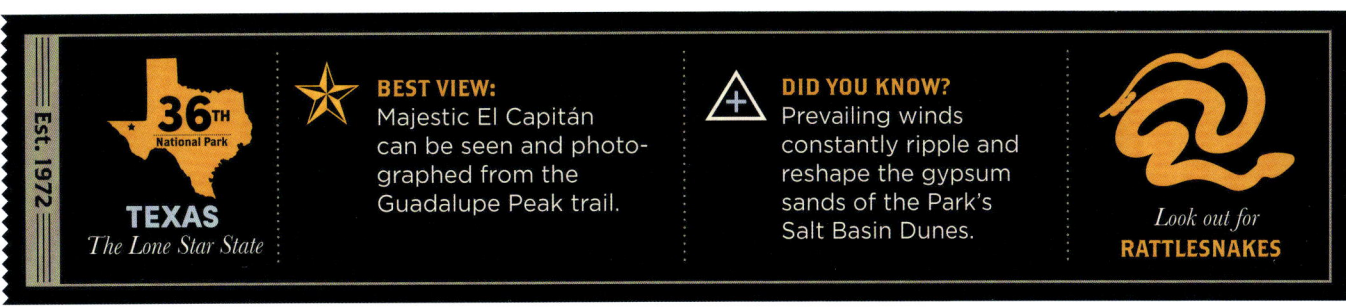

Est. 1972 · 36TH National Park · TEXAS *The Lone Star State*

BEST VIEW: Majestic El Capitán can be seen and photographed from the Guadalupe Peak trail.

DID YOU KNOW? Prevailing winds constantly ripple and reshape the gypsum sands of the Park's Salt Basin Dunes.

Look out for **RATTLESNAKES**

<GUADALUPE MOUNTAINS 18" X 24" Poster art created in 2013 by Michael Korfhage & Joel Anderson

HALEAKALĀ

YOU STAND in the silent twilight atop a dormant volcano. Sleep stings your eyes as you squint into the expanse. A cloud quilt lies rumpled over the yawning valley below. You shiver in the wind, glancing at the bleary-eyed tourists around you, all awaiting the arrival of the morning star. And slowly the silken cloud sea begins to glow orange and yellow. Jagged cliff silhouettes darken as the sky ignites, and the Pacific sparkles in the new light. Morning has dawned. Welcome to Haleakalā, the House of the Sun.

Hawaiian legend has it that the demigod Maui once heard his mother sigh and say that the island days were too short, that the sun did not stay up long enough for her laundry to dry. Clever Maui happened to know that the sun lived atop Mount Haleakalā, and he climbed up to the mountain's summit. Using his sister's hair, he made a lasso and yanked down the sun. He would only let go if the sun agreed to cross the sky more slowly. The sun pled for mercy and agreed that he would make the days longer in the summertime. Satisfied, Maui released the star and descended the mountain. Sun has generously splashed his rays on the islands ever since. Playful silversword plants laugh in the breeze, blooming beneath clear mountain skies. Down the mountainside, in verdant Kīpahulu Valley, waterfalls shimmer and tumble into the coves.

Haleakalā National Park is divided into two wholly distinct areas: the exalted moon-desert summit, and the lush beach jungles of **Kīpahulu.** No road connects the two regions, so it's best to take a few days to fully enjoy this diverse display of Hawai'ian wilderness. The summit is actually two volcanic valleys that melded after erosion ate away the mountain's peak. This supervalley formed a "crater" basin 2,720 feet deep. Ambitious hikers may now descend into this steep depression via **Halemau'u** and **Sliding Sand Trails.** Most Park guests are content to simply watch the sunrise from the crater rim at **Pu'u'ula'ula Summit**.

If you're not into high-altitude volcanic wastelands, you're in luck. Haleakalā features an incredible ocean-side Eden at Kīpahulu. While you cannot actually swim in the ocean here, water-lovers can splash in the sumptuous pools of **'Ohe'o Gulch.** Many of these jungle baths are formed by Kīpahulu's magnificent waterfalls, of which the greatest is 400-foot **Waimoku Falls**. Access the misty wonder of Waimoku from the luscious **Pipiwai Trail**, considered one of the best hikes in Hawai'i. Walk through thick bamboo forests and breathe in the island air. Volcanoes and waterfalls await you on this jewel of Maui. Escape the mundane and savor the sunshine at Haleakalā National Park.

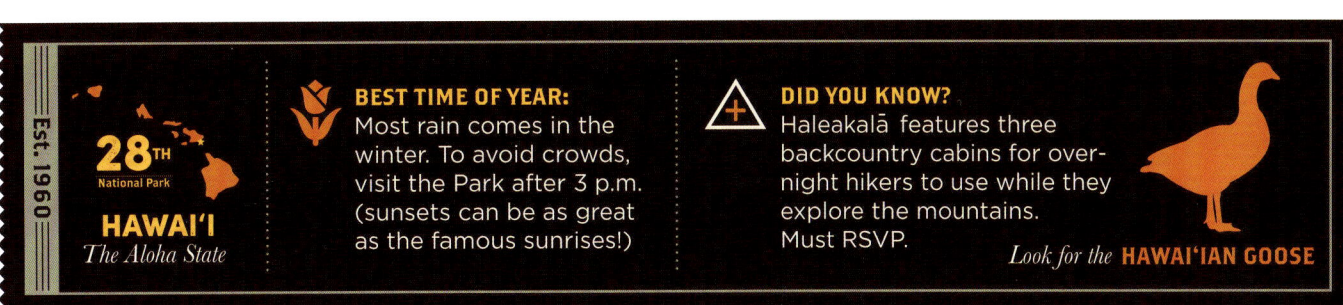

<HALEAKALĀ 18" X 24" Poster art created in 2015 by Michael Korfhage & Joel Anderson

HAWAI'I VOLCANOES

NATIONAL PARK

HAWAI'I VOLCANOES

LAVA and ocean intertwine at Hawai'i Volcanoes National Park. Huddled on the southeastern corner of the island of Hawai'i, this Park is governed by the volatile cycle of destruction and renewal. Hawai'i itself is a product of this volcanic process, and the Earth's red-hot magma that formed the islands continues to create new land in the South Pacific. Hawai'i Volcanoes is a place as steeped in history as it is in volcanic debris: Polynesian immigrants have occupied the islands for over 1,500 years. The Park has petroglyphs etched in lava by ancient Hawai'ians and fossilized footprints of native soldiers killed by a volcanic eruption. A more recent historical figure would bring national (and tourist) attention to the South Pacific. Mark Twain's clever and lurid accounts of the island helped spark an interest in preserving Hawai'i's mountains of fire.

Two mountain behemoths dominate the Park. **Mauna Loa** lies on the northern end, a sheer monster of volcanic rock. The base of the mountain sits at the bottom of the Pacific Ocean and rises some 50,000 feet from the ocean floor (13,679 feet above sea level). When measuring Mauna Loa's sheer girth, it is one of the largest mountains on the planet. Hawai'ians of old paid reverence to their volcano goddess Pele at **Kīlauea**, the second and most active of the Park's

two volcanoes. Kīlauea erupted as recent as 1983, and has stayed in a grumbling, cantankerous state ever since. Always up for a new adventure, Mark Twain once stayed at the Volcano House Hotel on Kīlauea's summit. At night he would watch as lava lit up the night sky:

"I turned my eyes upon the volcano again…. For a mile and a half in front of us and half a mile on either side, the floor of the abyss was magnificently illuminated … like the campfires of a great army far away…. It looked like a colossal railroad map of the State of Massachusetts done in chain lightning on a midnight sky. Imagine it — imagine a coal-black sky shivered into a tangled network of angry fire!"

Hawai'i Volcanoes National Park has several trails from which to explore the island's multidimensional landscape. Rainforest, desert, lava fields, arid mountaintops, and volcanic beaches can all be experienced here. And since the Park rests on an active volcano, it is constantly changing. Witness the smoldering activity of Kīlauea from the **Kīlauea Iki Trail**. Pay close attention to trail and road closures as lava flow and noxious gases can make parts of the Park inaccessible. If open, drive the scenic **Crater Rim Drive** for a (safe) observation of the tumultuous **Halema'uma'u Crater** from the **Jaggar Museum**. Follow in the footsteps of Twain and the ancient Hawai'ians as you gape at the power of this land on fire.

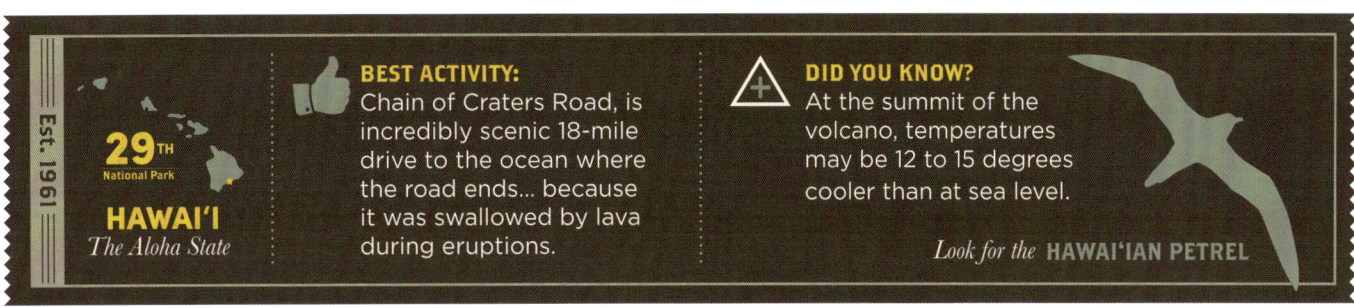

Est. 1961 — 29th National Park — **HAWAI'I** The Aloha State

BEST ACTIVITY: Chain of Craters Road, is incredibly scenic 18-mile drive to the ocean where the road ends… because it was swallowed by lava during eruptions.

DID YOU KNOW? At the summit of the volcano, temperatures may be 12 to 15 degrees cooler than at sea level.

Look for the HAWAI'IAN PETREL

<HAWAI'I VOLCANOES 18" X 24" Poster art created in 2013 by Michael Korfhage & Joel Anderson

HOT SPRINGS

A STEAMY reservoir of mineral water boils beneath the porous hills of central Arkansas. For centuries this basin has accumulated rainwater, slowly creating a deep underground well where water is boiled pure and spouted back out via geothermal energy. Forty-seven springs flow out of Hot Springs Mountain. A National Park-protected resort town now circles the mountain, and health- and beauty-conscious individuals have been bathing in this "fountain of youth" for almost 200 years.

Both the Spanish and the French ventured into this region way before Arkansas became a state. Native Americans introduced the explorers to this "Valley of the Vapors," which America acquired through the Louisiana Purchase in 1803. President Thomas Jefferson sent scientists to explore this fabled hot springs region soon after. The men found the springs, and the dream of a hot springs health spa began. People started moving in to build log bathhouses, claiming the healing powers of the boiling streams for themselves. This led the Arkansas Territory to ask President Andrew Jackson to set aside the Hot Springs region as a national reservation in 1832.

The mineral waters now belonged to the U.S. government, but that did not stop ambitious entrepreneurs from building hotels and bathhouses to tap into this moneymaking stream. By the late 1800s, Hot Springs was a bustling resort town containing opulent Victorian bathhouses, an elegant park for strolling, and underground pipes to keep the hot water flowing. The town's heyday ran well into the 1940s when as many as 24 bathhouses were open for business, giving more than a million baths in a single year! Celebrities, famous and infamous, poured into town to soak and sweat in the mineral baths all along Bathhouse Row. Al Capone was one notable repeat visitor. Director of the National Park Service Stephen Mather was also a regular at the bathhouses and commissioned the construction of a free bathhouse for all of the town's guests. He also persuaded Congress to redesignate the town as a National Park in order to protect Hot Springs Mountain's precious resource.

With the advancement of medicine, the hot springs of Arkansas are no longer worshipped as miraculous, but they are certainly still enjoyed by those seeking relaxation. Walk the **Grand Promenade** up to one of the most sumptuous bathhouses, **The Fordyce**, which now serves as a museum and the Park visitor center. Guests needing a break from the baths may climb the mountain reservoir itself on a trail up **Hot Springs Mountain** where a tower offers panoramic views of the Ouachita Mountain range. Tranquility is the norm in the nation's smallest National Park. Whether you prefer a stroll through the woods or a soak in the tub (or both), you will find a relaxing escape at Hot Springs National Park.

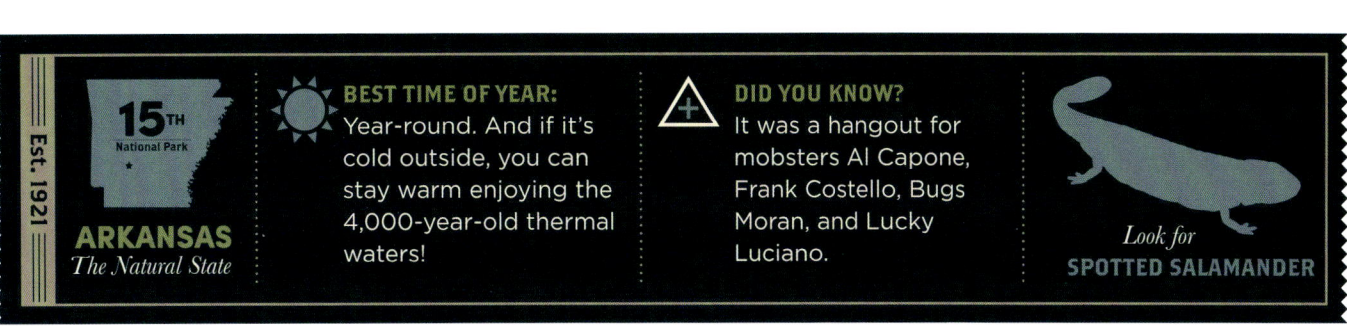

- Est. 1921 — 15TH National Park — **ARKANSAS** *The Natural State*
- **BEST TIME OF YEAR:** Year-round. And if it's cold outside, you can stay warm enjoying the 4,000-year-old thermal waters!
- **DID YOU KNOW?** It was a hangout for mobsters Al Capone, Frank Costello, Bugs Moran, and Lucky Luciano.
- *Look for* **SPOTTED SALAMANDER**

<**HOT SPRINGS** 18" X 24" Poster art created in 2013 by Michael Korfhage & Joel Anderson

INDIANA DUNES

LEFT IN THE MELTING wake of the mile-thick Wisconsin glacier, Indiana Dunes is an ecological wonder of the American Midwest. Only an hour from Chicago, few may realize that nestled against 15 miles of shoreline is an impressive collection of ecosystems: tumbling sand dunes knitted together by marram grass, black oakwood savannas, wildflower and bird-rich bogs and marshes, tranquil river forests, and the incessant waves and wind of Lake Michigan. Migratory birds enjoy an idyllic sanctuary here. Over 50 miles of trails provide ample opportunities for hikers, birders, backpackers, and wildflower enthusiasts to savor all this conveniently-located National Park has to offer.

In 1889, botanist Henry Cowles submitted a study to the University of Chicago regarding the wonderful variety of flowers and plants that flourished along the slim lakeshore of northwestern Indiana. Cowles soon realized he had uncovered a natural treasure sitting dangerously close to the booming industries of Chicago and northern Indiana. Mills and power plants took notice, especially the glass manufacturers. Local businesses such as the Ball Brothers from Muncie, Indiana (known for producing the iconic "mason jars"), took a keen interest in the mountains of quartz and silica-rich sand abounding in their own backyard. Meanwhile, across the lake, Cowles and a small group of like-minded conservationists rallied to form the Prairie Club of Chicago with the primary goal of establishing a Sand Dunes National Park.

Support grew in the Windy City and soon caught the attention of the National Park Service's first director Stephen Mather. Visiting Chicago in 1916, Mather held a public forum to discuss the possibility of establishing the Midwest's first National Park. "Save the Dunes" picket signs and banners began popping up across the region. Park fever was soon checked, however, by America's entrance into the First World War (making glass production and other industries an essential factor to winning the war). A small state park was eventually founded in 1926 but the Prairie Club kept pushing for federal protection. It wasn't until JFK's landmark decision to purchase-and-protect Cape Cod National Seashore that dune supporters saw their big chance. The President's Kennedy Compromise program linked national wealth with natural health—giving a noticeable nod towards Lake Michigan. This drove Illinois Senator Paul H. Douglas to bargain tirelessly with Congress that if a Port of Indiana waterway was necessary for industry, so was an unspoiled National Lakeshore. Indiana Dunes National Lakeshore was finally established in 1966, and, having expanded four times since then, now exceeds 15,000 acres. Congress approved the establishment of Indiana Dunes National Park on February 15th, 2019.

Honor the memory of Senator Douglas's efforts on **Paul H. Douglas Trail** with its impressive duneviews. Channel your inner botanist along the **Cowles Bog Trail System**. Enjoy a shoreline promenade via the paved **Portage Lakefront and Riverwalk**. Catch some rays and build a sandcastle at **Kemil Beach** before taking a ranger-guided sunset hike to the top of windswept **Mount Baldy**. Indiana Dunes also protects a **curious collection of retro houses** from the 1933 Chicago World's Fair—moved here soon after to promote a high-end housing community. Check the Park website to see when you can join a Park Ranger to explore these vintage abodes.

America's **61ST** National Park — **INDIANA** *The Hoosier State* — Est. 2019

DID YOU KNOW? Indiana Dunes has more native species of orchids than the state of Hawai'i.

GREAT ACTIVITY Take the 1.5-mile Three Dune Challenge to ascend the Park's tallest sand dunes: Mt. Jackson, Mt. Holden, and Mt. Tom.

Look for the **RED FOX**

<INDIANA DUNES 18" X 24" Poster art created in 2019 by Derek Anderson & Joel Anderson

ISLE ROYALE

ABOARD a ferry ship, you find yourself on a vast inland sea blanketed in thick fog. You cannot see more than a dozen feet ahead in any direction. The chill of mist and the unknown tingles your spine as the seconds, minutes, hours pass … and then, there in the ghost cloud, a lighthouse looms. The yellow-white light is faint but familiar, guiding the ferry on a hidden pathway towards harbor. More than 25 ships lost sight of the light, running aground or sinking in the treacherous Northern waters of Lake Superior. As the lighthouse takes form, you are aware of a lushly wooded shoreline. All is still. You have entered Isle Royale National Park.

Isle Royale is the most remote National Park in the lower 48 states, floating just below the Canadian border in the northwest corner of Lake Superior. The island is a 45-mile long, 9-mile wide stronghold of wildlands, a remote hermitage for moose, gray wolf, red fox, and loon. The lake's notoriously rough waters secure the island's seclusion from the casual passerby, but hardy backpackers and kayakers now have access to this guarded gem by way of ferry or seaplane. While the average visit to most National Parks is 4 hours, guests visiting Isle Royale commit to the long haul. An average visit to Isle Royale lasts 3.5 days, including the 4 to 6-hour ferry ride to and from Michigan's mainland. No automobiles ever reach the island; to visit Isle Royale is to give yourself over to the northern wilderness, where hikers share the trails with the island's untamed residents.

The primal nature of the isle has remained constant thanks to Detroit reporter Albert Stoll, who, in the 1920s, campaigned for the island's admission as a National Park. Greedy mining and lumber companies eyed the island as a prime source for copper and hardwood. For over a decade, Stoll fought off their greedy axes from his post at Detroit News, writing fiery articles that campaigned for Isle Royale's federal recognition. Finally, as Americans crawled out of a financial crisis in 1940, President Franklin D. Roosevelt used money generated by the New Deal to purchase the island, sustaining the mysterious archipelago for the next generation of explorers.

A trek to Isle Royale requires preparation, flexibility, and commitment. The Park is not easy to access or leave. Ferries from Minnesota and Michigan tow Park guests over precarious Lake Superior, with trips usually lasting around 2-6 hours each way. On the island, hiking is your only means of transportation. Trails such as **Greenstone Ridge, Stoll Memorial,** and **Rock Harbor** wind through the conifer forests and along Isle Royale's scenic ridgelines. Over 36 campgrounds dot the backcountry, providing multiple opportunities to take in the Park's unmarred solitude overnight. Kayaking is also very popular along the shoreline. Explore tiny islets off the main coast at **Five Finger Bay** or a north shore estuary at **McCargoe Cove**. For those with warm blood and a taste for nautical history, dive into the depths of frigid Lake Superior on a SCUBA tour into a watery shipwreck graveyard. The lonesome wilderness of Isle Royale awaits.

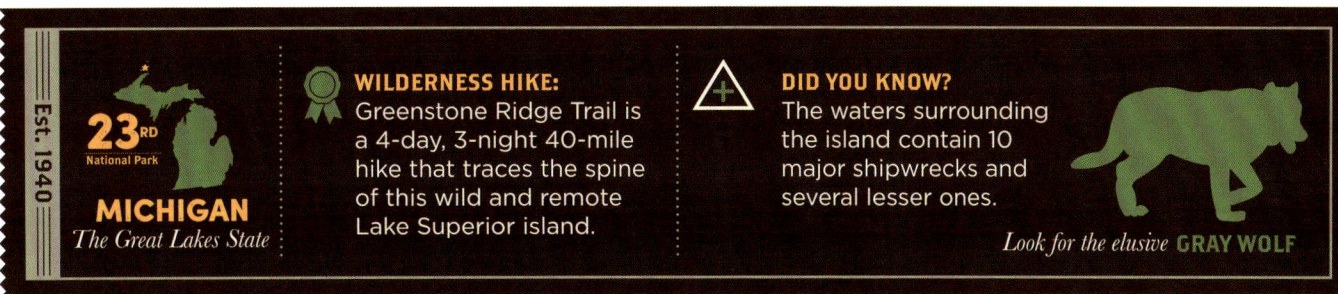

Est. 1940 · 23RD National Park · MICHIGAN *The Great Lakes State*

WILDERNESS HIKE: Greenstone Ridge Trail is a 4-day, 3-night 40-mile hike that traces the spine of this wild and remote Lake Superior island.

DID YOU KNOW? The waters surrounding the island contain 10 major shipwrecks and several lesser ones.

Look for the elusive **GRAY WOLF**

<ISLE ROYALE 18" X 24" Poster art created in 2015 by Michael Korfhage & Joel Anderson

JOSHUA TREE

IN SOUTHERN California, two deserts converge to form a strange and wonderful landscape. The "high" Mojave Desert tumbles down into the "low" Colorado, mingling each ecosystem's plants and wildlife. The result is a lustrous desert ecosystem rich with smooth rocks, cacti and yucca plants, and an endlessly adaptable population of birds, reptiles, and mammals. Joshua Tree National Park is named after its most iconic resident, the Joshua Tree. This yucca plant, with its quirky limbs, looks like a Dr. Seuss illustration come to life. The Joshua Trees thrive in the Mojave region of the Park where they reminded early Mormon settlers of the Biblical hero Joshua as he led the Israelites into the Promised Land with outstretched arms. Joshua Tree now welcomes over two million visitors each year: rock climbers, painters, hikers, and stargazers all find a unique blend of solace and adventure here in the arid wilderness.

Originally home to violent cattle rustlers, ranchers, and gold miners, Joshua Tree captured the imagination of a well-to-do Southern woman from Mississippi named Minerva Hoyt. Growing up in high society, Hoyt married a doctor and moved to Pasadena in the early 1900s. There she involved herself in a number of civic clubs and nature groups, among them a society to protect the austere beauty of California's deserts. As a gardener in Southern California, Hoyt showed particular interest in Joshua Tree's 800 species of plants and flowers that thrived in the arid basins. She respected their ability to flourish when the odds were permanently set against them. This lesson took on new meaning when she lost both her husband and her infant son. Thousands of miles from her Southern roots, she turned to the desert for consolation. Joshua Tree too was in anguish as hundreds of motorists cruised through the valley, uprooting cacti for their homes and burning the "grotesque" Joshua Trees for sport. Minerva Hoyt cried out for the suffering forests. She awoke to what would be her life-long calling, and with indomitable resolve organized worldwide botanical events. She introduced Southern California's distinct plant life to nature-lovers in New York, Boston, and London. Friends began calling her "the apostle of the cacti." Her impassioned articles and reports soon reached Washington, where Hoyt had the opportunity to speak directly with Franklin D. Roosevelt. Hoyt's zeal won him over, and Roosevelt commissioned Joshua Tree National Monument in 1936. President Bill Clinton added 200,000 protected acres and elevated the monument to a full-fledged National Park in 1994.

The San Andreas Fault, along with hundreds of other fault lines, stripe Joshua Tree National Park. These cracks in the Earth's crust have revealed a miscellany of strange rock formations. Smooth and pocked monoliths scattered throughout the Park make this region one of the country's finest destinations for crack, slab, and steep face rock climbing and bouldering. Climbers of all ages and skill levels will find a route suitable for them here. Joshua Tree National Park boasts over 8,000 individual climbing routes and hundreds of natural gaps to try your chalky hands at. This Park even has a designated Climbing Ranger who will be happy to answer any

54TH National Park · Est. 1994 · **CALIFORNIA** *The Golden State*

BEST VIEW: Stargazing: city dwellers are astounded when they get their first glimpse of the night sky in its natural state.

DID YOU KNOW? The famous San Andreas Fault bounds the south side of the Park and can be observed from Keys View.

Look for **JACK RABBITS**

<**JOSHUA TREE: JACK RABBIT** 18" X 24" Poster art created in 2020 by Aaron Johnson & Joel Anderson

of your questions regarding route closures and which areas are best suited for your skill level.

Not in the mood for bouldering? Joshua Tree features numerous nature trails that are both short and scenic, offering access to dramatic desert views, abandoned homesteads, and bizarre landmarks without requiring you to become part camel. Few trails gain much in elevation, making them ideal for families with small children. Squeeze your way through granite walls as you climb up to a massive boulder shaped like a human skull on **Skull Rock Trail.** Do not overlook **Hidden Valley.** This outstanding one-mile hike is brimming with Joshua Trees and cacti, piles of popcorn-like boulders, and desert wildlife scurrying about in the evening. Miner-rancher Bill Keys and his wife Frances raised a family here amongst the stones for six decades. You can learn more about Joshua Tree's most determined family at **Keys Ranch** and explore **Queen Valley** to see the abandoned mine in their sprawling backyard. Take in the endless California desert at sunset from atop **Keys View,** one of the best vistas in the Park. **The Cholla Cactus Garden** is another curious nature walk,

this one loaded with painfully spiny vegetation. Be sure to stay on the trail!

Backpackers longing for desert silence will not be disappointed. The three-mile **Ryan Mountain Trail** is a tough hike but the payoff is a commanding view from 5,000+ feet up. You'll never take water for granted again after a 7.2-mile trek out to the **Lost Palms Oasis.** Learn about the travails of the 49ers and inspect a well-preserved gold mine on a hike to **Lost Horse Mine.** At the end of a long day, pop your tent at **Jumbo Rocks, Indian Cove,** or **Cottonwood Spring** for sunset in the painted desert and a quiet night beneath the vivid starlight.

Four-wheeling on Joshua Tree's backcountry roads is one of the best ways to explore a large amount of the Park in a short time. Enormous Joshua trees, juniper, and pinyon pine flail in the wind as you bump along dirt roads in **Covington Flat.** Make the 3.8-mile trip out to **Eureka Peak** where a 5,516-foot summit offers a westward perspective on posh Palm Springs. Take a crash course in geology by mountain bike or 4WD on the **Geology Tour Road** to **Pleasant Valley.** Your only homework will be to return to your campground in one piece.

JOSHUA TREE: DESERT SUNRISE 18" X 24" Poster art based on an oil painting created in 2017 by Kai Carpenter >

KATMAI

THE RIVERS RUSH WHITE down the great Alaskan mountain ranges. Glistening in the sun, sockeye salmon wriggle their way towards their nesting grounds. They leap out of the strong currents, progressing up the stair-step waterfalls that impede their way home. The salmon are tired and desperate. Lurking around the slippery river staircase is the salmon's second obstacle: a barricade of hungry brown bears, fur matted and streaming with beads of frigid mountain water. They stand in the gushing current and wait. A mother glances towards shore to eye her two cubs wrestling in the shallows. She turns back to the foamy falls as a silver flicker darts past. Another slaps her nose. She bares her yellow fangs and licks her lips. A third bounces from the water and she snatches it by the tail. It writhes and squirms. The mother cranes her neck and flicks the fish to its broad side, securing it in her mouth. Cameras click and tourists ahh. The mother clears her nostrils and lumbers back to her cubs. Just another summer day at **Brooks Falls** in Katmai National Park.

Away from the fishing frenzy, a quiet stone valley slopes gently up to Katmai's volcano range. The Aleutian volcanoes of Alaska were formed by two layers of ocean crust shoved together by seismic force, forming a volatile island chain. In 1912, the peninsula of Katmai shuddered in torment as the rocky cap burst off the top of **Novarupta Volcano.** Ash and flaming rock spewed out, burying the valley in 700 feet of debris and suffocating all life in the atmosphere. Seattle residents, 1,500 miles to the south, washed their sidewalks of Novarupta's sooty remains. The National Geographic Society sent a team of scientists into the volcano range to examine the devastation four years later. What they found was astonishing and deadly. Poisonous gases curled up from the rubble blanket through fumarole vents. Gas masked scientists crept into the cooling basin. The lethal vapors made quite an impression on botanist Robert Griggs, who dubbed the desolate landscape: **Valley of Ten Thousand Smokes**. Griggs brought his findings back to Washington, and Congress created Katmai National Monument in 1918. In 1980, Katmai would be included in the Alaska National Interest Lands Conservation Act and become a National Park. Today, hikers may safely explore the volcanic ravine's 40 square miles, where ebullient rivers have since carved pathways into this valley of destruction.

Air taxis carry thousands of people into Katmai each year. This region is home to some of the best animal watching in the National Park System. Strategically placed porches and secure campgrounds are available for guests to feel safe while they observe the Park's 2,000 brown bears. Whether you hike, fish in the crystal streams, or simply sit and watch the furry locals, you'll never forget a day spent here on the Alaskan coast.

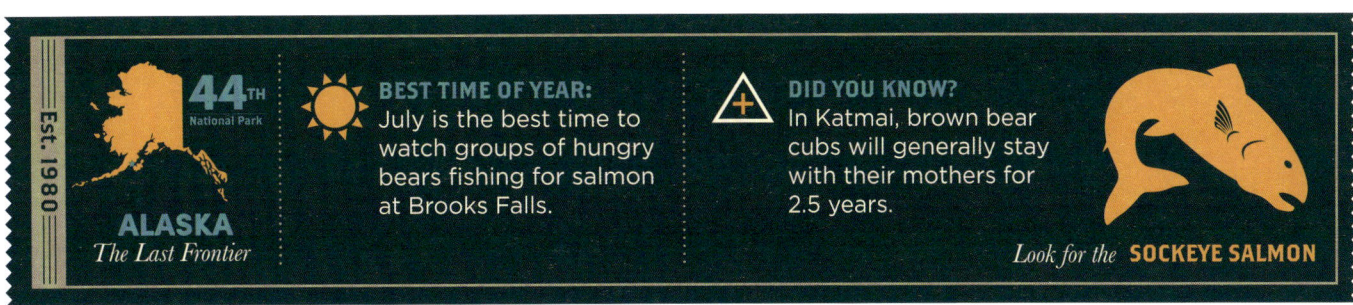

44TH National Park — Est. 1980 — **ALASKA** *The Last Frontier*

BEST TIME OF YEAR: July is the best time to watch groups of hungry bears fishing for salmon at Brooks Falls.

DID YOU KNOW? In Katmai, brown bear cubs will generally stay with their mothers for 2.5 years.

Look for the **SOCKEYE SALMON**

<KATMAI 18" X 24" Poster art created in 2015 by Aaron Johnson & Joel Anderson

KENAI FJORDS

SOLID RIVERS OF BLUE ice flow through Kenai Fjord's granite mountains and crumble into the sea. Glaciers are busy hewing Alaska's southern coast, leaving cavernous fjords in their wake. Dramatic slate-colored cliffs swarming with seabirds wall the fjord inlets. The most notable residents are the clown-faced puffins, air-to-water acrobats that collect fish with their brightly colored beaks. The fjords are also home to thousands of seals and sea lions. You can find whole communities splayed out together on the sloping shorelines. Mountain goats in their creamy white coats scamper along the dark ridges. Waterfall rivulets dance down mountain faces. These streams flow from the slowly receding ice of the highland glacier fields.

The ice king of Kenai Fjords is the indomitable **Harding Icefield**, the largest glacier field in the country. The icefield's vast frozen ocean stands more than a mile high and covers more than 300 square miles with blue-white waves. Thirty-eight glaciers stream down from this single arctic reservoir. Each glacier has quietly sculpted Kenai's terrain over time. As the glaciers melt away, their work is revealed in smooth cliffs and new meadows. Hosts of tour boats enter the Park via **Resurrection Bay** from the nearby town of Seward just to gaze at the evolving artwork of Kenai Fjords. The rich aquatic life and stunning fjord vistas make this National Park a boater's delight.

Visitors who wish to see Kenai Fjords on foot may drive up from Seward and park their cars beside Harding Icefield's little toe, **Exit Glacier**, in the northeast corner of the Park. Stretch your legs on a paved trail up to the overlook of this small but impressive icefield extremity. Willing hikers may climb further up into conifer forests and frozen wastelands on the arduous yet rewarding **Harding Icefield Trail**. The Park also features a myriad of inlets and islands to explore by kayak. A 9-hour ferry ride will bring you to the pristine **Northwestern Lagoon**, a frosty coastal paradise for the adroit kayaker. Rustic campsites dot the shore where weary paddlers spend their evenings beneath crisp Alaskan starlight. Slightly closer to civilization is **Aialik Bay,** its shoreline riddled with forested coves, perfect for a day of adventure. The frozen earth is alive at Kenai Fjords National Park. Grab a paddle and enjoy this watery world of Alaskan splendor.

<KENAI FJORDS 18" X 24" Poster art created in 2015 by Aaron Johnson & Joel Anderson

KINGS CANYON

THE VENERABLE redwood trees of Kings Canyon populate the thick forests just north of Sequoia National Park. A diminutive scrap of this region was initially set aside as General Grant National Park in 1890. This small thumb of a Park included the **General Grant Tree**, the second largest tree in the world, and the illustrious grove of sequoias harboring this giant. Kings Canyon National Park would spring from this patch of revered woodlands and grow into a prime destination for a Californian backcountry adventure.

The vision for an "extended" Sequoia began as early as the 1880s but would not come into fruition until 1940. On a jaunt through the Sierras, Secretary of the Interior Harold Ickes was shaken by the timelessness of Kings Canyon. The elderly trees, laughing rivers, yawning caves, and solemn canyons inspired him beyond words. This unadulterated freshness felt different from other Parks. By this time, roadways laced several of America's National Parks. Families could drive up and through these natural wonders within a few hours. Ickes desired to establish a Park that would be left undeveloped, impenetrable to the meandering automobile. He wanted a place that would require its guests to get out of their cars and onto the trails: a landscape of stillness, of nature's song uninhibited by the noise of mankind. Ickes saw this exquisite possibility up here in the Sierra Nevada and endorsed Kings Canyon as a National Park, to be left as it was found. Only a single, curvy road descends into the canyon.

The undeveloped nature of Kings Canyon remains to this day. Sequoia trees still grow wild on the slopes of the Sierras, especially in **Redwood Canyon**. **Grants Grove** stands taller than ever, quietly stretching heavenward in the southwest corner of the Park. **Zumwalt Valley** alone is worth the potential nausea from your car ride. This emerald of the Sierra is tucked into the floor of the canyon and fed lavishly by the Kings River. Lakes dot the Park like alpine puddles after a winter's thaw. Leave your car at **Road's End** and begin a refreshing journey into the High Sierra along **Rae Lakes Loop**, where concealed glacial beauty waits to be uncovered. Kings Canyon seems to exist outside of time, as it was intended. Enter in and get lost for a while.

Est. 1940 — **22ND** National Park — **CALIFORNIA** *The Golden State*

BEST TIME OF YEAR: Mid-September and October are the best times to visit, with smaller crowds and pleasant weather.

DID YOU KNOW? Kings Canyon has the world's most extensive remaining stand of giant sequoias with over 15,800 trees.

Look for **SIERRA NEVADA FOX**

∧ **KINGS CANYON: BEARS** 18" X 24" Poster art created in 2018 by Derek Anderson & Joel Anderson
< **KINGS CANYON** 18" X 24" Poster art created in 2015 by Michael Korfhage & Joel Anderson

KOBUK VALLEY

ABSOLUTE, DESOLATE wilderness awaits the brave at Kobuk Valley National Park. This is a backpackers' toughest challenge: the merciless and unpredictable landscape of northwestern Alaska. There are no roads here. There are no visitor centers here. You may enter the Park only by plane or boat. You must carry in everything you need to survive on the endless tundra. It is the least visited National Park in America, averaging just about 3,000 visitors per year. And with good reason. Like its neighbor, the Gates of the Arctic National Park, Kobuk Valley lies completely above the Arctic Circle. It is a land of extremes: winter temperatures steadily stay below freezing and the chilling arctic winds make it feel even colder. Summer is the best time to visit, but be prepared for the nefarious swarms of mosquitoes.

You may be wondering, *Why on earth did we turn this place into a National Park?* Though barren and isolated, this region is an ancestral home to one of Alaska's most majestic creatures, the caribou. Native Inuit tribes have lived off these herds for nearly 10,000 years. And for travelers seeking an escape from developed America, this is about as far away as you can get.

Kobuk Valley lies between two mountain ranges: the **Baird Mountains** to the north, and the **Waring Mountains** to the south. The wide, placid **Kobuk River** flows gently across the valley floor. This is the region's lifeline, the heart of the region's wildlife activity. The most prolific residents of Kobuk Valley are the wooly caribou. Numbering more than half a million, vast herds of caribou cross the Kobuk River twice each year, migrating to and from their breeding grounds. Within the Park's 2 million acres reside about a dozen small Inuit communities. With time-honored tradition and respect, the natives still hunt the caribou during the caribou's migration period. The Inuit rely on the meat to feed their families and the skins to keep warm throughout the harsh winters. Park guests may witness the mass exodus of the caribou at a river bend called **Onion Portage**, a ford where the herds have crossed for millennia.

To the south of the Kobuk River, at the foot of the Waring Mountains, is **Great Kobuk Sand Dunes.** Sometimes referred to as "the Sahara of the Arctic", this rippling desert stretches out for over 25 square miles. The dunes are a mountainous collection of ancient dust, by-product of glacial grinding from the last Ice Age. The caribou herds must cross this gusty desert twice each year. Incessant wind, like an Alaskan Etch-a-Sketch, quickly erases all evidence of the caribou's migration. Park visitors can experience the lonely solitude of the dunes on a round-trip 4-hour hike as part of their weeklong rafting excursion across the Park. The 80 miles of river will carry you from the eastern town of Ambler to Kiana in the west, with plenty of hiking opportunities along the way. A trip like this will require extensive planning, but few wilderness encounters can match the solitary communion with nature found at Kobuk Valley National Park.

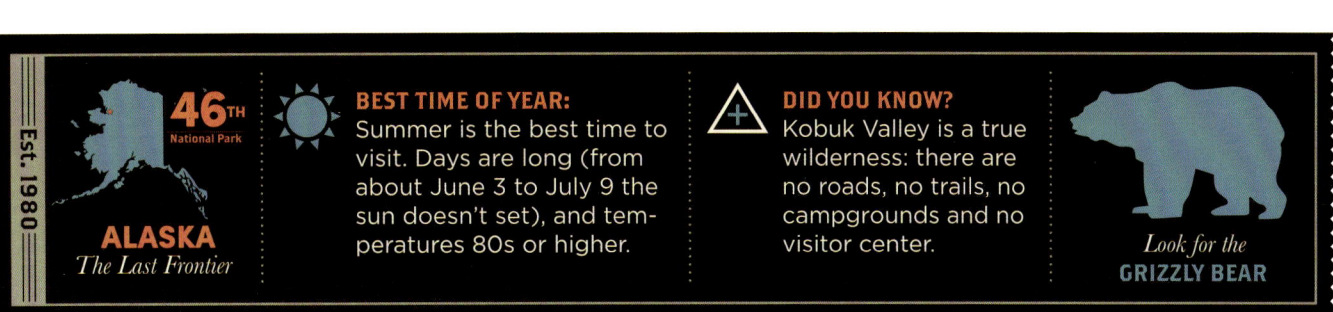

BEST TIME OF YEAR: Summer is the best time to visit. Days are long (from about June 3 to July 9 the sun doesn't set), and temperatures 80s or higher.

DID YOU KNOW? Kobuk Valley is a true wilderness: there are no roads, no trails, no campgrounds and no visitor center.

46TH National Park · Est. 1980 · ALASKA *The Last Frontier* · *Look for the* **GRIZZLY BEAR**

<**KOBUK VALLEY** 18" X 24" Poster art created in 2015 by Joel Anderson

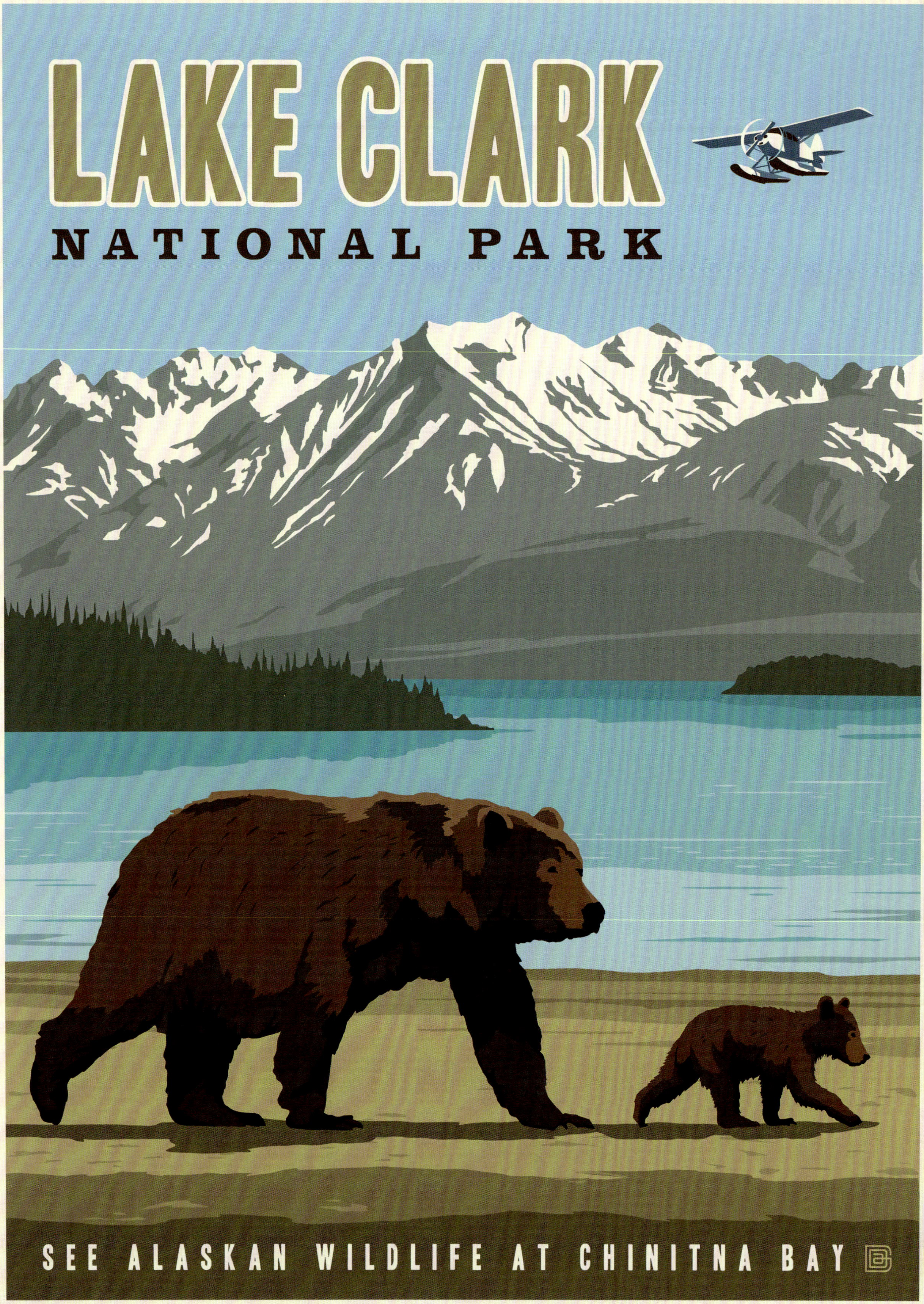
LAKE CLARK
NATIONAL PARK
SEE ALASKAN WILDLIFE AT CHINITNA BAY

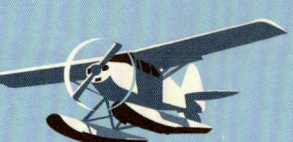

LAKE CLARK

FOUR MILLION ACRES of the best Alaskan countryside await you at Lake Clark National Park. Bush pilots from Anchorage fly visitors into the Park via seaplanes. These small aircraft provide their passengers with an awe-inspiring aerial view of Lake Clark's glory. Cerulean lakes, glacier-flooded mountain passes, thick coastal rainforest, fish-filled rivers, and wind-swept tundra all play their part in the natural symphony that is Lake Clark. Three distinct mountain chains, peppered with secluded lakes and streams, unite within Park boundaries. Two active volcanoes, **Iliamna** and **Redoubt**, regularly vent reminders of their presence. Fishermen from all over the world cast their lines into Lake Clark's streams each summer. This Park is an anglers' paradise; rainbow trout, arctic grayling, northern pike, and five different types of salmon can all be caught within Lake Clark. The native Dena'ina Athabascan people have worked, played, lived, and died here for thousands of years. Their name for this region is Qizhjeh Vena, "a place where people gathered." Protected by the National Park Service, the Athabascan way of life continues to this day. Park visitors too can now gather together to enjoy this serene slice of Alaskan coastland.

A log cabin on the shore of **Twin Lakes** stands as a testament to Alaska's hardy, self-reliant residents. Richard L. Proenneke, a nature writer and master craftsman, built his lakeside cottage by hand in the 1960s. For the next 3 decades he lived alone in this cabin, exploring, filming, and writing about Lake Clark's unrefined grandeur. He was a man who did everything by hand, living solely off the land and streams with

simple tools. In his journals, collected in Sam Keith's book *One Man's Wilderness: An Alaskan Odyssey*, Proenneke wrote: "I enjoy working for my heat. I don't just press a button or twist a thermostat dial. I use the big crosscut saw and the axe, and while I'm getting my heat supply I'm working up an appetite that makes simple food just as appealing as anything a French chef could create." This wry, do-it-yourself attitude, paired with a deep admiration for nature's power, allowed Proenneke to preach the message of wilderness conservation to millions of readers. He is remembered to this day by the National Park Service as a champion steward of Alaska's natural resources. Park visitors today can visit his log cabin and read his joyful, down-to-earth recollections of daily life in remote Alaskan backcountry.

In a Park so rich in outdoor activities, opportunities abound for an intimate connection with Lake Clark's wilderness. Try your hand at salmon fishing on the **Tlikakila River,** or take a wild whitewater-rafting trip down the **Chilikadrotna.** A more peaceful boating tour sails on the turquoise waters of **Lake Clark** itself, where steep mountain slopes hem you in from both shores. Hire a guide and trek into the hilly Alaskan outback via **Telaquana Trail,** a path used by the Athabascan people for centuries. The grand wilderness of southwestern Alaska lies wide open before you at Lake Clark National Park. Enter in and enjoy the many charms of this arctic utopia.

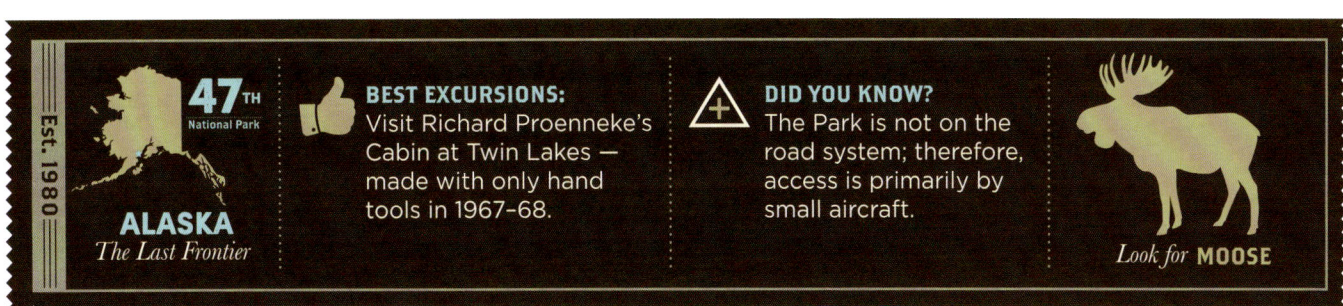

<LAKE CLARK 18" X 24" Poster art created in 2015 by Michael Korfhage & Joel Anderson

LASSEN VOLCANIC

A VOLCANO quietly seethes at the dragon-tail end of the Cascade mountain range in California. Birds sing in the breezy conifers while black bears roam the fields beneath this gray pyramid peak. Tranquil scenery plus a lack of tourism make this small Park a serene getaway. All seems calm now, but the silent mountain has a savage history. In 1915, Lassen exploded, firing off a series of eruptions that devastated the surrounding area. An awe-struck photographer named B.F. Loomis caught the explosion on film and documented the dangerous scene:

"The eruption came on gradually at first, getting larger and larger until finally it broke out in a high roar like thunder. The smoke cloud was hurled with tremendous velocity many miles high, and the rocks thrown from the crater were seen to fly way below the timberline ... they were followed by a comet-like tail of smoke which enabled us to tell definitely the path of their flight."

This volcanic outburst cloaked the forest in ash. Fortunately, no one in Loomis's party was seriously hurt. Their survival story paired with Loomis's photographs of the destruction brought national attention to Lassen. Congress converted the then-National Monument into a full-fledged National Park in 1916. Though Lassen Volcanic was now a Park, the government did not see fit to fund it. One senator explained, "it should not cost anything to run a volcano." Lassen Peak ominously rumbled for another five years.

The Park is lightly visited throughout the year with snows closing off many of the main trails in the wintertime. Similar to Yellowstone, Lassen Volcanic contains several strange geothermic features, bubbling up through the Park's thin crust. Follow the boardwalk through **Bumpass Hell** to see roiling mudpots, smelly hot springs, and the ghastly shore of **Cold Boiling Lake**. Take in the Park's dramatic vistas from the **Juniper Lake** region or lace up your hiking boots to climb the dormant **Lassen Peak** itself.

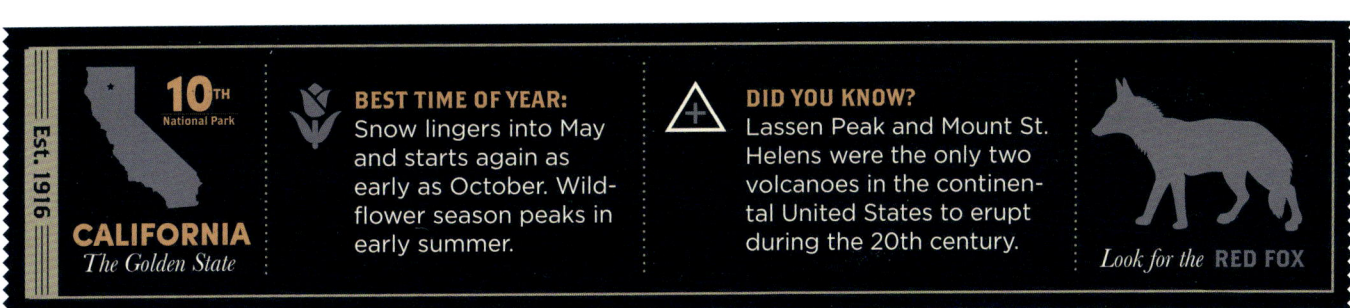

Est. 1916 — **10TH** National Park — **CALIFORNIA** *The Golden State*

BEST TIME OF YEAR: Snow lingers into May and starts again as early as October. Wildflower season peaks in early summer.

DID YOU KNOW? Lassen Peak and Mount St. Helens were the only two volcanoes in the continental United States to erupt during the 20th century.

Look for the **RED FOX**

<LASSEN VOLCANIC 18" X 24" Poster art created in 2015 by Michael Korfhage & Joel Anderson

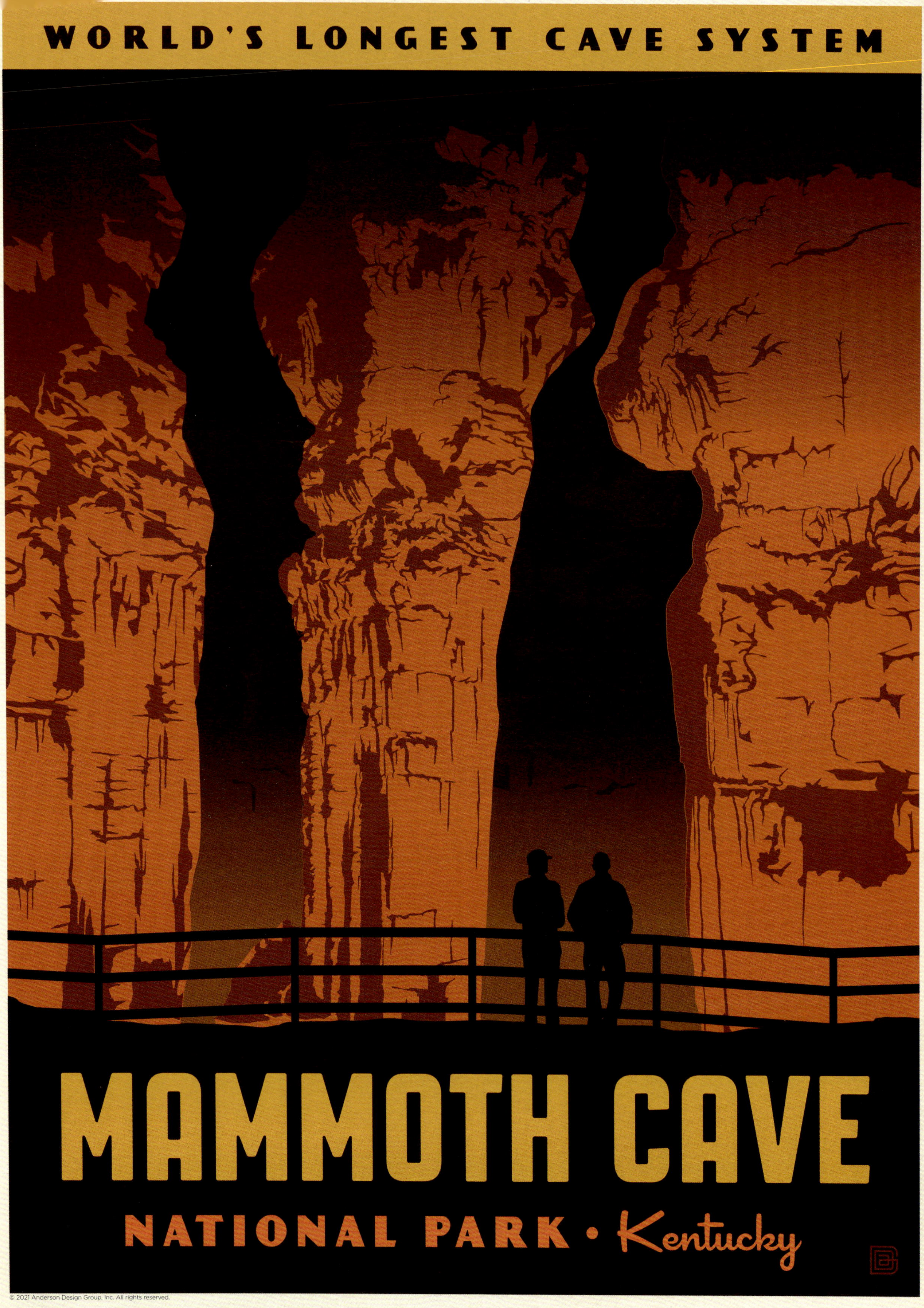

MAMMOTH CAVE

DRIVING up I-65, you would never know the longest cave system on Earth lies just below the rolling Kentucky hills. Mammoth Cave is gargantuan. Carved into porous limestone, the cave is over 400 miles long. And scientists believe there's still plenty more to discover. Despite its immensity, Mammoth Cave somehow maintains a humble disposition, instilling in its spelunking guests a simple giddiness for exploration. It is not garish (no "mood" lighting or music). The lighting installed along the underground trails reveal only what it is: a wondrous labyrinth of stone. It is also a place that epitomizes the American struggle for freedom.

Mammoth Cave played a pivotal role in protecting America's existence in the War of 1812. Mammoth contained large deposits of saltpeter, which could be mined out and easily converted into gunpowder. In fact, Park Rangers will tell you that a majority of the American ammunition used in the war came straight from this cave. Sadly, the miners of Mammoth Cave's minerals were slaves, people who would be unaffected by an American victory over England. Slaves worked in the damp darkness of the cave 10 to 12 hours a day, mining for a precious resource that would keep them in their squalor. All Americans today owe our enslaved forefathers a great debt, for through them Mammoth Cave (and the freedom to enjoy it) would be protected.

You cannot visit Mammoth Cave without hearing the name Stephen Bishop. Stephen was a Kentucky slave in the 1830s and one of the cave's first and greatest tour guides. He was bright, witty, and brave; working with a Louisville cartographer, he mapped out roughly 10 miles of the cave he had explored from memory. Park visitors can still purchase a copy of his extraordinary "memory map" in Mammoth's Visitor Center. When the nephew of the cave's wealthy owner foolishly left Stephen's tour group looking for a lost hat, Stephen went back for him. The young man was lost in the dark for 38 miserable hours before Stephen found him. With his trademark enthusiasm, Stephen named many of Mammoth's key landmarks and passages, and you can still see his signature written in ash on walls throughout the underground Park.

Mammoth is not your typical cave. You won't find many stalactites dripping from the ceiling or glittery quartz in the walls. The beauty lies in its simplicity. It is a tunnel of stone: vast, cool, and deep. Inviting wisps of mist rise from the cave's mouth throughout the hot Southern summer. About 15 miles of the cave is open to the public. Park Rangers, brimming with anecdotes and geology lessons, lead tour groups along the trails. Tours include a family-friendly saunter to **Frozen Niagara** and the fascinating **Historic Tour**. Mammoth Cave even has something for guests with an adrenaline itch: the pitch-black, belly-crawling, why-did-I-sign-up-for-this **Wild Cave Adventure**.

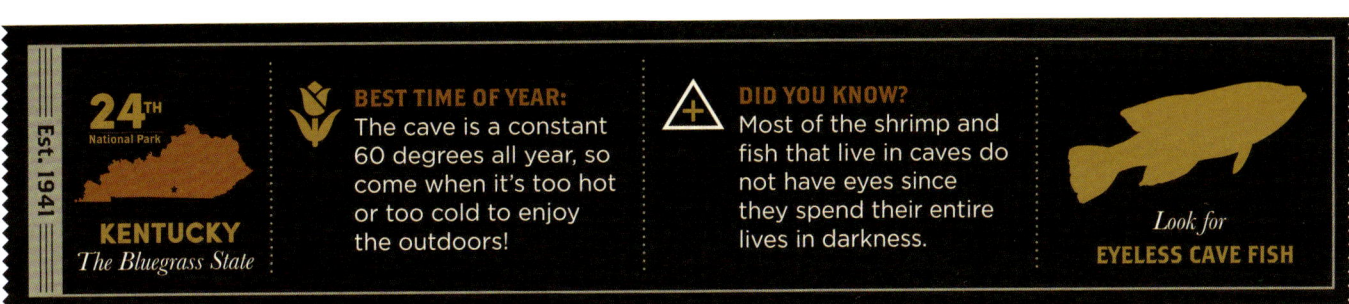

Est. 1941 — **24TH** National Park — **KENTUCKY** *The Bluegrass State*

BEST TIME OF YEAR: The cave is a constant 60 degrees all year, so come when it's too hot or too cold to enjoy the outdoors!

DID YOU KNOW? Most of the shrimp and fish that live in caves do not have eyes since they spend their entire lives in darkness.

Look for **EYELESS CAVE FISH**

<**MAMMOTH CAVE** 18" X 24" Poster art created in 2015 by Michael Korfhage & Joel Anderson

MESA VERDE

UNDER the infinite skies of southwestern Colorado, an Ancestral Puebloan city called Mesa Verde ("Green Table") has slept in the canyon walls for almost a thousand years. The ghostly remains of this metropolis help us understand where these ancient people worked, what they ate, how they worshipped, and where they slept. It also highlights the ingenuity of their 12th century architects, who designed homes of all shapes and sizes into the soft rock. As such, this Park was the first one established to protect a manmade prehistoric site. The priceless artifacts found at Mesa Verde National Park challenged us to value pre-Columbian antiquity and to protect it from plundering.

Quaker cowboys were the first to excavate the Puebloan cliff dwellings. The Wetherhills, five brothers from Kansas, were a curious group of young men who stumbled across Mesa Verde while tending their cattle in 1889. It didn't take long for them to realize the rich significance of the place and their obligation to protect it. Al Wetherhill wrote: "To know you are the first to set foot in homes that had been deserted for centuries is a strange feeling. It is as though unseen eyes watched, wondering what aliens were invading their sanctuaries and why."

As novice archaeologists, Al and his brothers did their best to dust off ancient pottery and utensils, carefully labeling the artifacts and noting where they had found them. Their digs soon became a full-time job, led by their ambitious eldest brother Richard. Unfortunately, word spread of their findings, and their precious site became host to vandals and treasure hunters. The brothers reached out for help from the Smithsonian and the U.S. government to no avail. Meanwhile, an enthusiastic Swedish scientist named Gustaf Nordenskiöld taught the brothers how to properly dig and preserve the artifacts (and took some back home with him in the process). Activist groups arose, lead by the Colorado Cliff Dwelling Association, to highlight the prehistoric city's need for protection. And in 1906, President Theodore Roosevelt would sign the bill, preserving Mesa Verde for future generations as a National Park.

Ranger-led tours of the Puebloan homes are offered throughout the summer. The regal **Cliff Palace** contains 150 individual rooms. This structure alone hosted about 100 people, and many of their living spaces and ceremonial rooms (called "kivas") are still intact today. There are 5,000 known archaeological sites in the Park, and 600 of them are cliff dwellings. Tours into the **Balcony House** and **Long House** are also excellent ways to understand how the Puebloans lived out their daily lives.

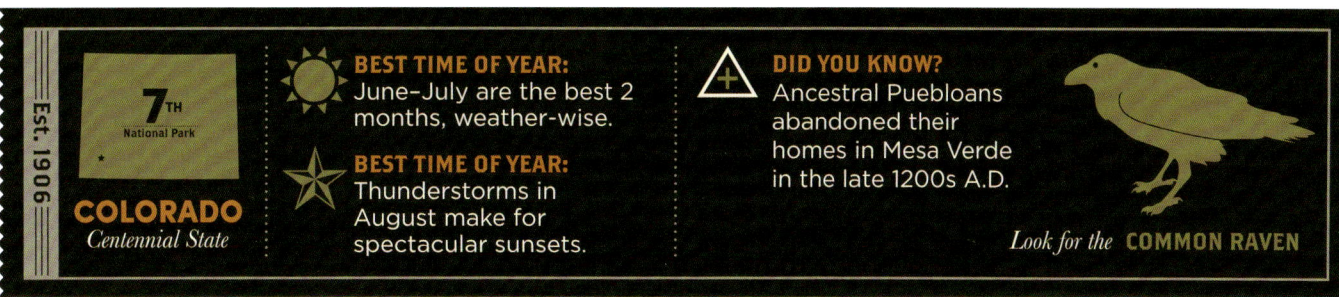

- **BEST TIME OF YEAR:** June–July are the best 2 months, weather-wise.
- **BEST TIME OF YEAR:** Thunderstorms in August make for spectacular sunsets.
- **DID YOU KNOW?** Ancestral Puebloans abandoned their homes in Mesa Verde in the late 1200s A.D.

Est. 1906 · 7TH National Park · **COLORADO** *Centennial State*

Look for the **COMMON RAVEN**

<MESA VERDE 18" X 24" Poster art created in 2014 by Michael Korfhage & Joel Anderson

MT RAINIER

NATIONAL PARK

MOUNT RAINIER

VOLCANO AND GLACIER, fire and ice: **Mount Rainier** is a poetic duality. The almighty colossus of the Cascade Range, Mount Rainier stands nearly three miles tall. Before the American expansion westward, Rainier was a sacred place to nearly a dozen native tribes who called the mountain Tahoma - "the great mountain where the waters begin." The snowy crown of the Great Mountain glowers over Washington's verdant valleys and lower mountain heads. Rivers of ice course down the steep slopes. The Park hosts 25 major glaciers, an icy cover-up for the layers of magma and ash that once poured out of the Rainier volcano, just 50 miles southeast of Seattle. The occasional earthquake reminds visitors that the primeval Rainier is still potent. Its last eruption was only 120 years ago after all. Despite the mountain's potential fury, the mood most visitors encounter at Mount Rainier National Park is one of

> "Climb the mountains and get their good tidings. Nature's peace will flow into you as sunshine flows into trees. The winds will blow their own freshness into you, and the storms their energy, while cares will drop off like autumn leaves."
> *-John Muir*

ebullient bliss. Cheerful woodlands and meadows wreathed in foliage cause many to consider this region of the Cascades "the American Alps."

The Park contains a glorious blend of alpine lakes, evergreen forest, brilliant wildflowers, and heavy snowfall. Walk through this extensive montane dreamscape on a week-long backpacking trip along **Wonderland Trail**. This 93-mile trail circles the entirety of Mount Rainier and provides quiet communion with wilderness at the foot of such overwhelming grandeur. Park rangers built and completed this beloved pathway in 1915, utilizing it as an efficient (and scenic) route to traverse the thick Rainier backcountry and protect the land from poachers and vandals. Rangers built patrol cabins along the way, some of which are still used today. In 2015, Mount Rainier National Park celebrated the 100th anniversary of Wonderland Trail. It is a

<MOUNT RAINIER 18" X 24" Poster art created in 2020 by Derek Anderson & Joel Anderson

prized possession of the National Park System that has taught self-reliance and a deeper appreciation for nature for over a hundred years.

In the late 1800s, Mount Rainier's thick forest groves were caught in the center of a conservation war. Under the Forest Reserve Act, Presidents could set woodlands aside for national protection without hindrance from Congress. Rainier's forests came under U.S. protection in 1893. The question was: how should "protection" be defined? Chief forester Gifford Pinchot believed in the "conservation by use" philosophy, that through responsible cutting American forests could be preserved. Pinchot proposed to implement this theory on the lush forests of Rainier. The ever-vigilant John Muir stood in his way. Muir refused to see this rejuvenating land used for anything other than enjoyment and quickly called for the establishment of a National Park. Support came from a variety of parties with a variety of motives. The National Geographic Society wanted to study Rainier's volcanoes and glaciers. The Northern Pacific Railroad Company saw a National Park as an opportunity for more tourism and train ticket sales. Despite the fanfare for converting Rainier into a National Park, the federal government was hesitant to give its blessing and overrule Pinchot. Congress had to be assured Rainier would never be suitable for farming or mining and that they wouldn't have to spend another dime to manage it. The bill finally passed in 1899 and Rainier became the Pacific Northwest's first National Park.

The Park itself circles the base of the mountain, providing magnificent views of the mountain centerpiece from many different angles. Plunge into the rainforests and hike along smooth-stone glacial streams at **Carbon River.** Walk beneath thousand-year-old trees at the **Grove of the Patriarchs** or enjoy a picnic beside the subalpine lakes in the **Sunrise region.** Abundant bouquets of wildflowers are enjoyed throughout the summer in the busy **Paradise area.** And for those that are willing, Mount Rainier invites you to climb straight up its 14,410 foot slope and look down upon this Alpine Elysium.

"Few National Parks in the contiguous United States provide the diversity of resources that Mount Rainier offers. From walks through old growth 'rain forests' along crystal clear streams to high alpine glacier climbing — and everything in between. This Park has it all for visitors." — Bill Wade, Retired Park Ranger at Mount Rainier from 1967-1970 (total years of NPS service: 30)

MOUNT RAINIER 18" X 24" Poster art created in 2013 by Michael Korfhage & Joel Anderson ∧
MOUNT RAINIER: FLORAL FOX 18" X 24" Poster art based on an oil painting created in 2015 by Kai Carpenter >

National Park OF AMERICAN SAMOA

AN ISOLATED diamond in the South Pacific, American Samoa is one of the most picturesque as well as hardest to reach Parks in the system. The five volcanic islands are nothing more than tiny dots on a map, some 2,600 miles southwest of Hawai'i. Its remote location and tradition-focused inhabitants preserve the island's laid-back culture. Though convenience isn't a theme here, unadulterated natural beauty certainly is. These islands are the only National Park (or U.S. property of any kind) below the equator, and they host five distinct rainforest ecosystems: lowland, montane, coast, ridge, and cloud. The Samoan fruit bat and a variety of tropical birds flit through the trees. Out in the water, coral reefs line the coast, concentrated especially around the **island of Ofu**. These reefs are home to over 950 species of fish.

As distinct as the islands themselves, the bilingual Samoan people are both proud and conscientious of their land. They have partnered up with the National Park Service to protect many of Samoa's rainforests, coral reefs, and beaches. Laws were passed to prevent non-Samoan investors from exploiting the land to build resorts and timeshares. Though there are a few hotels on the main island of **Tutuila**, the National Park of American Samoa provides travelers with a unique lodging experience that cannot be found anywhere else: the **Homestay Program.** For a modest fee, guests can live, eat, and play alongside a Samoan family while learning about the rich cultural history of the native people. Sort of like a bed-and-breakfast, island family style. The host families set the cost of accommodations and activities, regulated by the National Park. This is a highly recommended experience for curious travelers comfortable with stepping out of their comfort zones.

Though much of the protected region is still inaccessible, there are a few trails from which to explore American Samoa's volcanic coastline. North of the primary city of Pago Pago is the trailhead to scenic **Mount 'Alava.** Resting in nearby Vai'ava Strait, the beloved **Pola Island** receives lots of photographic attention from hikers. Snorkeling is another way to experience the island's abundance. Though unpopulated and difficult to reach, the island of Ofu has some of the most beautiful (and secluded) reefs and beaches in the Park. **Si'u Point from Ta'u Island** dazzles visitors with emerald sea cliffs towering over the brilliant blue South Pacific.

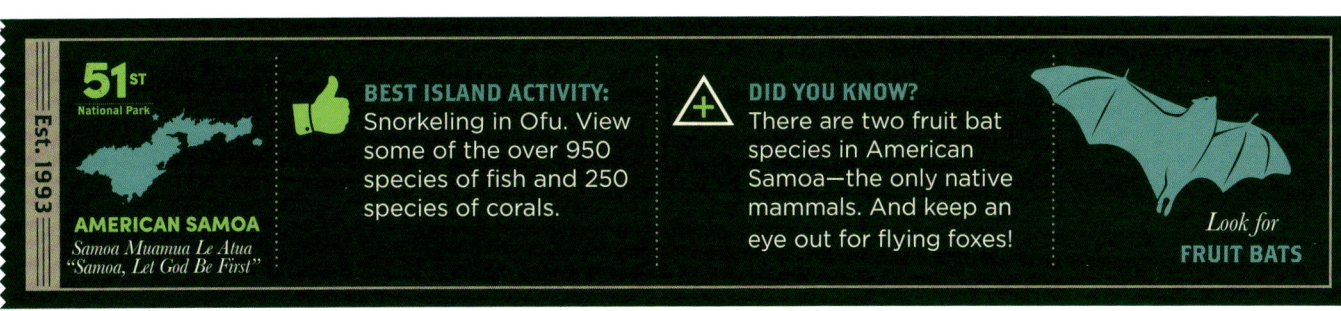

51ST National Park
Est. 1993
AMERICAN SAMOA
Samoa Muamua Le Atua
"Samoa, Let God Be First"

BEST ISLAND ACTIVITY: Snorkeling in Ofu. View some of the over 950 species of fish and 250 species of corals.

DID YOU KNOW? There are two fruit bat species in American Samoa—the only native mammals. And keep an eye out for flying foxes!

Look for **FRUIT BATS**

<AMERICAN SAMOA 18" X 24" Poster art created in 2015 by Michael Korfhage & Joel Anderson

NEW RIVER GORGE

TWO FORCES run through New River Gorge National Park and Preserve: the river and the railroad. You cannot visit this section of the Appalachian Mountains without hearing both. Freight and coal-bearing trains rumble along the meticulously-graded railways, coursing through steep mountain passes. White water roars in the bottom of the gorge, blasting through narrow, boulder-strewn channels in search of calmer, wider stretches. West Virginia is a state known for its storied past in coal mining and its exciting future in outdoor recreation. History and possibility, like the river and the railroad, run through New River Gorge, inviting a new generation of Americans to explore and enjoy the nation's 63rd National Park.

The New River is a stream of life, action, and power. Originating from the Blue Ridge Mountains of North Carolina, this north-running waterway is considered one of the oldest rivers in North America, having existed before the Ice Age as a tributary of the ancestral Teays River system. The river's notorious **"Lower New"** section of class IV to V whitewater rapids is a magnet for paddle-toting thrill-seekers worldwide. But the raging river is also a resounding reminder of how water (and it's erosive power) never stops shaping the Earth. A sediment-loaded stream has been flowing through this region for time immemorial, slowly and forcefully deepening the New River Gorge. As the river tore away its banks, hidden layers of ancient rock were revealed, including the lofty sandstone walls now lining the canyon. The rugged Nuttall sandstone of New River Gorge draws thousands of seasoned outdoor rock climbers each year.

Running almost parallel to the New River is the Chesapeake and Ohio railroad line, a feat of America's unheralded backbone: the working class. Irish Catholic immigrants and African Americans, now freed from slavery, began building this section of railway in 1869. Anxious to create new lives for themselves and their families, these men faced a monumental task: to connect the Virginia coast to the Ohio River by rail. One of the most arduous obstacles to this already enormous challenge was through the rugged New River Gorge. Armed only with hand tools and explosives, the railroad crews hacked, hammered, blasted, and dug their way through the Appalachians for three long years, grading and leveling the land before hammering the rails into place. Tales of legendary strength and skill would be told about these builders, the story of John Henry perhaps the most memorable. Their completion of the railroad brought prosperity and accessibility to West Virginia, particularly for the coal and lumber industries. Company-created boomtowns and mining camps popped up along the New River; Park visitors can visit one of these now-abandoned boomtowns at **Thurmond** and learn about the legend of John Henry at the **Great Bend Tunnel.**

At 876 tall and over 3,000 feet wide, the New River Gorge Bridge is the awe-inspiring centerpiece of this National Park. Snap some photos of this lofty giant at **Canyon Rim Boardwalk** and **Fayette Station.** Thick rhododendron and eastern hardwood forests coat the slopes of New River Gorge. Plunge into these lush woodlands on **Endless Wall Trail** (don't forget to catch your breath at **Diamond Point**), or explore the wildflower-laden **Grandview Area**. Built by the Boy Scouts, the 13-mile long **Arrowhead Trail** is a premier destination for mountain biking. And, if battling the mighty rapids by raft isn't your thing, a quiet trip to **Sandstone Falls** is a wonderful way to spend some quality time in the West Virginia wilderness.

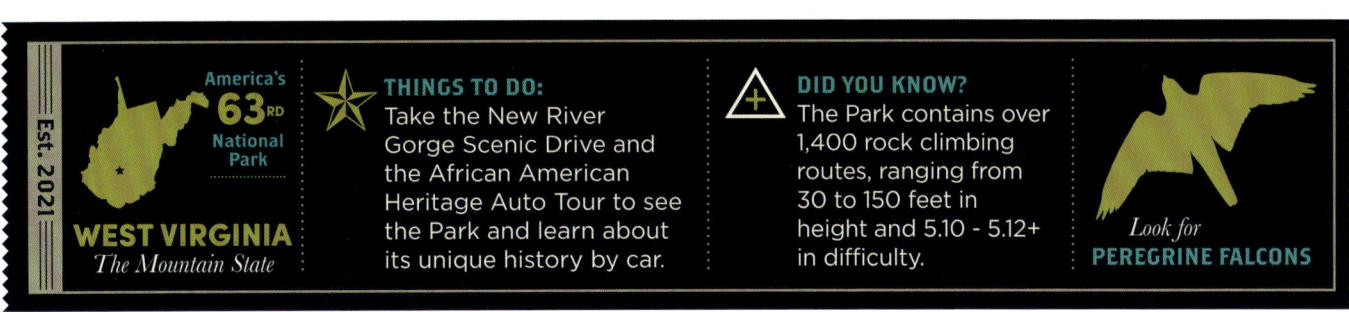

America's 63RD National Park — Est. 2021 — **WEST VIRGINIA** *The Mountain State*

THINGS TO DO: Take the New River Gorge Scenic Drive and the African American Heritage Auto Tour to see the Park and learn about its unique history by car.

DID YOU KNOW? The Park contains over 1,400 rock climbing routes, ranging from 30 to 150 feet in height and 5.10 - 5.12+ in difficulty.

Look for **PEREGRINE FALCONS**

<NEW RIVER GORGE 18" X 24" Poster art created in 2021 by Aaron Johnson & Joel Anderson

NORTH CASCADES

PEER UP INTO the snowy chiseled peaks of the American Alps. Breathe in the pure air, seasoned with hints of cedar and snowmelt. You feel like you are the last human on Earth here. The solemn mountains surround you, hemming you in with their glacial glory. Over 300 glaciers still work their craft in this Park today, patiently shaping and molding the Cascade Range in the Pacific Northwest. These mountains received their name from the innumerable waterfalls that rush down their rocky slopes, feeding the Park's cerulean lakes. North Cascades National Park is a wonder, a continuous work of wilderness art. It is a paradise locked away from civilization by its own design: the Cascades are notoriously difficult to access here, making this Park one of the least visited in the lower 48 states. Still, the invitation to explore is especially tantalizing in a place like this. With over 400 miles of wooded and river-laced trails, the opportunities abound to unlock the treasures of the Cascades.

Today, a single highway spans North Cascades National Park. Travelers are regaled with angular, seemingly inaccessible mountain beauty as they drive through **Rainy** and **Washington Pass** in the Park's northern region. Even the hardiest fur trappers grew pale at the feet of these harrowing Cascade giants in the early years. "A more difficult route to travel never fell a man's lot," growled trapper Alexander Ross in 1814. Mountain names such as Mount Despair, Damnation Peak, and Mount Terror attest to the area's daunting character.

Nonetheless, the Cascades' fearless inhabitants went to work, uniting old miner roads and exploration routes to form the stunning **North Cascades Highway,** completed in 1972. This road pierces the Cascade Range by way of the **Skagit River,** which feeds into the Park's cherished lake system. Canoes, kayaks, and ferries carry passengers across the chilly waters of **Lake Diablo** and **Lake Ross** (both belonging to the North Cascades' Ross Lake Recreational Area). The gravelly **Cascade River Road** brings you into the Park's rugged southern region, where day hikers find a rejuvenating thrill in the climb to **Cascade Pass.**

Keep a sharp eye out for the North Cascades' lighthearted mascot, the mountain goat. These furry rock climbers thrive on the ridgelines. Salmon leap up the Skagit River to their spawning beds each fall. This annual spectacle draws a gawking host of tourists and bald eagles, eager to catch (and eat) a piece of the action. Though only a few hours from Seattle, this magnificent region remains a well-kept secret within the Park system, where undefiled wilderness awaits you. Climb up and enter the solitude of North Cascades National Park.

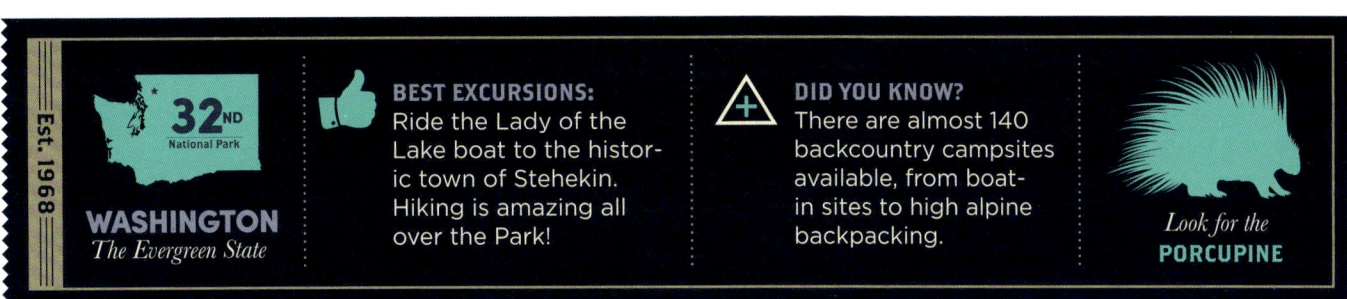

Est. 1968 — 32ND National Park — WASHINGTON *The Evergreen State*

BEST EXCURSIONS: Ride the Lady of the Lake boat to the historic town of Stehekin. Hiking is amazing all over the Park!

DID YOU KNOW? There are almost 140 backcountry campsites available, from boat-in sites to high alpine backpacking.

Look for the PORCUPINE

<NORTH CASCADES 18" X 24" Poster art created in 2015 by David Anderson & Joel Anderson

OLYMPIC

A TEMPERATE rainforest practically spills into the Pacific Ocean from the northern peninsula of Washington state. Blankets of moss drape the old forests, sumptuously clothed before the regal Mount Olympus. Drinking around 200 inches of precipitation each year, the trees at Olympic National Park are dripping with life. Thirteen rivers ring around the mountain, bubbling beneath untouched groves of western hemlock, red cedar, and giant sitka spruce. These woodlands house a large community of wildlife: black bears and Roosevelt elk, mountain goats and marmots, beavers and salamanders, osprey and bald eagles. Olympic also boasts 73 miles of pebbled Pacific coastline, dotted with intertidal ecosystems. Purple crab and sprawling starfish lounge in the shallows. Further out, gray whales breach in the springtime. This is a Park where ocean meets forest, and the whole Earth seems to rejoice at this union.

Olympic National Park swells with opportunities to explore, and people have gravitated towards the pristine mountains and beaches for millennia. Native Americans have occupied the Olympic peninsula for over 12,000 years. Five distinct tribes still dwell alongside the Park's rugged coast. Western explorers floated by these shores for centuries, slowing their ships to marvel at the mesmerizing peak of Mount Olympus. A lieutenant named Joseph P. O'Neil sought a closer encounter with Olympus, and led an expedition into Olympic's rainforests from the town of Port Angeles in 1885. His month-long, 17-mile journey brought him to **Hurricane Ridge**, an overlook that is now arguably the most scenic vista in the Park. Today, Park visitors can reach this gusty ridgeline by car, and the view continues to refresh and reward those who venture up.

Highway 101 now circles the Park, providing outlets to the various regions around Mount Olympus. Given the impassibility of the Olympic mountain range, there are no roads that cross over. Be sure to allow yourself a few days (or trips) to fully enjoy all that Olympic National Park has to offer. **Hurricane Ridge Road** pierces the northern border of Olympic National Park from Port Angeles, approximately following the same route blazed by Lieutenant O'Neil. The 17-mile drive is beloved by many for its astounding alpine views as it climbs up into the cradle of Mount Olympus. Snowhounds will delight in the various arctic activities available here in the wintertime. Cross-country and downhill skiing, sledding, tubing, and snowshoeing opportunities are all available to individuals with 4WD and the weekend off (the Ridge road is closed on winter weekdays). Accessibility to the trails and roadways on Hurricane Ridge drastically improves in the summer. Satisfy your lust for life (and conquer your fear of heights) by traversing **Obstruction Point Road** from the Hurricane Ridge Visitor Center. Trailheads in these highlands lead

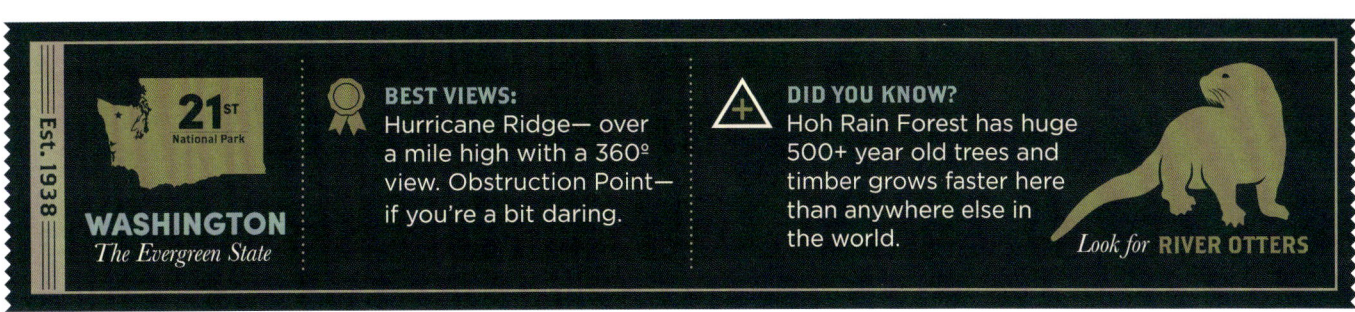

Est. 1938 — 21ST National Park — **WASHINGTON** *The Evergreen State*

BEST VIEWS: Hurricane Ridge— over a mile high with a 360º view. Obstruction Point— if you're a bit daring.

DID YOU KNOW? Hoh Rain Forest has huge 500+ year old trees and timber grows faster here than anywhere else in the world.

Look for **RIVER OTTERS**

<OLYMPIC 18" X 24" Poster art created in 2013 by Michael Korfhage & Joel Anderson

to glacial lakes and knee-weakening views of mountains upon mountains.

Nestled on the northwestern slopes of the Olympic range is the shimmering **Lake Crescent.** Just off the 101, Lake Crescent is a favorite destination among anglers as native Beardslee and Crescenti trout thrive below the surface. Vacationers can enjoy the refreshing stillness of this glacial lake by boat or by paved trail as the old **Spruce Railroad** bed hugs the shore. The water is a crystal clear blue thanks to a lack of nitrogen and little algae growth. A bird's eye view of this azure beauty can be reached from a World War 2 spotting tower on **Pyramid Peak Trail.** Lodging at Lake Crescent is a smart way to visit both the beaches and mountains of Olympic National Park, due to its central location.

Just to the south, **Sol Duc**'s leafy forest and hot springs are a boon for weary mountain climbers. Forests fed by constant rainfall make for pleasantly cool ambles alongside the river. One such route leads to the effervescent **Sol Duc Falls.** Backpackers unsatiated with the majestic Mount Olympus and her highland kingdom will enjoy a hike on the 18.2-mile **High Divide Loop / Seven Lakes Basin Trail** which begins here too.

Further to the southwest is a rain-soaked emerald paradise called **Hoh Rain Forest.** The Hoh forest splays out between the Pacific Ocean to the west and the Olympic Mountains to the east. This perfect location means milder winters and LOTS of rain. Between 140 and 170 inches

of precipitation douse the Hoh forest each year (that's 12 to 14 FEET of water). An evergreen explosion seems to have erupted here, blanketing everything in sight with moss and thick foliage. A prodigious herd of rare Roosevelt Elk saunter through these woods, enjoying the bottomless food supply. Stroll through the **Hall of Mosses** for a deeper understanding of what a true Pacific Northwest jungle looks like or enjoy a waterfall-strewn journey towards Mount Olympus on **Hoh River Trail.** Don't forget to pack your rain jacket.

Head west on US-101 towards the crashing breakers of the Pacific. You will have entered Olympic's wild and rambling coastline. A 73-mile beachfront haunted by seastacks runs from **Ozette** to **Kalaloch.** The dramatic **Shi Shi Beach** awaits in seclusion at the very top of this stretch (you will need a Recreation Pass from the local Makah tribe to visit). The north central **Mora** region is a destination for oceanfront photography. The weatherworn **Hole-in-the-Wall natural arch** on **Rialto Beach** is a perennial favorite. Bleached driftwood litters the shoreline like old whalebones up and down the coast. Clamber over a horizontal forest to reach **Second Beach** in **La Push** and breathe deep the salty air. Further down the shore is **Ruby Beach** on the northern end of Kalaloch, a delightful region for tide pools laden with starfish and sea anemones. Orcas migrate here in the springtime, adding an extra splash of drama to this already impressive waterfront.

OLYMPIC: MAGIC MOMENT 18" X 24" Poster art based on an oil painting created in 2016 by Kai Carpenter >

PETRIFIED FOREST

THE ANCIENT and sleepy wonders of Petrified Forest National Park rest only a few miles off I-40 and Route 66 in northeastern Arizona. Though now a silent fossilized wasteland, scientists believe that this area was once a lush subtropical jungle. Fossils of some of the world's earliest dinosaurs have been found here, while the wood-turned-stone trees still lie scattered about (rather than a 'standing' forest, as might be expected). For those who enjoy anthropology, the remains of an ancestral Pueblo neighborhood lie on the north end of the Park. Though much remains unknown, stories told by these ancient people are etched into nearby rock walls. Driving through the sleepy Route 66 towns to reach this Park reminds you that this was once a place of vitality. It is now a detour into the past. As with the trees themselves, a heavy sense of nostalgia sprawls across the hills of **the Painted Desert**, inviting you to reflect on ages long gone.

Americans have John Muir and President Theodore Roosevelt to thank for preserving the remarkable antiquities of the Petrified Forest. If it were not for the efforts of these two men, the remaining 250 million-year-old trees would have been picked apart bit by bit until none remained. Opportunists found all sorts of ways to turn the crystallized wood into a souvenir: from paperweights and bookends to stools, lamps, even tabletops. Gem collectors would blast logs of the petrified wood in search of precious crystals. John Muir noticed this while exploring the area in 1906. With his trademark ability to frustrate businessmen, Muir began a new crusade to save the fossilized forest. Thanks to his close friendship with President (and fellow nature enthusiast) Theodore Roosevelt, Petrified Forest was declared a National Monument in 1906 and became a National Park in 1962.

One 28-mile main road takes you from the north entrance to the south with a visitor center on each end. The petrified wood, **Crystal Forest**, and **Agate Bridge** can be found in the

southern section of the Park while the Painted Desert, **Blue Mesa**, **Pueblo villages**, and **petroglyphs** are located in the north. The crystal sarcophagi of primeval trees await your inspection throughout Petrified Forest National Park. Take the time to wander through their final resting places, and watch as their colors awaken in the rain.

Photo by Joel Anderson

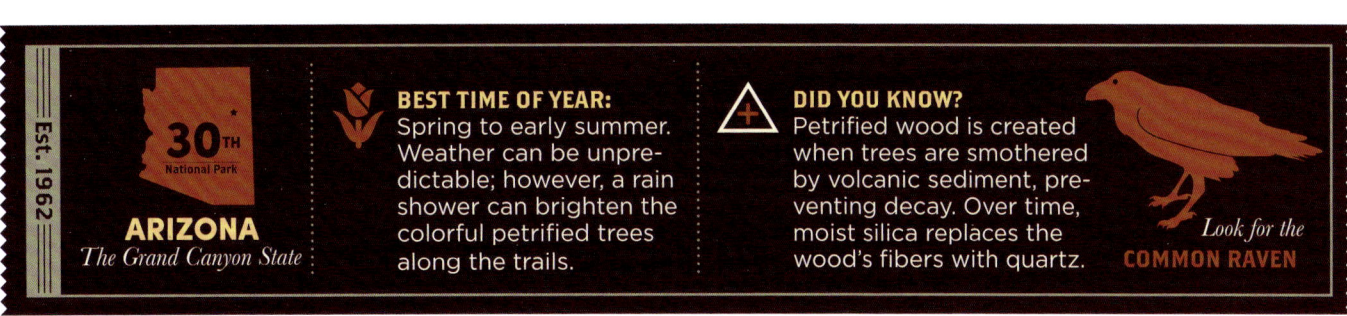

Est. 1962 · 30TH National Park · **ARIZONA** *The Grand Canyon State*

BEST TIME OF YEAR: Spring to early summer. Weather can be unpredictable; however, a rain shower can brighten the colorful petrified trees along the trails.

DID YOU KNOW? Petrified wood is created when trees are smothered by volcanic sediment, preventing decay. Over time, moist silica replaces the wood's fibers with quartz.

Look for the **COMMON RAVEN**

<PETRIFIED FOREST 18" X 24" Poster art created in 2015 by Michael Korfhage & Joel Anderson

PINNACLES

A REFUGE of ancient beauty is carved into the hills of coastal California. Copper spires and castles of volcanic rock crown the tumbling bluffs in glory. Only an hour outside Monterey, Pinnacles National Park looks and feels like Middle Earth, a land fit for an epic tale of adventure. Condors, like kings of old, spread their massive wings and levitate over their dominion: prehistoric remains of a volcano fractured by the San Andreas Fault. The windy gusts these condors glide on have fashioned the stone palisades and fortresses for thousands of years. Merry streams trickle down from the highlands and churn into basins and narrow canyons. Earthquakes transformed some of these canyons into talus caves, deep gorges roofed by toppled boulders that wedged into the fractures. Fourteen species of bats inhabit these caves. In **Bear Gulch Cave** and **the Balconies**, the soft darkness is especially vibrant with these furry colonies. Out in the sunshine, bees and butterflies busy themselves in the swaths of spring wildflowers that pop up out of the scrubby chaparral. Pinnacles National Park is a realm of joyful and unblemished solitude.

Native Chalon and Mutsun tribes have delighted in the valleys and colonnades of Pinnacles for centuries. They lived off the landscape's abundant provision; acorns, wildflower seeds, rabbit, deer, and elk kept the natives clothed and well-fed, while the region's unique plant and tree species provided a variety of medicines. Through small fires and strategic harvesting, these early Californians cultivated the lavish landscape. In time, Spanish monks and homesteaders settled the surrounding countryside, forever altering the natives' way of life. Their population dwindled as European diseases ravaged the coast.

A century later, a young Michigan transplant named Schuyler Hain moved into Pinnacles with his family. Fascinated by the dream-like stonework, Hain began leading tours into **Bear Valley** and the nearby caves. He wrote articles and letters, proclaiming the wonders of this stone garden: "Here the cliffs of many-colored rock rise hundreds of feet in sharply defined terraces, great domes or pinnacles. Beyond, and scattered over an area of some six square miles, is a mass of conglomerate rocks wonderful in extent and in fantastic variety of form and coloring." Hain's letters attracted the attention of Stanford University, whose president helped him connect with National Forester Gifford Pinchot. Through Pinchot's recommendation, President Theodore Roosevelt established Pinnacles National Monument in 1908. CCC groups developed Hain's dream in the 1930s, building trails into the stone walls and paving roadways. One hundred and five years after Roosevelt's initial protection, President Barack Obama designated Pinnacles as America's 59th National Park. Today, a breathtaking ascent to **High Peaks** will introduce you to this serrated land of mythical grandeur, crafted by nature for the permanent enjoyment of all mankind.

59TH National Park — Est. 2013 — **CALIFORNIA** *The Golden State*

BEST TIME OF YEAR: February–early June.

BEST HIKE: Don't miss the Balconies Cave Trail and the Bear Gulch Cave Trail.

DID YOU KNOW? The California condor—a species of vulture with a nine-and-a-half-foot wingspan—was reintroduced to Pinnacles in 2003.

Look for the **ACMON BLUE BUTTERFLY**

<PINNACLES 18" X 24" Poster art created in 2018 by Derek Anderson & Joel Anderson

PETRIFIED FOREST

THE ANCIENT and sleepy wonders of Petrified Forest National Park rest only a few miles off I-40 and Route 66 in northeastern Arizona. Though now a silent fossilized wasteland, scientists believe that this area was once a lush subtropical jungle. Fossils of some of the world's earliest dinosaurs have been found here, while the wood-turned-stone trees still lie scattered about (rather than a 'standing' forest, as might be expected). For those who enjoy anthropology, the remains of an ancestral Pueblo neighborhood lie on the north end of the Park. Though much remains unknown, stories told by these ancient people are etched into nearby rock walls. Driving through the sleepy Route 66 towns to reach this Park reminds you that this was once a place of vitality. It is now a detour into the past. As with the trees themselves, a heavy sense of nostalgia sprawls across the hills of **the Painted Desert**, inviting you to reflect on ages long gone.

Americans have John Muir and President Theodore Roosevelt to thank for preserving the remarkable antiquities of the Petrified Forest. If it were not for the efforts of these two men, the remaining 250 million-year-old trees would have been picked apart bit by bit until none remained. Opportunists found all sorts of ways to turn the crystallized wood into a souvenir: from paperweights and bookends to stools, lamps, even tabletops. Gem collectors would blast logs of the petrified wood in search of precious crystals. John Muir noticed this while exploring the area in 1906. With his trademark ability to frustrate businessmen, Muir began a new crusade to save the fossilized forest. Thanks to his close friendship with President (and fellow nature enthusiast) Theodore Roosevelt, Petrified Forest was declared a National Monument in 1906 and became a National Park in 1962.

One 28-mile main road takes you from the north entrance to the south with a visitor center on each end. The petrified wood, **Crystal Forest**, and **Agate Bridge** can be found in the

southern section of the Park while the Painted Desert, **Blue Mesa**, **Pueblo villages**, and **petroglyphs** are located in the north. The crystal sarcophagi of primeval trees await your inspection throughout Petrified Forest National Park. Take the time to wander through their final resting places, and watch as their colors awaken in the rain.

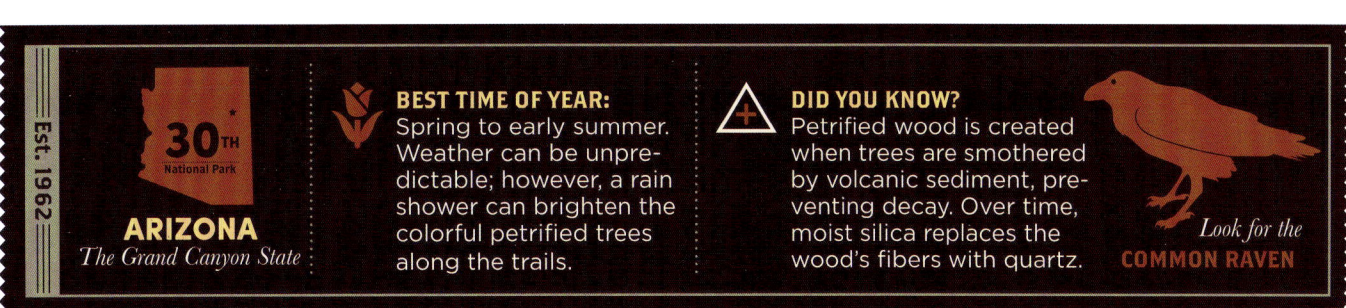

Est. 1962 — **30TH** National Park — **ARIZONA** *The Grand Canyon State*

BEST TIME OF YEAR: Spring to early summer. Weather can be unpredictable; however, a rain shower can brighten the colorful petrified trees along the trails.

DID YOU KNOW? Petrified wood is created when trees are smothered by volcanic sediment, preventing decay. Over time, moist silica replaces the wood's fibers with quartz.

Look for the **COMMON RAVEN**

<PETRIFIED FOREST 18" X 24" Poster art created in 2015 by Michael Korfhage & Joel Anderson

REDWOOD

DENSE MORNING FOG rolls slowly over a lush grove of coastal redwoods. The sun filters through the tree mist, shedding a smattering of sunlight across the forest floor. Roosevelt elk call out to one another in the meadow as sleepy sea lions slip out from their coves in search of breakfast. Gloomy and alive, Redwood National Park encompasses 133,000 acres of Pacific coastland. Old

> "The redwoods, once seen, leave a mark or create a vision that stays with you always."
> *-John Steinbeck*

growth forest once dominated this landscape. As late as 1850, over 2 million acres of thick redwood coated Northern California. Today, the Park protects what remains of these resplendent woodlands. Some of the world's tallest and oldest trees grow in this forest. Despite their shallow root systems, the redwoods can grow taller than the Statue of Liberty (many already have) and live for more than two millennia. The tallest tree in Redwood is **Hyperion**, towering 379 feet high as a spectacular example of undisturbed growth. The Park's proximity to the Pacific Ocean keeps the region cool and foggy, a near-perfect environment for the long life of a thirsty giant. While this Park now contains a landscape of prehistoric serenity, it was once in danger of being logged completely bare. Conservationist groups would struggle for decades to salvage what was left of these mossy behemoths.

Native American tribes thrived within the redwood forests for over 3,000 years. Using the wood from fallen trees, the natives built entire villages and fleets of canoes. They lived off the land, picking berries, hunting elk, and fishing for salmon off the shores of the Pacific. Evidence of their complex and harmonious societies can still be found along the coast. When gold became king in the 1850s, settlers and prospectors swarmed into Northern California, wiping out many of the Native American villages and pushing the people onto reservations. Some natives resisted, hiding in the redwood groves. Their ancestors continue to live within the Park to this day.

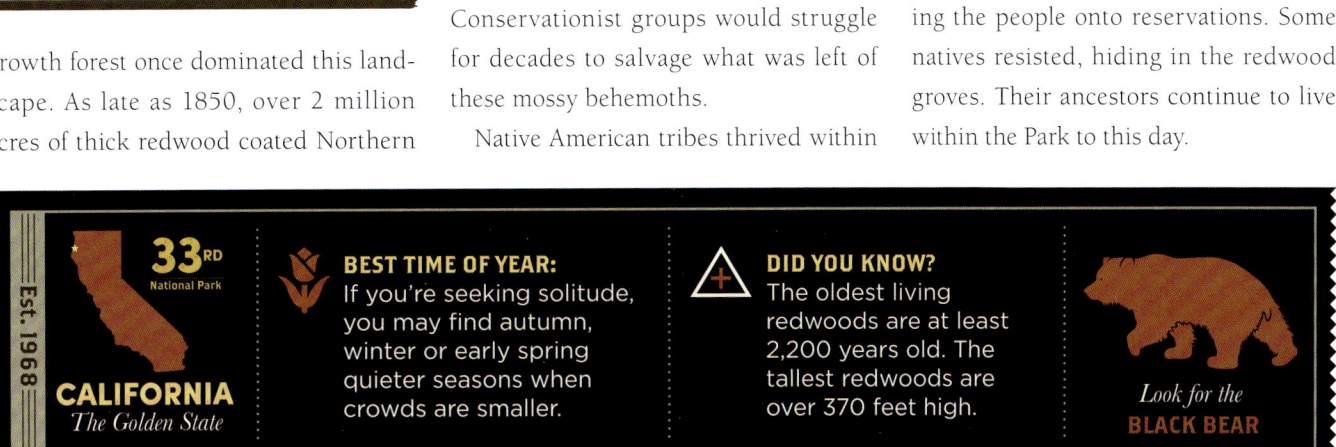

33RD National Park
Est. 1968
CALIFORNIA *The Golden State*

BEST TIME OF YEAR: If you're seeking solitude, you may find autumn, winter or early spring quieter seasons when crowds are smaller.

DID YOU KNOW? The oldest living redwoods are at least 2,200 years old. The tallest redwoods are over 370 feet high.

Look for the **BLACK BEAR**

<**REDWOOD: CHANDELIER TREE** 18" X 24" Poster art created in 2020 by Aaron Johnson & Joel Anderson

As unlucky gold miners lifted their eyes from their pans to the surrounding forests, a new lucrative scheme entered their heads. A logging mania overtook the region as wide swaths of old forest were harvested and sold up and down the booming West Coast. The incessant buzzing of the sawmills grabbed the attention of early 20th century conservationists. Alarmed at the rate of the forest's destruction, a group of naturalists formed the Save-the-Redwoods League. They rallied support from all over the country, and the state of California soon responded with the establishment of three state-protected Parks. The loggers kept chewing up trees until 1968 when President Lyndon B. Johnson commissioned Redwood National Park, finally silencing the saws once and for all.

The woods would need years to recover. Thankfully, a massive redwood replanting and cultivation project began in 1978 and continues today. Redwood National Park is now enjoyed by nearly half a million people each year. Many come just to see the tree kings that reign in this part of the country. Grab a permit and walk beneath the outstretched arms of these titans on the **Tall Trees Trail**. Enjoy a leisurely loop through the forest on the **Lady Bird Grove Trail** or spend an afternoon by the sea at **Crescent Beach**. In time, these wild forests will take back the barren patches and cloak the hills once more in fresh redwood glory.

"Every time I walked through a grove of redwoods I sensed the hushed majesty of these giant trees. I always felt as if I had entered a cathedral where all my senses were alive with the feeling of a timeless forest of the tallest trees in the world. I could sense the centuries these trees had stood and drew on this timelessness to strengthen my resolve to protect them."
— Bill Pierce, Former Superintendent of Redwood National Park from 2003-2006
(Total years of NPS service: 38)

REDWOOD: AMONG THE GIANTS 18" X 24" Poster art based on an oil painting created in 2015 by Kai Carpenter >

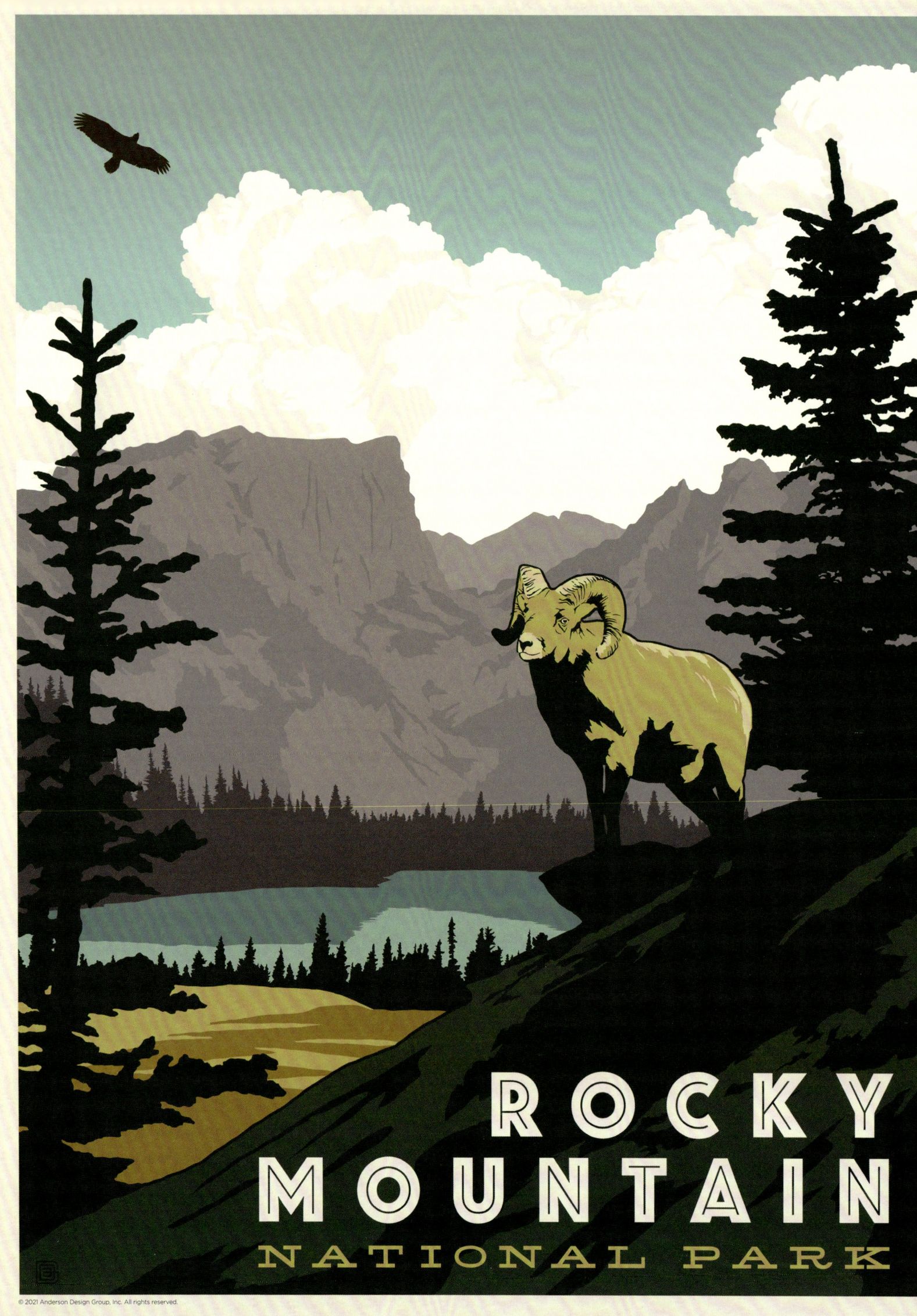

ROCKY MOUNTAIN

ALPINE bliss awaits you at Rocky Mountain National Park. This incredible mountain chain in Colorado epitomizes the West: lofty snowcapped peaks, crystal lakes, fields of elk and moose, rugged trails inviting high adventure. The Rocky Mountain's clean air and fresh wilderness have been cherished by Americans for centuries. The Park is only a two-hour drive from Denver, making it a favorite of local weekenders all year round. And, as to be expected in Colorado, there are a wide variety of activities in this relatively small Park: rock climbing, horseback riding, backpacking, fishing, camping, cross-country skiing, and of course hiking. So many ways to experience a Rocky Mountain High!

The National Park System exists because of a handful of tireless Americans who put their passion for nature ahead of personal gain or glory. The common, everyday people that saved the Parks for millions of others are often themselves left forgotten or unheralded. Enter Enos Mills. Enos was a clean-cut outdoorsman and nature writer who, as a sickly boy, had been transplanted to the Rockies in the late 1800s. As he grew up, he gained his strength from the pure mountain air at **Longs Peak**, the tallest of more than sixty 12,000+ foot peaks in the area. An avid spokesman and believer in nature's healing power, he opened an inn and led his guests on strenuous hikes to the heights of his beloved mountain range. The scourge of reckless logging, as well as a chance encounter with John Muir, motivated Enos to soon seek out public protection for his adopted home. He began a crusade to save the Rockies, pointing to the now-elderly Muir as his inspiration. When Muir died in 1914, his passion for conservation was remembered well; with the death of the "Father of the National Parks", Congress hastened to pass a bill establishing Rocky Mountain National Park, in memory of Muir.

Though the Park's size is one-eighth of Yellowstone, it receives just as many visitors each year. Utilizing a shuttle bus or early morning parking spot will get you away from the crowds and up into the tundra. One roadway that's worth the traffic is **Trail Ridge Road**. A winding 48-mile highway, it has been recognized as an All-American Road, one of the finest scenic byways in the United States. Gaining over 4,000 feet in elevation, Trail Ridge Road crests the Rocky Mountains at over 12,000 feet and connects the western and eastern halves of the Park. Similar to Glacier National Park's glorious Going-to-the-Sun Road, Trail Ridge is fully drivable only 3-4 months each year due to weather. The drive-by vistas, pullover spots, and hiking trailheads from this road alone make stomaching a summer crowd absolutely worth it (although it's advisable to visit during the week). You'll travel through quaking aspen and ponderosa pine forests, alpine meadows blooming with radiant wildflowers, snowpack feet-thick even in June, and the most glorious mountain panorama available anywhere.

Streams flow both east and west in Rocky Mountain National Park as the Continental Divide winds through **Milner Pass**, a stop along Trail Ridge Road. Trail Ridge runs from Estes Park in the east all the way to Grand Lake in the west, con-

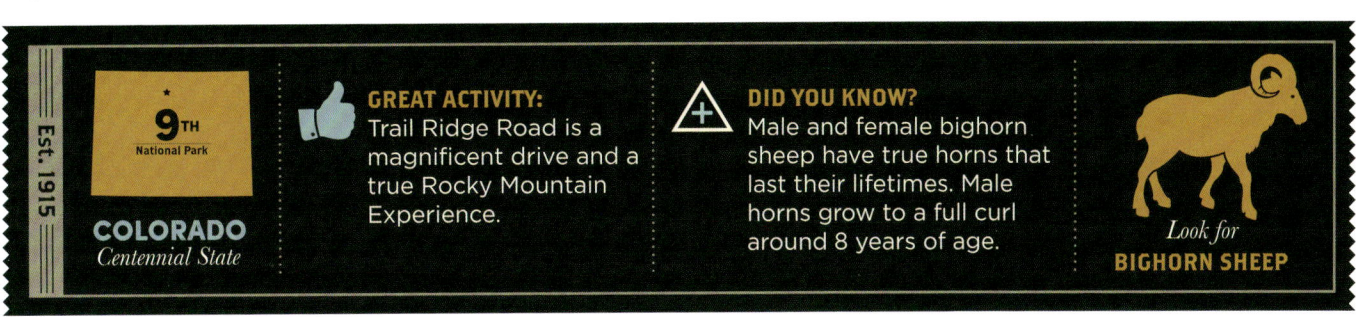

Est. 1915 — 9TH National Park — **COLORADO** *Centennial State*

GREAT ACTIVITY: Trail Ridge Road is a magnificent drive and a true Rocky Mountain Experience.

DID YOU KNOW? Male and female bighorn sheep have true horns that last their lifetimes. Male horns grow to a full curl around 8 years of age.

Look for **BIGHORN SHEEP**

<ROCKY MOUNTAIN 18" X 24" Poster art created in 2013 by Michael Korfhage & Joel Anderson

necting two halves of the National Park and the country. Animal activity is very common along this highway. Depending on the elevation and time of day, you're likely to see moose, bighorn sheep, elk, marmots, and pikas. These critters can cause sudden bumper-to-bumper traffic when sightseers stop to take pictures. When possible, be sure to pull fully off the roadway when stopping for nature shots.

Opportunities to enjoy the Rocky Mountains range from just a few steps out of your car to a 20-mile multi-day backpacking adventure. Day-hikes and short family jaunts abound along Trail Ridge Road and **Bear Lake Road.** Some of the most popular destinations in the Park are below the treeline, such as the exquisite collection of lakes from the **Bear Lake Trailhead.** This area's parking lots fill up quickly during the summer so be sure to come early. Short (less than 4 miles) trails provide access to a set of glacial beauties: Nymph, Dream, and Emerald lakes. A quick 2-mile trip from the nearby Glacier Gorge Trailhead will fill your lungs with fresh mountain air as you enjoy a picturesque Colorado moment at Alberta Falls. Ambitious hikers will be well-rewarded if they choose to continue on to the secluded **Sky Pond** or **Black Lake.**

Ready to climb some mountains? This Park has a few for aspiring mountaineers to choose from, ranging from moderate to extremely strenuous in difficulty. One of the more pleasant peaks to summit on foot is **Deer Mountain.** Topping out over 10,000 feet, the 3-mile trail gains

just over a thousand feet in elevation and makes an ideal spot for a picnic and a nap as you are blanketed with sweeping alpine scenery. The **Twin Sisters Peaks** are more difficult to ascend but the 360° views at the top are astounding. From the 11,400-foot summit, the rolling woodlands of Roosevelt National Forest lie at your feet to the south. The gargantuan Longs Peak looms still higher westward. The trail to the top of Longs Peak is a 16-mile test of endurance, will, and skill. Only the well-prepared and well-conditioned should attempt to summit this "14er" (hiker lingo for a mountain taller than 14,000 feet). If you complete the hike, you will have reached the roof of Rocky Mountain National Park, and the sweeping kingdom below will be yours to fully enjoy.

Though summer is peak season in the Rockies, the winter should not be underestimated. Many hiking trails, especially on the west side of the Park, remain open to snowshoers and cross-country skiers throughout the winter months. Many of the Park roads are closed until spring, meaning far less people and plenty of solitude in this snow-mantled paradise. Animals are much easier to spot with a pure white backdrop as they hunt for food. Park Rangers are available for snowshoe and ski tours of their favorite snowbound trails. Whether you visit with the multitude in mid-summer or alone in the dead of winter, there really is never a wrong time to explore these incredible highlands in the heart of America.

ROCKY MOUNTAIN: LONGS PEAK 18" X 24" Poster art created in 2013 by Michael Korfhage & Joel Anderson ^
ROCKY MOUNTAIN: MOOSE IN THE MORNING 18" X 24" Poster art based on an oil painting created in 2017 by Kai Carpenter >

SAGUARO

THE ROYAL KINGS of all cacti, the saguaro reign over the Sonoran Desert in southern Arizona. This cactus species is synonymous with the American Southwest and a seemingly ever-present prop in Western films. Flanking the eastern and western sprawl of Tucson's suburbs, Saguaro National Park protects over 1.5 million of these spiked monarchs. They are as benevolent as they are regal: the sweeping arms of the saguaro cactus protect many of the region's vulnerable wildlife from the harsh desert climate. Woodpeckers, elf owls, warblers, and Harris hawks all build their nests to this cactus kingdom is humanity.

Students and faculty at the University of Arizona first showed interest in protecting their needled neighbors back in 1920. Tucson was then a quiet frontier town, and ranchers allowed their cattle to rummage through the fragile cacti forests just 15 miles away. Tourists removed young saguaro plants as souvenirs, while locals uprooted the saguaros for their own home landscaping purposes. Teenagers carved their names into the waxy trunks. Grazing cows stamped the soil solid, preventing the diminutive saguaro seeds from germinating.

Park continued to take shape. CCC teams built scenic roads in the 1930s. President Kennedy added 25 more square miles of dense saguaro forest from the Tucson Mountains in 1961. Finally, in 1994, Congress declared Saguaro a National Park.

"The tall Saguaro cactus may be one of the most iconic symbols of the West. Yet, it has limited range and is only found in key ecosystem niches in Arizona and northern Mexico. It is really the symbol of the Sonoran Desert, the majority of which lies in Mexico. In places in this Park are found the best and largest specimens living within an area that ranges from lush desert to high islands in the sky peaks. The Park bookends the East and West sections of the Tucson metropolitan area offering not only a place to hike and escape to but a reminder of a rich desert heritage that needs constant protection."
— Robert Arnberger, Superintendent of Saguaro from 1983-1987 (total years of NPS service: 34)

on or inside the hollow cacti. The saguaro's ruby-red fruit feeds nocturnal foragers such as the pig-like javelina, fox, and desert tortoise. Each spring, the saguaro plants are adorned with brightly colored blossoms that bloom in the setting sun, to the delight of timely Park visitors. These cacti are desert Goliaths, growing up to 50 feet tall and weighing up to 16,000 pounds. Their waxy skin and spongy flesh take advantage of the rare Arizona rainstorms, absorbing and storing 200 gallons of water inside their rigid frames. When the saguaro flourish, the wilderness rejoices. The only threat

Something needed to be done before this desert forest was irreparably damaged. University of Arizona's president Homer L. Shantz, a botanist, championed the cause, envisioning an outdoor laboratory for students in the university's own backyard. With the help of Tucson newspaperman Frank Hitchcock, Shantz drew national recognition to the plight of the cacti. Hitchcock's political connections in Washington paid dividends in 1933 when Herbert Hoover invoked the Antiquities Act to set aside Saguaro as a National Monument. In the care of the U.S. Forest Service, the framework for a National

Enter the realm of desert splendor on the **Cactus Forest Drive** in the eastern **Rincon Mountain district**. You can cool off from the desert heat on a hike up into the Rincon Mountains via **Tanque Verde Trail**, where groves of ponderosa pine and Douglas fir shelter black bear and white-tailed deer. Take a family stroll along the **Desert Discovery Trail** in the Park's western **Tucson Mountain district**. Here you can learn all about the unique survival skills of the plants and wildlife in this arid landscape. The outstretched arms of the saguaro welcome you into Saguaro National Park.

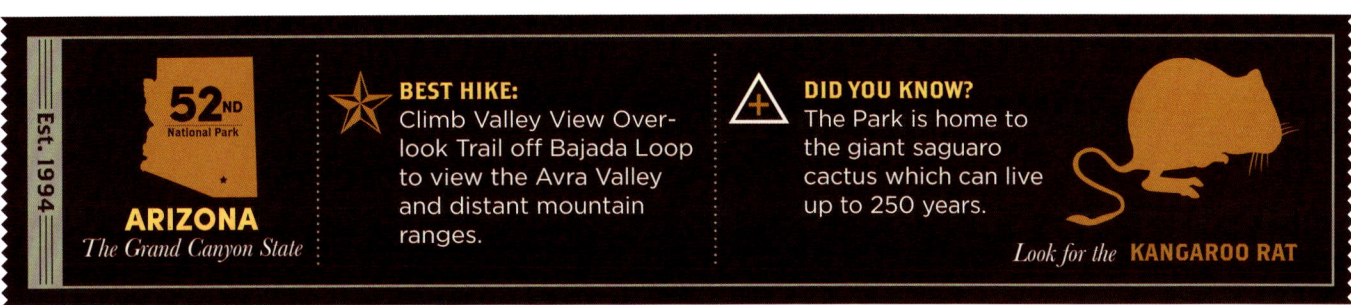

Est. 1994 | 52ND National Park | ARIZONA *The Grand Canyon State*

BEST HIKE: Climb Valley View Overlook Trail off Bajada Loop to view the Avra Valley and distant mountain ranges.

DID YOU KNOW? The Park is home to the giant saguaro cactus which can live up to 250 years.

Look for the **KANGAROO RAT**

<SAGUARO 18" X 24" Poster art created in 2014 by Michael Korfhage & Joel Anderson

SEQUOIA

THE SOLEMN forest of Sequoia National Park rests on the western slope of the Sierra Nevada Mountains in California. As the second oldest National Park in the system, Sequoia set a precedent for America's "best idea," the preservation and enjoyment of our natural wonders. Roads are few here. This is a backpacker's paradise, an area of ancient beauty where some of the world's grandest trees live and grow. It is also home to the tallest mountain in the lower 48 states, **Mount Whitney**. The giant in American conservation, John Muir, once wandered these woods. Much of his zealous early writing was charged from the abuse he saw amongst these trees.

In 1876, Muir described the Sequoia tree groves as "God's First Temple." This wooded cathedral was Muir's refuge from the rapidly developing world of California. And, like a prophet disgusted with man's treatment of the holy temple, so Muir reacted to the careless and greedy actions of encroaching enterprisers. Sheepherders were burning down swaths of forest to create pasture, while loggers, understandably impressed by the immense size of the trees, took to chopping them down by the square mile. Two-thousand-year-old trees were ripped from the ground to build rocking chairs and make room for more sheep to graze. Muir would not let this temple be desecrated by ignorance. Logger-turned-conservationist Walter Fry would aid in Muir's dream, using his first-hand experience with the fragile trees to advocate their need for protection. Congress set aside Sequoia as a National Park in 1890, and Fry would go on to become one of Sequoia's most enthusiastic Park Rangers.

Sequoia groves punctuate the western slopes of the Sierras, with Sequoia and Kings Canyon National Park protecting some of the densest and most dramatic copses. These Parks are home to the world's two largest trees. **General Sherman**, the emperor of the evergreens, can be approached in Sequoia National Park. **General Grant**, the second largest, reigns in the southwest corner of Kings Canyon. Though the paved, downhill trail to General Sherman is by far the busiest section of the Park, it is worth hustling through the crowds to stand in the shadow of the world's largest tree. Thousands of photos are taken in front of the General Sherman sign each year, but no camera has yet been able to truly capture the reverence (not to mention the sheer girth) of this specimen. Thanks to the construction

2ND National Park
Est. 1890
CALIFORNIA *The Golden State*

BEST TIME OF YEAR: Fall generally lasts from mid-September through November in Sequoia. The Park is less crowded in the autumn months.

DID YOU KNOW? The General Sherman Tree is calculated to weigh 6,000 tons, and it is 275 feet tall, making it the largest tree in the world.

Look for the **BLACK BEAR**

<SEQUOIA: AT THE FOOT OF SHERMAN 18" X 24" Poster art created in 2020 by Aaron Johnson & Joel Anderson

of the Generals Highway, a few of these most celebrated groves are accessible by car and a short hike, such as the **General Sherman Grove, Giant Forest,** and **Big Trees Trail.**

Notice the soft, almost styrofoam-like bark of the Sequoia. The tree's spongy exterior helps it to absorb massive amounts of water despite the dry climate of Central California. The thick bark also serves as armor against frequent forest fires. Patches of fire-blackened trees seemingly roasted by a ferocious dragon are scattered throughout Sequoia and Kings Canyon National Parks. Despite their ugly, charred exterior, many of these trees continue to grow and thrive, slowly covering their old scars with new life. In fact, natural wildfire helps the Sequoia trees reproduce by burning away brush on the forest floor, clearing a sunlit space for their tiny seeds to someday become titans.

Sequoia National Park's trees may be spectacular, but so are its rocks. Scaling **Moro Rock** will provide you with otherworldly views of both the jagged Sierra Nevada skyline and the glistening San Joaquin Valley. Over 350 steps and steel handrails mark the trail to the top. It is a terrifying climb on a windy day but the summit views are phenomenal. The stairs are steep and the way is narrow, and you will have to squeeze against the wall to allow descending hikers to pass. For those who would prefer to keep their shoes on solid ground (especially with little kids in tow), try a family-friendly spelunk at

Crystal Cave. A Park Ranger will lead you through a marble tunnel bedecked with dripping stalactites, liquid-like veils of pallid stone, and other strange subterranean sculptures.

For a rigorous education in all that Sequoia National Park has to offer, backpackers have two epic courses to choose from: a plunge into the remote **Mineral King region** or an ascent to the top of **Mount Whitney,** the tallest mountain in the lower 48 states. The Mineral King valley is famous for its untouched wilderness: pristine lakes, alpine meadows, and the glacial-crafted Sierra Nevada mountains. In a world of instant gratification, reaching this paradise requires great patience and a steady hand on the steering wheel: nearly 700 hairpin curves plague the 25 mile-long **Mineral King Road** as it winds 7,500 feet up to the valley from the town of Three Rivers. **Monarch Lake** and **Eagle Lake** are two fabulous destinations for a quiet day-hike in the Mineral King backcountry. Located in the far eastern end of the Park, Mount Whitney looms a staggering 14,494 feet above Sequoia National Park and Inyo National Forest. **Whitney Portal** is the shortest route the top, a 10.7-mile trail stemming from the eastern slope of the Sierras. All hikers seeking to summit Whitney must obtain a permit before arrival at the trailhead. From the tallest trees to the highest mountain, Sequoia National Park features one of the finest collections of natural wonders in North America.

SEQUOIA: NATURE'S CATHEDRAL 18" X 24" Poster art based on an oil painting created in 2017 by Kai Carpenter >

SHENANDOAH

FAWNS grazing in the quiet hollows of Virginia's Shenandoah hearken a simpler time, when communion with nature was a daily occurrence in our young country. This Park, tucked away in the tumbling Blue Ridge Mountains, is only 75 miles from Washington D.C. It has served as a sylvan retreat from Eastern cities for over a century. The main artery of the Park is **Skyline Drive**, a 105-mile ribbon of road that laces through a narrow sheet of protected forest, mountain, and meadow in the Blue Ridge highlands. Atop these mountain peaks are crowns of lichen-clad boulders, providing climbers a breathless view of the Virginia valleys below. Four seasons circulate the Park's scenery each year, drawing over a million annual visitors to watch the endless transformation. A sea of burning orange, yellow, and red foliage ignites the forest each fall, and delicate new life blooms from the snowmelt in spring. Time has the ability to move and stand still simultaneously here. Change and changelessness, these are the unique traits of Shenandoah.

The Park itself has a rich American history, and it played an important role in one of our poorest decades. The region was at one time a patchwork of private land, over a thousand independent tracts owned by farmers, loggers, posh resort proprietors, even the President of the United States. With such close proximity to the capital, Shenandoah hosted a wide variety of political galas, weekend getaways, and private conferences for Washington's elite. However, when the stock market crashed in 1929 and the nation hurtled into the Great Depression, the Park also became a haven of renewal. President Hoover, along with hundreds of the area's residents, handed over their homes and their land to the state of Virginia. The state then placed Shenandoah National Park under federal protection in 1935. During the bleak 1930s, President Franklin D. Roosevelt commissioned ten CCC camps to facilitate and enhance the Park for all people to enjoy. They went to work blazing trails, building visitor centers and facilities, and fashioning walls and guardrails along Skyline Drive. FDR envisioned this Park as a place of "recreation and re-creation". Shenandoah rose from the ashes of the Depression and became a natural refuge for so many weary Americans.

Although Shenandoah's most prominent feature is Skyline Drive, it is by no means the only highlight. The main road connects visitors to several of the Park trailheads, from which 200,000 acres of pristine woodlands and meadows can be accessed and explored. Opportunities to camp, hike, birdwatch, and ride horseback abound here, and the 511 miles of trails vary from a family-friendly nature walk at **Fox Hollow** to the heart-pounding ascent of craggy **Old Rag**. Visit the abandoned homesteads of Shenandoah's former residents on **Limberlost Trail**. You can dine like an aristocrat on a chic-rustic retreat to **Skyland Resort** or sleep like a black bear under the oak and hickory trees along the **Appalachian Trail** (which runs straight through Shenandoah). Whether high above the misty hills or deep within the valley, the sights and sounds of Shenandoah National Park will instill in you a sense of gratitude and love for this beautiful country.

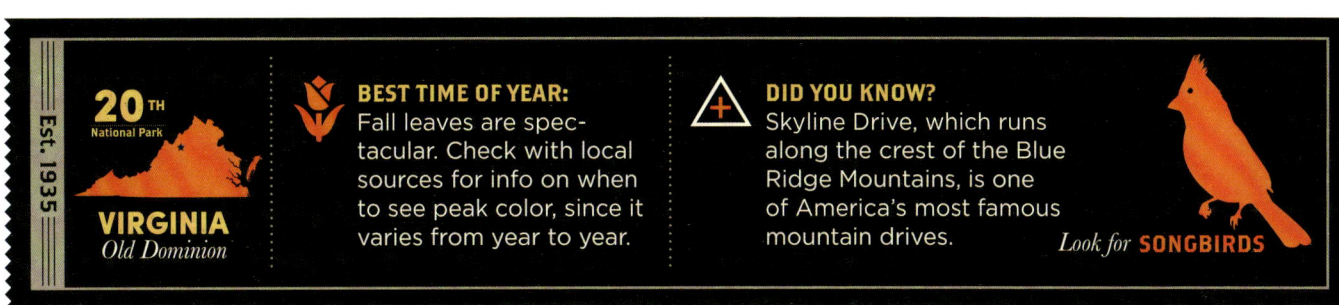

BEST TIME OF YEAR: Fall leaves are spectacular. Check with local sources for info on when to see peak color, since it varies from year to year.

DID YOU KNOW? Skyline Drive, which runs along the crest of the Blue Ridge Mountains, is one of America's most famous mountain drives.

Look for **SONGBIRDS**

Est. 1935 · 20TH National Park · **VIRGINIA** Old Dominion

<**SHENANDOAH: DARK HOLLOW FALLS** 18" X 24" Poster art created in 2017 by Michael Korfhage & Joel Anderson

THEODORE ROOSEVELT

ONE OF THE STRONGEST personalities in American history found his calling here in the Badlands of North Dakota. The landscape is pure Western prairie wilderness, home to wild horses, prairie dogs, buffalo, and pronghorn. The broken hills and weathered rock formations give testament to the region's incessant wind erosion, creating a strange and timeless aura to the Park. It is a near perfect place to feel connected and refined by unpolished nature. The **Little Missouri River** churns through colorful canyons and

> "I never would have been President if it had not been for my experiences in North Dakota."
> *-Theodore Roosevelt*

buttes across the valley floor, leaving a lush cottonwood and juniper-dotted riverbed in its wake. It was here, near the banks of the Little Missouri, that a young and sickly boy named Theodore Roosevelt became a man, finding a hidden toughness and respect for the wild. Roosevelt sought healing on the plains of North Dakota, and the vitality this region brought him changed the course of National Park history forever.

Theodore Roosevelt first arrived in Medora, North Dakota, in 1883. He was a skinny, bespectacled 25-year-old rich kid from New York City with one thought on his mind: to bag a bison. Stepping off the train, TR was immediately enamored with the cowboy lifestyle of the West. Though the local ranchers made fun of his city slicker background, Roosevelt's limitless energy soon impressed his peers and he bought into the rigorous life of a cattle rancher. His homestead at **Maltese Cross Ranch** is preserved to this day as a capsule to TR's development as a man in the Badlands. In 1884, back in New York City, TR lost both his wife and his mother on the same day. Overwhelmed with grief, TR returned to the northern plains where he built **Elkhorn Ranch** and faced a brutal North Dakota winter that wiped out more than half of his cattle. Though suffering great loss on all accounts, Roosevelt discovered an inner strength and a deep passion for America's wilderness that would alter the course of his life. The lessons he learned in North Dakota, and the ability to connect with the common man, eventually transformed the young Roosevelt into the President of the United States and a founding father of the National Park System. In his memory, this Park was established in 1978, preserving forever the rugged landscape that shaped an incredible life.

Opportunities for solitude abound at Theodore Roosevelt National Park. Explore the grassy hills and curved canyons on horseback, just like TR did 100 years ago. This Park is one of the few in the country that is almost completely accessible for horses, and a great place to saddle up is at **Peaceful Valley Ranch.** If you'd prefer an air-conditioned perspective, take the **Scenic Loop Drive** that winds through some of the most breathtaking regions of the North and South units of the Park, including the much-loved **Prairie Dog Towns.** Be sure to stop and stretch your legs at the **Caprock Coulee Pullout** for a glimpse of some eerie mushroom-shaped hoodoos along the trail. Let the wild winds of the northern plains reinvigorate you, just as they did for our resilient 26th President, Theodore Roosevelt.

Est. 1978 — **39TH** National Park — **NORTH DAKOTA** *Rough Rider State*

BEST TIME OF YEAR: Summer is the most popular time to visit since the North Dakota daylight is very long then.

DID YOU KNOW? The Park is home to animals such as bison, prairie dogs, wild horses, mule deer, elk, pronghorn and numerous bird species.

Look for **FERAL HORSES**

<**THEODORE ROOSEVELT: ELK** 18" X 24" Poster art created in 2021 by Aaron Johnson & Joel Anderson

VIRGIN ISLANDS

A JEWEL NECKLACE of emerald isles graces the neck of the Caribbean. Each gem is a living paradise, a divine getaway for thousands of visitors each year. Sugar-white beaches, thick leafy jungles, and a lustrous coral reef teeming with colorful fish crown the tropical dreamscape known as the Virgin Islands. Within this lovely archipelago is St. John's Island, home to Virgin Islands National Park. Though seemingly flawless today, the sugar mill ruins on St. John's Island give testament to a darker time, when these islands were populated with slaves rather than sun-starved tourists. The Park protects these monuments of the past, reminding us of an ugly era in human history. And yet, just as jungle reclaims the abandoned sugar fields, new life replaces the old. Virgin Islands National Park seems to redeem this once-exploited land and promote hope in all who wash up on its ivory shores.

On a voyage to the West Indies, Christopher Columbus first christened the numerous and undefiled Virgin Islands in 1493. Opportunistic Europeans set sail for this mythical island chain soon after.

Danish sugar planters laid claim to St. John's and turned the island into a sugar- and rum-producing powerhouse. More than 80 plantations smothered the island, choking out native plants and animals to cultivate the sugar stalks. African slaves tended these fields for 150 years. Relics of these plantations, factories, and mills are scattered throughout the Park, serving as reminders of the Danish sugar empire and the plight of the Africans forced to run it. The sugar boom ended in the mid-1800s with tired island soil and the emancipation of the slaves. At the height of World War I, the United States purchased St. John's and 50 other Virgin Islands to protect the mainland from German naval attacks. The war ended and vacationers soon discovered the tropical appeal of these isles. Developers began building posh resorts as more and more tourists flocked to the sunny Caribbean. Once again, the island's forests were threatened by commercialization. In the 1950s, billionaire conservationist Laurance Rockefeller purchased 5,000 acres, or half of St. John's Island, and donated it to the U.S. government as a National Park.

Today, Virgin Islands National Park is a nature haven for a large variety of birds, sea turtles, dolphins, forests of seagrass, palm, and the coral reef's bustling fish communities. Safe from exploitation, the land and sea now flourish with life. Investigate the vivacious coral reefs firsthand by snorkel or SCUBA in **Waterlemon Cay.** Experience the rich history of St. John's along the **Reef Bay Trail,** and finish off with a refreshing dip in the cove. Pop a tent on the shores of **Cinnamon Bay** for one of the most idyllic campgrounds in the United States. Reconnect yourself to nature and spend a day in the sand at Virgin Islands National Park.

27TH National Park
Est. 1956
VIRGIN ISLANDS
United in Pride & Hope

BEST TIME OF YEAR: Anytime of the year is great for visiting this tropical paradise.

DID YOU KNOW? Most of St. John's original vegetation was clear-cut in the colonial period for sugar-cane production. Fortunately, it has all grown back!

Look for the **BOTTLENOSE DOLPHIN**

<**VIRGIN ISLANDS** 18" X 24" Poster art created in 2013 by Michael Korfhage & Joel Anderson

VOYAGEURS

A SPIRIT of adventure pulses through the web of waterways at Voyageurs National Park. This was once an 18th century fur trappers' paradise, and the French Canadian "voyageurs" were masters of these channels. They romped across the region's 30 lakes singing merry songs and smoking pipes, camped out beneath the stars of the North Country, and hunted for beaver, whose pelts were then at the pinnacle of European fashion. Only the hardiest sailors could travel with the voyageurs, as the trappers often paddled up to 16 hours a day and endured the brutal Minnesota cold each winter. But these explorers were responsible for charting much of the continent's northwestern territory, and their zealous energy pervades the Land of 10,000 Lakes to this day.

Modern day paddlers still find never-ending adventure among the 900+ islands of this National Park in northern Minnesota. Though remote, Voyageurs was once in danger of losing its natural features to land development. Loggers ravaged the region's timber and miners blasted for gold. Dams were built, suffocating the lake country in the noose

> "Nature is always lovely . . . All scars she heals, whether in rocks or water or sky or hearts."
> *-John Muir*

of progress. In the 1930s, a local conservationist named Ernest Oberholtzer stepped in to save what was left of these pristine lakelands. As a founder and councilman of the nationally-recognized Wilderness Society, Oberholtzer's cries for preservation soon reached federal ears. Park recognition would take decades, but in 1975, Congress created Voyageurs National Park to permanently protect this Minnesota treasure.

With less than 10 total miles of roadway, this Park is meant to be explored by boat. Beavers, bald eagles, gray wolves, loons, and moose can all be encountered through kayaking the inlets or hiking along the island trails. Don't forget your fishing pole; this Park has some of the best fishing in the Midwest. Explore the Park's 4 major lakes (**Kabetogama, Namakan, Rainy,** and **Sand Point**) and end your day unwinding in one of the 200 shoreline campsites. Reenact the voyageur life in a 26-foot canoe and learn about these hardy French Canadian sailors on a free Ranger-led **North Canoe Voyage**. Test your boating skills, enjoy the summer sunshine, and experience the ultimate lake country at Voyageurs National Park.

37TH National Park · Est. 1975 · **MINNESOTA** *The Gopher State*

BEST TIME OF YEAR: June is the best time to see orchids, loon chicks, and eaglets.

DID YOU KNOW? The Park lies in the southern part of the Canadian Shield, some of the oldest exposed rock formations in the world.

Look for **RIVER OTTERS**

<**VOYAGEURS** 18" X 24" Poster art created in 2015 by Michael Korfhage & Joel Anderson

WHITE SANDS

AN ETHEREAL, even disorienting, landscape lies in the deep southern wilderness of New Mexico. Trapped between the Sacramento and the San Andres Mountain ranges is the bowl-like Tularosa Basin and a celestial sea of crushed gypsum. With texture more like powdered sugar than beach sand, this ghost-colored dunefield covers over 275 square miles: the largest gypsum dunefield in the world. White Sands National Park protects this windy "sandscape" and the creatures that inhabit it.

As in most cases of natural phenomena, water (and the lack thereof) played a crucial role in the formation of these dunes. The mineral-rich Permian Sea once covered this land, leaving thick deposits of gypsum on the ocean floor. As the Earth's tectonic plates shifted, mountains formed and the sea was dammed, leaving behind the isolated Lake Otero. The region warmed, the winds picked up, and the lake began to evaporate, revealing the rich deposits of buried minerals. Strong and frequent gusts of wind crushed and shaped the gypsum crystals into the powder dunes we enjoy today.

Scientists have deemed this arid ecosystem "a desert Galapagos" for the fascinating amount of short-term evolution that has occurred here. Several species of plants, animals, and fungi have become lighter in color to survive in this uniquely white environment. Humans have scratched out a life here as well. Archaeologists have discovered 10,000-year-old Paleoindian arrowheads, hinting at a time when large game wandered these lands. Another discovery is the plastered fire-pits (known as "hearth mounds") built by the Archaic people four to six thousand years ago. Americans began to wander out to these remote dunes in the late 1800s, some trying unsuccessfully to profit off the resale of unprocessed gypsum sand. Local

residents began to write their Congressmen about the merits of their peculiar backyard during this time, too. Congress eventually took notice and President Herbert Hoover established White Sands National Monument in 1933. Congress also designated a large portion of this region as a military base and missile testing ground in the 1940s. After decades of negotiations with the U.S. military, New Mexico's most-visited national monument became a National Park in 2019.

The eight-mile **Dunes Drive** pierces the center of White Sands via Highway 70, providing the only way in and out of the Park. Five hiking trails and various vistas stem from this solitary roadway as it snakes through the seemingly eternal hills of gypsum. As with all National Parks, the landscape is equally interactive and dangerous. Sunscreen and sunglasses are as essential as water here in this white desert. While the gypsum sand is mercifully heat-resistant (safe to touch even on scorching summer days), the reflective nature of the sand can be blinding and cause sunburn if you're not prepared. Visitors are invited to explore and enjoy the endless dunes but must be careful to stay near the designated trails; getting lost is very easy to do here. The silky smooth texture of crushed gypsum means that **sand sledding** is a very popular activity. Be sure to stop by the Visitor Center to purchase a sled and ask a Park Ranger where the best sledding spots are. For a slightly less sandy experience, take an elevated jaunt over the dunes on the **Interdune Boardwalk**: an easy 0.4-mile trail that includes educational signposts and a shaded canopy. Intrepid outdoor enthusiasts can spend the night under the stars at a rustic campsite on **Backcountry Camping Trail** (permit required). **Photography** is phenomenal here, especially during the "golden hours" of dusk and dawn. **Alkali Flat Trail** is not an easy hike but will provide stunning photo opportunities among the Park's tallest dunes.

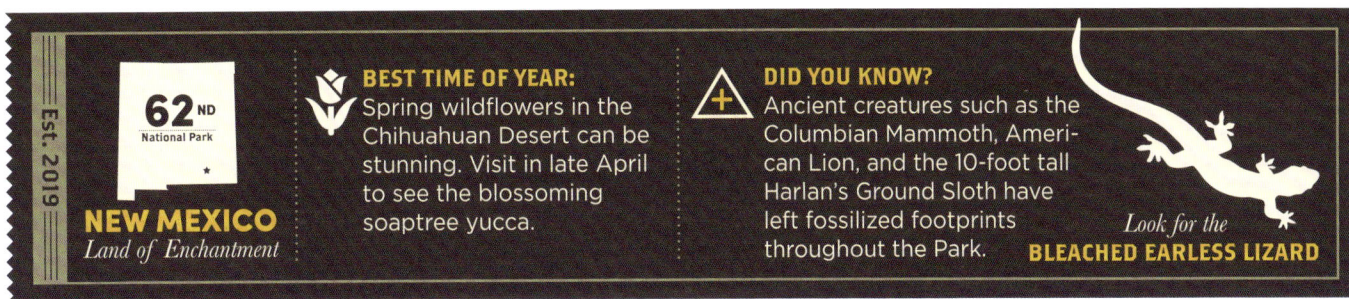

62ND National Park — Est. 2019 — **NEW MEXICO** *Land of Enchantment*

BEST TIME OF YEAR: Spring wildflowers in the Chihuahuan Desert can be stunning. Visit in late April to see the blossoming soaptree yucca.

DID YOU KNOW? Ancient creatures such as the Columbian Mammoth, American Lion, and the 10-foot tall Harlan's Ground Sloth have left fossilized footprints throughout the Park.

Look for the **BLEACHED EARLESS LIZARD**

<WHITE SANDS   18" X 24" Poster art created in 2019 by Derek Anderson & Joel Anderson

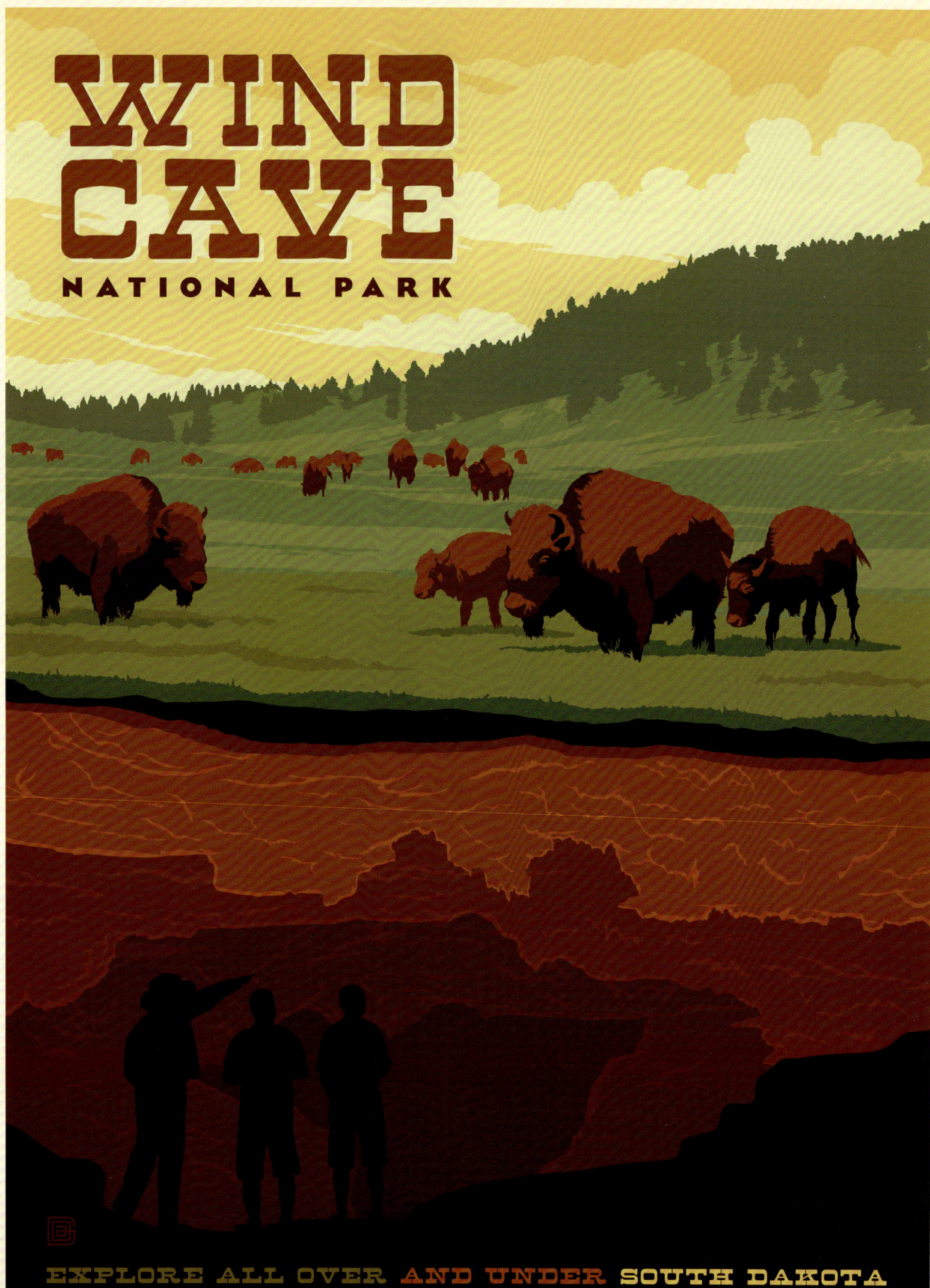

WIND CAVE

ACCORDING to Lakota Sioux legend, the world's first bison stepped out the mouth of Wind Cave. Wind Cave National Park is still home to many of America's bison today, though you probably won't find any milling about underground. While the Park is named after its whistling subterranean chasm, the gorgeous Black Hills of South Dakota should not be missed. Though (or because) the Park is small, the concentration of wildlife is great. In fact, Wind Cave is one of the most photo-friendly places in the Park System. Bison, prairie dogs, elk, falcons, and the black-footed ferret all dwell on the plains and in the ponderosa pines of the Black Hills. And of course, there's the cave itself.

Thanks to its quirky ability to knock off hats, Wind Cave was rediscovered by a pair of brothers in 1881. The "cave wind" is created by uneven air pressure: when the cave's air becomes more pressurized than the atmosphere outside, great bursts of wind will rush out the cave's only entrance. News of this cave spread, and the South Dakota Mining Company laid claim to the area a few years later, hiring J.D. McDonald to live above ground and mine for gold below. No gold was found, but the resourceful McDonald and his 16-year-old son Alvin began offering cave tours. Alvin kept finding new passageways while his dad saw that there was money to be made in tourism.

In 1891, the McDonalds partnered with a local businessman named John Stabler to start a cave improvement company, building staircases and walkable trails along the known passageways. They also built a hotel and facilitated a stagecoach taxi service that carried guests to and from the cave mouth. Tragedy and discord soon broke the partnership, however. Alvin McDonald died of typhoid at the age of 20, and Stabler began to make claims of the land previously leased to the McDonalds. Stabler tried to drive J.D. out of the partnership altogether, and the feud caused such a ruckus that the U.S. Department of the Interior got involved. The government found that neither party had legitimate claims to the cave and instead had the land established as a National Park in 1903.

Much like Mammoth Cave in the Southeast, Wind Cave is a relatively dry cave with few stalagmite or stalactite formations. The tunnels do contain a wide variety of strange mineral formations, including the rare boxwood, which looks like a freakish wasp's nest of calcite. You can go back in time and explore the cave by **candlelight tour**: Park Rangers lead a small group of visitors along the old trails of Alvin McDonald with only a candle bucket to guide you. If you'd prefer the sunlight, above-ground trails at **Boland Ridge** and **Lookout Point** will give you excellent views of the gentle Black Hills.

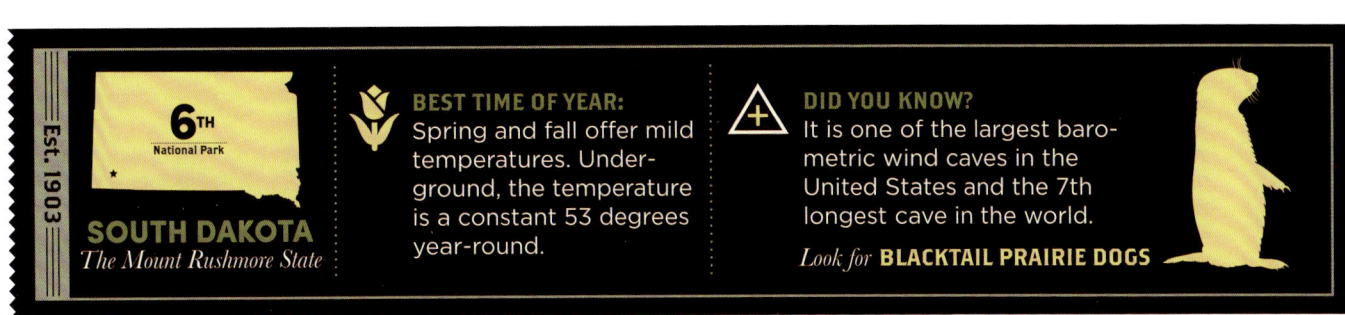

Est. 1903 — 6TH National Park — **SOUTH DAKOTA** *The Mount Rushmore State*

BEST TIME OF YEAR: Spring and fall offer mild temperatures. Underground, the temperature is a constant 53 degrees year-round.

DID YOU KNOW? It is one of the largest barometric wind caves in the United States and the 7th longest cave in the world.

Look for **BLACKTAIL PRAIRIE DOGS**

<**WIND CAVE** 18" X 24" Poster art created in 2015 by Michael Korfhage & Joel Anderson

WRANGELL-ST. ELIAS

THE ALASKAN COLOSSUS of Wrangell-St. Elias National Park is as big as it gets. Looming over the Canadian Yukon border in southeastern Alaska, the sweeping 13 million acres of Wrangell-St. Elias has it all. Sawtooth peaks claw at the infinite sky. Deep chasms puncture fields of blue ice. Gluttonous glaciers swallow up entire mountain ranges in frozen excess. Foaming streams and alpine lakes sparkle in the summer sun. Boreal forests of spruce, aspen, and poplar furnish the leafy foothills. Bison, moose, grizzlies, Dall sheep, gray wolves, bald eagles, and caribou all thrive in this virgin wilderness, broadly untouched and unexplored by mankind. It is America's largest National Park, six times the size of Yellowstone. And, unlike many of its Alaskan counterparts, Wrangell-St. Elias is accessible by car. Two gravel roads bring Park visitors into the midst of incomprehensible majesty. They also quietly remind guests of the region's rich history in copper and gold mining. Today, the **Nabesna** and **McCarthy Roads** run past the remains of desolate mining villages and into a vast undisturbed kingdom of water, tree, and stone.

Three monstrous mountain ranges form the backbone of this National Park. The glacier-gutted **Wrangell Mountains** lie to the north, the **Chugach range** to the south, and the **St. Elias range** to the east. Nine of the 16 tallest peaks in America stand in these three lustrous mountain ranges. North America's second largest is the Park's southeastern peak Mount St. Elias. Russian explorers were some of the first non-natives to enter Wrangell-St. Elias, arriving in the early 1700s. Hired by the Russian Czar, Danish adventurer Vitus Bering led a fleet of Russian ships across the channel from Siberia to Alaska (the route is now known as the Bering Strait). On the feast day of St. Elias, Bering and his men laid their eyes on a magnificent snow-capped pinnacle tumbling down into **Icy Bay.** Overwhelmed by the peak's sheer magnitude, Bering named the mountain "St. Elias" in honor of the day it was discovered.

A century later, Russian governor and naval officer Baron Ferdinand Petrovich von Wrangel governed the Russian colonies in Alaska. Life was never easy for Wrangel as he battled three native tribes to maintain control of the **Copper River region**, an area rich in fish, furs, and minerals. The feisty baron kept the colonies intact until 1867, when Russia sold their Alaskan territory to America once and for all. Wrangel's memory would be left in the rocks so to speak: the Park's primary mountain range, along with several landmarks and an island along the coast, are named after the Russian governor. (American settlers would eventually add an extra "L" to Wrangel's name in regards to the mountain range.)

There is no better way to experience the sweeping icy expanse of Wrangell-St. Elias than on a **flightseeing tour.** Small bush planes carry passengers over some of the most exquisite landscape on earth, sights Bering or Wrangel could only dream of. Like other Alaskan Parks, WSE also hosts some of the finest fishing spots on the continent: Copper River is a premier destination for anglers looking to land the big one. Come and explore the nation's largest National Park, now part of our American heritage forever.

Est. 1980 — 48TH National Park — **ALASKA** *The Last Frontier*

BEST TIME OF YEAR: May is prime time for mountaineering excursions.

DID YOU KNOW? Parts of the Park are so remote and unexplored that mountains, glaciers, and passes remain unnamed.

Look for **MOUNTAIN GOATS**

<**WRANGELL-ST. ELIAS** 18" X 24" Poster art created in 2015 by Michael Korfhage & Joel Anderson

YELLOWSTONE

MASSIVE. Strange. Iconic. These are just a few of the many superlatives belonging to America's first National Park. With over 2.2 million acres of real estate, Yellowstone is enormous. It is a Park bubbling (figuratively and literally) with life. Due to its convenient location above an active supervolcano, the Yellowstone Caldera, the Park possesses over 10,000 geothermal features within its boundaries. Perhaps most famous of these are the geysers, with household names like **Old Faithful**. The Park also contains a vast array of otherworldly wonders: technicolor hotpots of emerald green and Tahoe blue, pasty gray cauldrons of boiling mud, bleached-white terraces of sulphuric springs, and a canyon made of golden rock.

John Colter, an explorer formerly associated with Lewis and Clark, came across the Yellowstone region in the first decade of the 1800s while trapping for the Missouri Fur Trading Company. Colter's tales of the steaming pools, evil-smelling bowls of boiling mud, and

gushing fountains were laughed off by many. Yet the myth of "Colter's Hell" spread, drawing Ferdinand Hayden, head of the Geological and Geographical Survey of the Territories, and his ambitious team of scientists into the region in 1871.

Fully prepared for what he might find, Hayden made sure to bring along landscape painter Thomas Moran and photographer William Henry Jackson to document the team's discoveries. Through the eyes and hands of these artists, the world saw Yellowstone. Moran painted dreamscapes of color: water, rock, and light dancing together. Jackson's dramatic black and white photographs of bursting geyser fountains and hot springs revealed an untamable wilderness. Through the diligent practice of art and science, Hayden's team brought national attention to the region.

Hayden convinced Congress that the elevated, volcanic land would never be good for mining or agriculture. A pub-

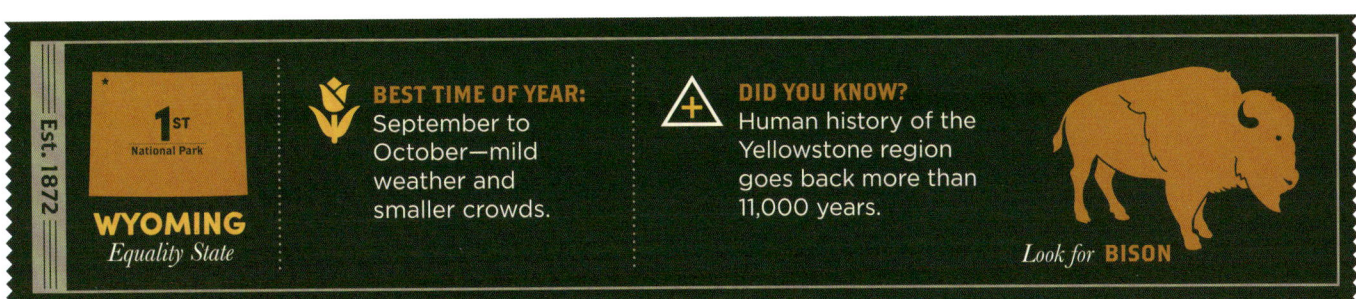

Est. 1872 · **1ST** National Park · **WYOMING** *Equality State*

BEST TIME OF YEAR: September to October—mild weather and smaller crowds.

DID YOU KNOW? Human history of the Yellowstone region goes back more than 11,000 years.

Look for **BISON**

<**YELLOWSTONE** 18" X 24" Poster art created in 2010 by Julian Baker & Joel Anderson

Photo by Joel Anderson

lic park, one protected from exploiters and profiteers, would be more suitable. Without government protection, however, Yellowstone would become a commercialized tourist attraction, and its strange grandeur would be diminished. Congress was convinced, and President Ulysses S. Grant signed the first National Park into existence on March 1, 1872.

Exploring Yellowstone is a meditation on the odd, a journey that requires time but produces a type of awe that few other places on Earth can. In the early years, the Park was protected by the U.S. military, who built roads while staving off lawless poachers and prospectors. These access roads were eventually united into the single **Grand Loop Road**, a 142-mile figure eight that connects guests to all of Yellowstone's most popular regions. From this sweeping roadway, visitors experience the natural panorama of Yellowstone. Steamy geyser basins such as **West Thumb**, **Midway**, and **Norris** line the south and middle regions, displaying a wide variety of color, form, and volatility. Boardwalks lead to the world-famous Old Faithful geyser on the **Upper Geyser Basin**. The **Grand Canyon of the Yellowstone** is another wonder, a heart-stopping display of power as the Yellowstone River dashes into the golden-walled gorge below. The eerie **Mammoth Hot Springs** lie on the north end of the Park.

While geothermal abnormalities abound in this unconventional ecosystem, plants and animals of all shapes and sizes do too. Outside of Alaska, Yellowstone has the densest concentration of non-human mammals in the United States. Over 67 different species of mammals populate the Park, ranging from bison and grizzly bears to gray wolves, big horn sheep, moose, elk, lynx, and wolverines. The hot springs act as a beachside resort for the tiny thermophile ("heat-loving") organisms and lichens that flourish in and alongside the boiling-hot basins. The Park has also become a safe place to bring back the dead: the gray wolf, nearly eliminated from the lower 48 states, was reintroduced to Yellowstone National Park in 1995.

"I always think of Yellowstone as North America's Serengeti. No other place in the lower 48 has such an amazing variety of wildlife. The geysers, hotsprings and mudpots are the bonus visitors get when traveling through this amazing place. It truly deserves the distinction of being the world's first National Park."
— Rick Smith, Retired Seasonal Ranger in Yellowstone from 1959-1969
(total years of NPS service: 31)

YELLOWSTONE FALLS 18" X 24" Poster art based on an oil painting created in 2015 by Kai Carpenter ^
YELLOWSTONE LAKE 18" X 24" Poster art created in 2018 by Derek Anderson & Joel Anderson ^
BISON CROSSING 18" X 24" Poster art based on an oil painting created in 2015 by Kai Carpenter >

YOSEMITE

SO MUCH of John Muir's work was inspired by the mystic grandeur of Yosemite National Park. His psalms of creation welled up from the base of **Yosemite Falls** and echoed off the granite face of **El Capitan**. He attempted to describe the indescribable. Muir's passion for places like Yosemite left an indelible mark upon America, teaching us how to hold on to a beautiful space: not too tight and not too loose, to savor and to share. We are left with his legacy in writing and in the preservation of 1,190 square miles of picturesque Sierra high country. One of the country's oldest National Parks, Yosemite is now a place of solace, inspiration, and adeventure for families and backpackers from all across the world. The National Park System's healthy tension between preservation and tourism began here. This tension is still felt today as the mile-wide, 7-mile long **Yosemite Valley** welcomes millions of visitors each year who begin their wilderness adventure from the valley floor.

Yosemite, a shapely diamond in the Sierra's mountain crown, was first the sacred home to the Ahwahneechee tribe. A battalion of soldiers seeking them stumbled across the untarnished majesty of Yosemite Valley in the 1850s. Whispers of such beauty would draw men with varying ideas on how to use it. Former gold miner James Mason Hutchings saw that there was money to be made and began heading up tours and nature trips into the valley in 1855. He soon built a ramshackle hotel to house his guests. Galen Clark was also enamored by Yosemite's glory but instead sought to protect it from commercial abuse. His letters to Congress were eventually backed by California Senator John Conness, and President Lincoln would place Yosemite Valley and **Mariposa Grove** under state control in 1864.

Est. 1890 — **3RD** National Park — **CALIFORNIA** *The Golden State*

BEST TIME OF YEAR: Winter— least busy and most beautiful when covered in snow.

BEST PHOTO: Half Dome at sunset

DID YOU KNOW? The Merced River runs 81 miles through the Park, winding right through Yosemite Valley.

Look for the **INCENSE CEDAR**

<YOSEMITE 18" X 24" Poster art created in 2010 by Andy Gregg & Joel Anderson

Clark became the Park's first caretaker while Hutching's squatting tourist business became illegal. Hutchings kept at it, however, and eventually hired a wandering shepherd named John Muir to run his sawmill. Muir found a home among the tall trees of Yosemite, building a cabin at the foot of Yosemite Falls. He too was fascinated by Yosemite's wonders and would accompany Hutchings' few customers on hikes when not tramping through the wilderness alone. Soon Muir was an attraction himself, and Park visitors followed Muir around to try and see the Sierras through his eyes.

Tourism grew by leaps and bounds as the years went on, and the ever-changing state government began to neglect the protection of Yosemite. Land was leased to farmers, loggers, and ranchers. Tourists built enormous bonfires and spilled them down the cliff face at **Glacier Point** to create "fire falls." Muir was outraged. He realized that the only way to save Yosemite was through Washington: "Through all the wonderful, eventful centuries since Christ's time -- and long before that -- God has cared for these trees, saved them from drought, disease, avalanches, and a thousand straining, leveling tempests and floods; but He can-

> "I have here seen the power and glory of a Supreme Being; the majesty of His handy-work is in that 'Testimony of the Rocks.'"
> -Dr. Lafayette Bunnell, Yosemite: 1851

not save them from fools -- only Uncle Sam can do that." Muir got his wish in 1890 when Congress designated Yosemite as a National Park.

Muir would rejoice knowing the vast backcountry of Yosemite still remains unspoiled today. Visitors can experience many of the same views and vistas that Muir once described with such reverence. Popular hiking routes spring from the busy Yosemite Valley, such as **Mist Trail**, which leads visitors up to classic viewpoints at **Vernal** and **Nevada Falls** and eventually to the very peak of spectacular **Half Dome**. **Tunnel View** is a must-see for photographers. There are many ways to dive in and escape the huge summer crowds. Drive into the heart of the Sierras via **Tioga Road** to access the exquisite lakes and alpine meadows of the high country. From **Hetch Hetchy Backpackers Camp**, see the notorious dam that filled the one valley Muir loved most but could not save. And don't forget to visit the sleeping giants at Mariposa Grove, where the mighty sequoia continue to grow thanks to the efforts of John Muir, Galen Clark, and the National Park Service.

"I never tired of going to work and looking up at the walls of Yosemite Valley. Depending on the season or the time of day, no two views were the same. How fortunate we are as Americans that those who came before us had the wisdom and foresight to preserve and protect this wonderful place. We would be poorer as a nation had they not done so." — Rick Smith, Retired Park Ranger at Yosemite from 1971-1976 (total years of NPS service: 31)

YOSEMITE VALLEY: HORIZONTAL 24" X 18" Poster art created in 2017 by Derek Anderson & Joel Anderson ^
YOSEMITE VALLEY MIST 18" X 24" Poster art based on an oil painting created in 2015 by Kai Carpenter >

ZION

> "Wherever we go in the mountains, or indeed in any of God's wild fields, we find more than we seek."
> *-John Muir*

CENTURIES before Mormon settlers discovered this lush oasis in southeastern Utah, Zion National Park was known to the natives as "Mukuntuweap" or "straight-up land." Unlike the Grand Canyon where visitors usually view the spectacular rock formations from above, the Navajo Sandstone giants of Zion are mainly experienced from the ground up. These cliffs, sculpted by incessant wind and rain, surround your periphery as the effervescent **Virgin River** flows between canyon walls and across the valley floor. You cannot help but feel a little unworthy in this sacred tabernacle of natural beauty. The mountains themselves seem to have been dramatically summoned from the dry landscape, called to protect an American slice of Eden.

Up until the 20th century, Zion was too remote a destination for tourism. Only through sheer determination did Native Americans and Mormons traverse and settle scant portions of this rugged landscape. With only old wagon trails for roads, this natural sanctuary remained an enigma until 1904 when a traveling painter named Frederick S. Dellenbaugh permanently changed that. His dreamscape portrayals of cream- and red-colored canyons caught the country's attention at the St. Louis World's Fair. In only a few years' time, President Taft would declare the region a National Monument. President Wilson and the U.S. Congress would add more land and declare the protected area a National Park in 1919. With the same awe-filled determination of Zion's former residents, Zion National Park's new stewards paved roads and brought ease of access into the region. Though the Great Depression staggered the U.S. in 1929, it would soon create an incredible opportunity for unemployed Americans to cultivate Zion's matchless splendor. Teams of Civilian Conservation Corps tunneled through solid rock to carve out roadways that confound imagination. The CCC built new campgrounds, managed flood control of the Virgin River, and even blazed one of the most hair-raising hiking trails in the National Park

Photo by Joel Anderson

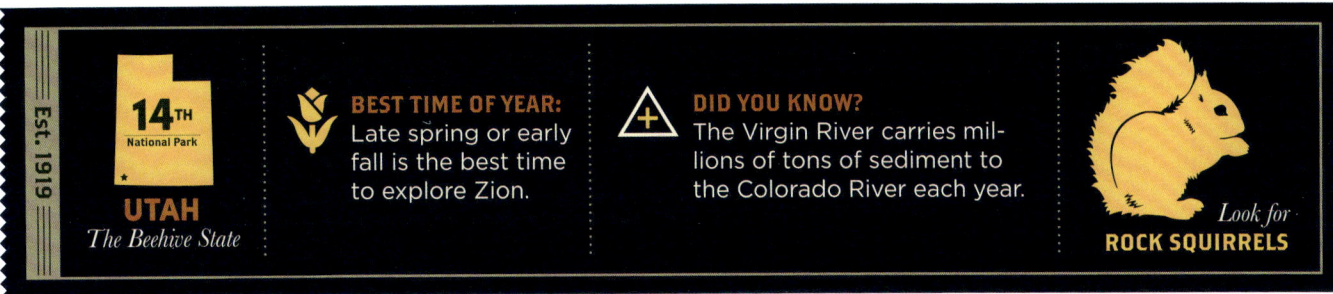

Est. 1919 · 14TH National Park · **UTAH** *The Beehive State*

BEST TIME OF YEAR: Late spring or early fall is the best time to explore Zion.

DID YOU KNOW? The Virgin River carries millions of tons of sediment to the Colorado River each year.

Look for **ROCK SQUIRRELS**

<ZION: ASCENT TO ANGELS LANDING 18" X 24" Poster art created in 2019 by Aaron Johnson & Joel Anderson

System. Thanks to the tireless efforts of CCC work crews, roads such as **Zion Canyon Scenic Drive** and **Zion-Mount Carmel Highway** now bring delight and wonder to millions of visitors each year.

Exploring the southern area of Zion is simple thanks to the Park's convenient shuttle bus system that carries guests from the visitor center to various trailheads along Zion Canyon Scenic Drive. You can imagine the painter Dellenbaugh setting up his easel across many of the roadway's fantastic vistas. The busy shuttles drive through this single asphalt artery into the heart of Zion National Park. A network of hiking trails stem from this road and lead guests through a living liturgy of wilderness psalms. The Virgin River whispers joyfully beneath the Park's storybook peaks and even invites you to enter the river on trails

> "Everybody needs beauty as well as bread, places to play in and pray in, where Nature may heal and cheer and give strength to body and soul alike."
> -*John Muir*

such as **the Narrows**. With walking stick in hand, you can splash through the shallow river and enjoy the stunning smooth-rock bluffs that bless each and every turn. A divine section of the Virgin River murmurs beneath the mountains at **Big Bend.** Here the riverbanks are strewn with colored stones, and visitors feel hemmed-in by the gigantic rock castles of **Heaps Canyon.** Look up and witness the spine-tingling climb to **Angels Landing** from below. This trail was crafted by the CCC and includes switchbacks, thousand-foot dropoffs, and a single chain handrail to lead you to the very roof of Zion National Park. Backpackers are rewarded with the astonishing glory of **Kolob Arch** in Zion's vast backcountry. Enter in and witness the splendor of this consecrated canvas on the Colorado Plateau.

"The scenic grandeur of Zion National Park has long brought a feeling of wonder and awe to those fortunate enough to have experienced it. The towering sandstone walls formed by the Virgin River were viewed as somewhat formidable by the early Southern Paiutes who named it Mukuntuweap or straight canyon. Issac Behunin, an early Mormon settler thought of the canyon as Little Zion, a place of reverence and peace. That name stuck and the Park now carries the name of Zion. Today's visitors can experience those same feelings as the Park preserves a sanctuary for them and for future generations, providing a place of life and hope."
— Donald A. Falvey, Former Superintendent of Zion from 1991-2000
(total years of NPS service: 28)

ZION: 100th ANNIVERSARY 18" X 24" Poster art created in 2018 by Derek Anderson & Joel Anderson ^
ZION: VIRGIN RIVER NARROWS 18" X 24" Poster art based on an oil painting created in 2015 by Kai Carpenter >

How the Art is Made...

WE WORK AS A TEAM of artists. As founder of Anderson Design Group, I (Joel) have had the great pleasure of collaborating with creative friends to accomplish artistic feats that none of us could do alone. I was trained as an illustrator so when possible, I enjoy rendering a poster from start to finish. But for this project, I realized the best way to produce 80+ National Park posters along with a book within 5 years was to act like the conductor of a chamber orchestra and write parts for each of my virtuoso players to perform. I started by creating a master list of poster themes. Then I assigned illustrations to different artists (many of whom I had trained as interns) who could draw, paint, and design in a classic style. During this process, several artists were always working on different posters at the same time. I would look at progress sketches and renderings, offer input and guidance, and then try to stay out of the way as much as possible to let everyone do what they were born to do. As soon as one of the illustrations was turned in, I would spend several hours on it adding finishing touches, creating continuity for the entire series of posters. Andy Gregg and Julian Baker created the first few poster designs for this collection back in 2010. Since then, Michael Korfhage, Kai Carpenter, Aaron Johnson, David Anderson and Derek Anderson have done the rest. Here is a behind-the-scenes look at how we create....

1. I sketch out the basic composition on the canvas and start blocking in rough color.
2. I usually work for 2-3 hours at a time (that's 3-4 of my favorite Tom Petty albums).
3. After the main composition and color palette are established, I add smaller details.
4. Working in acrylics allows me to work fast since the paint dries within half an hour.
5. Once I am satisfied with a painting, I shoot a high-resolution photo and add type and extra touches in Photoshop.

JOEL ANDERSON: I am an illustrator, designer, author, and the Creative Director / founder of Anderson Design Group. I was born in Denver, Colorado and spent my childhood living in places like Curacao, El Salvador, Texas, New York, South Carolina, and Florida. I studied illustration at Ringling School of Art & Design. I draw on a variety of influences for my work, notably 20th Century travel poster art and advertising art as well as American folk art. When I am not traveling to take reference photography for books or illustrated poster art, I enjoy mentoring and training up-and-coming artists who often become collaborators or full-time staff.

© 2021 Anderson Design Group, Inc. All rights reserved.

   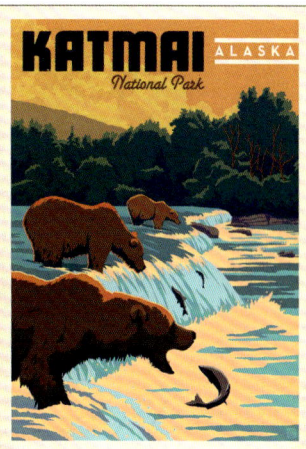

1. I created a rough sketch to show Aaron my vision for the poster composition.
2. Aaron took my concept, did some research, and expanded the idea in his own sketch.
3. Once we were happy with the composition, Aaron began rendering the illustration.
4. After experimenting with a few different sky colors, Aaron settled on a palette that bathed the scene in evening light.

AARON JOHNSON: Aaron graduated from Watkins School of Art, Design & Film in Nashville, TN. He worked as an intern before joining ADG as a staff artist. Aaron prefers to draw and paint on a tablet hooked up to an iMac computer. Using the same techniques and motions that he would normally use with pencils and brushes, his digital workspace allows for unlimited editing and experimentation with no paint to clean up afterwards! Aaron enjoys making art in different styles, and he can do anything from paintings and WPA-era posters to Art Nouveau and even comic book art.

Michael's process and techniques are very similar to Aaron's. He starts with a pencil sketch and then moves to the computer to render his art digitally. Like the rest of us, he is also a fan of old-school poster and advertising art from the early to mid-20th Century.

MICHAEL KORFHAGE: Michael works in Nashville as a free-lance illustrator and commercial artist. After graduating from Watkins College of Art, Design & Film, he started collaborating with us as an independent contractor helping me produce poster art. We love working with him because, after working together on more than 100 posters, he knows exactly what we are looking for. Michael also works for magazines, ad agencies, and small businesses. His work is inspired by folk art, mid-century design, and storytelling.

1. I supply photo reference I've shot to share my vision for the poster composition.
2. Derek does more research and expands the idea with a computer-rendering.
3. Once we are both happy with the composition, he begins rendering the illustration.
4. Derek adds typography and finishing touches to the composition. The finished poster design is ready for publication.

DEREK ANDERSON: Derek graduated from Watkins School of Art, Design & Film in Nashville, TN. He worked as an intern before joining ADG as a staff artist. Even though he shares the same last name as the company he works for, Derek is not actually related to Joel Anderson—but his style fits the Anderson Design Group look perfectly! Like his studio mate Aaron, Derek likes to design and illustrate on the computer.

1. After I tell Kai what I want to see, he creates some rough sketches of different scenarios.
2. Once we settle on a composition, he draws a tighter sketch showing specific details.
3. He then begins painting with oils on a canvas. See the progression of his work above.
4. Once the painting is dry enough to be handled, Kai takes it to a photographer to have a digital photo made.
5. I add some subtle changes in Photoshop to create an area for the typography which I overlay to finish the poster.

KAI CARPENTER: Kai grew up in the Pacific Northwest and works from his Seattle studio. I still recall the first time I saw his work: I felt like I was looking at magazine cover art from the 1930s or '40s. Kai's style and sense of lighting gives his art a look from a bygone era. I knew his paintings would be a great fit for the vintage-style poster series I was creating. A graduate of the Rhode Island School of Design, Kai has illustrated for numerous clients including Wizards of the Coast and Harper Collins. Kai draws his inspiration from artists of the late 1800s to the 1940s, particularly the Golden Age illustrators.

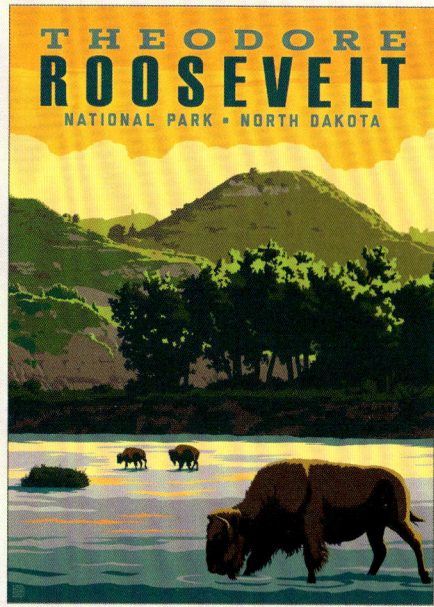

THE NP COLLECTION KEEPS GROWING all the time as we take trips that inspire us to produce new art. Each National Park is so big and diverse that one poster design cannot tell the whole story. Whenever we visit a National Park, we come back to the studio with fresh insights and new ideas about how to celebrate the unique aspects of that wonderful place. In addition to using our own adventures for inspiration, we also enjoy hearing from folks who tell us of places that are meaningful to them. (Wonderful wilderness experiences that were shared with someone special inspired some of our favorite posters!) We also get requests for new art from our licensing partners who work with Visitor Center gift shops around the USA to create souvenirs and collectibles. Items like postcards, magnets, mugs, journals, shirts, etc. become treasured keepsakes—mementos of a life-changing experience that Park visitors purchase to cherish or give as gifts. As long as we are inspired, and as long as there is a demand for more art, we will continue to create new illustrated National Park posters.

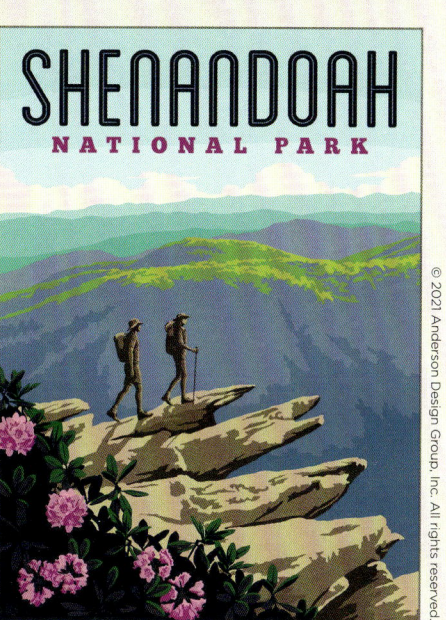

Top row from left to right: Yosemite by Aaron Johnson, Grand Canyon by Derek Anderson, Theodore Roosevelt by Aaron Johnson
Middle row: Horizontal Arches Print by Aaron Johnson
Bottom row from left to right: Bryce Canyon by Aaron Johnson, Grand Teton by Derek Anderson, Shenandoah by Aaron Johnson

INFORMATION SOURCES

All facts, figures, and quotes are derived from the sources below and the National Park Service website. They are listed in recognition of the authors and for your convenience as a reader.

Research is always easier when the topic excites you. My (Nathan) enthusiasm for the National Parks was matched (if not exceeded) by a few incredible adventurers, filmmakers, and authors. Their passion for the Parks and their attention to detail allowed me to write a narrative that, I hope, adds to this wonderful canon of National Parks travel writing. I relied on the following sources throughout the book:

• *Guide to National Parks of the United States*, 7th ed. by the National Geographic Society, 2012.
• *The National Parks: America's Best Idea* by Dayton Duncan and Ken Burns. New York: Knopf, 2009.
• *Your Guide to the National Parks* by Michael Joseph Oswald. Whitelaw: Stone Road Press, 2012.

Writing a solid research paper means bringing a posse, a collection of experts to back you up in your great chase for truth. The following folks backed me up, and I am grateful they wrote their thoughts down for the world to read and enjoy. The parenthetical page numbers indicate where we used the quote in our book:

• *Travels with Charley in Search of America* by John Steinbeck. New York: Penguin, 1980. (Page 4)
• "History" edited by Ranger Doug's Enterprises. Ranger Doug website. (Page 6)
• "What's the Difference between National Parks and National Monuments?" by Ashley M. Biggers. *Outside Online*. Outside Magazine website, 22 Apr. 2014. (Page 9)
• *Desert Solitaire: A Season in the Wilderness* by Edward Abbey. New York: Touchstone, 1990. (Page 19)
• *Bob Marshall in the Adirondacks: Writings of a Pioneering Peak-Bagger, Pond-Hopper and Wilderness Preservationist* edited by Phil Brown. Saranac Lake: Lost Pond, 2006. (Page 65)
• *RVing with Monsters: The Complete Guide to the Grand Circle National Parks* by Eric Henze. Gone Beyond Guides, 2014. (Page 76)
• *One Man's Wilderness: An Alaskan Odyssey* by Richard Proenneke and Sam Keith. Anchorage: Alaska Northwest, 1999. (Page 115)

Park Ranger quotes were provided by the following former NPS employees (in order of appearance) Rick Smith, Bill Wade, Bill Pierce, Roger Rudolph, Robert Arnberger, Donald Falvey, Fred J. Fagergren, Maureen Finnerty, Walt Dabney, and Cherry Payne. Their photos were supplied by the Rangers themselves and have been used with their permission. Thank you!

All stock photography was purchased from Deposit Photos and Shutterstock. Historic images are courtesy of the National Park Service and the Library of Congress. Photos of Joel Anderson are by Alyssa Adams Palumbo (Pages 7, 180). Where indicated, original photos are by Joel Anderson or Boundless Blue. Original oil paintings are by Kai Carpenter, on loan from the Anderson Design Group Collection. Original posters are by Anderson Design Group: Joel Anderson, David Anderson, Derek Anderson, Julian Baker, Andy Gregg, Aaron Johnson and Michael Korfhage. All original Park photos are by Joel Anderson.

OUR HISTORY: Anderson Design Group has been around since 1993. We started out producing CD and toy packaging, book covers, posters, and logos. In 2003, I (Joel) began leading my artists to create work in the classic poster art styles from the early 20th century. Our first poster series was the *Spirit of Nashville* collection—a group of prints that celebrated the history and charm of our hometown. Over time, we morphed into an illustration and design studio with a poster shop on the ground floor.

In 2010, after producing over 150 different Nashville designs, I started a new series of posters called *The Art & Soul of America*—a travel poster collection full of my favorite American destinations. It began as a small collection of prints depicting cities like Seattle, New Orleans, New York, and Chicago. The series was an instant success, and we soon received requests from all over the USA for new art depicting other places that were special to people—places where memories were made and souls were stirred.

As of 2021, we have produced over 2,000 different poster designs. Our art has been exhibited on every continent on the globe (except Antarctica). Our prints have been featured on movie and network TV sets, presented to diplomats, hung in embassies and galleries, published in design journals, and displayed on walls by travel poster lovers everywhere. What started in Nashville as a way to celebrate Music City and promote our little family-owned business has grown to become one of the largest bodies of decorative poster art ever assembled by one team of artists. We are still small, but our collection continues to grow. It's all available in the Anderson Design Group Studio Store located at 116 29th Ave. North, Nashville, TN 37203, or online at **www.ADGstore.com**.